ANDREA ROBINSON'S

2009 WINE BUYING GUIDE

for Everyone

**FEATURING MORE THAN 800 TOP WINES
AVAILABLE IN STORES AND RESTAURANTS**

Andrea Robinson

JGR Productions, LLC

PUBLISHED BY JGR PRODUCTIONS, LLC

www.Andreawine.com

First edition published 2002

Previously published in the United States by Broadway Books, an imprint of The Doubleday Broadway Publishing Group, a division of Random House, Inc., New York

The Library of Congress has cataloged the first edition as follows:
Immer, Andrea
[Wine buying guide for everyone]
Andrea Immer's wine buying guide for everyone /
Andrea Immer; edited by Anthony Giglio.—1st ed.
p. cm.
Includes index.
1. Wine and wine making. I. Title: Wine buying guide
for everyone. II. Giglio, Anthony. III. Title.

TP548 .I4624 2002
641.2'2—dc21   2002023077
ISBN-13: 978-0-9771032-4-9
ISBN-10: 0-9771032-4-2

ANDREA ROBINSON'S

2009 WINE BUYING GUIDE

for Everyone

From the library of
Dean Robert J. Trebar

Much loved, sorely missed

CONTENTS

ANDREA ROBINSON'S

2009
WINE
BUYING
GUIDE

for Everyone

INTRODUCTION

Although enjoying a good glass of wine is easy, all the types and confusing labels can make *shopping* for a bottle pretty hard. For the typical wine consumer, critics' scores and elaborate tasting reports of rare and exclusive bottlings aren't much help. That is why I wrote *Andrea Robinson's Wine Buying Guide for Everyone*. It is your road map to the *real* world of wine buying. Here is what you'll find inside:

Wines that are...

Broadly Available

This guide showcases more than 800 of the most popular and available wines on the market. That includes everything from the very best of the supermarket stalwarts to high-end boutique brands found mostly in restaurants. Putting it plainly, if the wine is in this book it is probably available in your favorite wine shops and restaurants or your supermarket.

Only the Best Quality

For this buying guide, I only include wines that I or my Web site tasting panel have rated as top quality. To give you "only the best" and still cover the most important wines in the world I start with all of the top selling wines in the US, I add "benchmark" wines that are important in a category, and I add wines with broad support from my tasting panel. I then cull down that list based on their ratings and mine to give you the best of the best. With limited space in this book and time on your hands, I prefer to use it telling you what you *should* buy, rather than what to avoid.

Great Value

I also only include wines that deliver good, very good or awesome value for the money. And the good news is you won't have to spend an arm and a leg to buy the wines in this guide. While some of the wines are expensive, most are popularly priced.

For each wine I provide:

Scores and Reviews

Each wine entry includes tasting reviews and scores from me and/or my tasting panel. For some of the most widely-rated wines I have included, in quotes, the consensus reactions of the tasters who review wines on my Web site. And if there's a great-tasting dish or cheese to pair with the wine, I share it.

When it comes to wine, I believe the voice of the wine consumer is more relevant than ever. So add yours! You can do so by adding your scores and comments to my wine rating database, on Andreawine. com. As always, you can set up a free profile to search the ratings database and add your own reviews. It also lets you share impressions directly with other wine lovers, and see a broader list of thousands of wines with up-to-date ratings. For each new edition, I invite my reviewers to submit their newest ratings and receive a free copy of the updated *Guide*.

I really believe wine quality, value and diversity will improve, the more winemakers hear the voice of not just a few critics, but of a broader group of people who taste and have an opinion about wines. In my database I categorize tasters in the following categories

- The Masters
- The Professionals
- The Expert Amateurs
- Everyone else

I and my Web site tasters assess the listed wines on two criteria:

- *Taste*—Does the wine deliver on taste?
- *Value for the Money*—Are you happy with what you got for the price you paid?

I keep the rating criteria simple, with taste scores listed on a 100-point scale. Past editions of the *Guide* presented ratings based on a 30-point scale. I have converted to the 100-point system because I believe it has become the industry standard. Over my years of teaching I have learned that even tasters who lack the experience to feel comfortable assigning a precise score to a wine, have an intuitive grasp of the quality category into which it falls. Here is how they are defined:

0–69 Poor (not included)

70-79 Fair (not included)

80-87 **Very good** - A good-quality, well-made wine that is pleasant to drink

88-94 **Excellent** - A wine that is delicious to drink, and is exemplary in its category and the world of wine

95-100 **Amazing** - A wine that rocks your world and seizes your senses with its utterly exciting complexity and expressiveness.

For value, on my Web site I use stars with the following scale

* Poor (not included)

** Fair (not included)

*** Good - the wine is priced fairly

**** Very good - the wine delivers more than you expect for the price

*****Awesome - The wine's quality equals that of wines that cost 2x as much, or more

In this guide I have only included wines with at least a Good (3-star) value rating. To keep the reviews easy to read, rather than publish the value scores, I have simply pointed out which wines have especially great value scores in the tasting notes.

Andrea's Favorites

Sometimes the rating of my tasting panel differs from mine, so I give my personal favorites a medal in this book. (You will see that the medals aren't always next to the highest-scoring wines.)

Match Your Palate

You know your taste, and it may not always synch with that of the uber-critics. It happens to me all the time. The "experts" often disagree because our individual palates are different. A wine that you love might not get a high rating from an expert and, if that's the case, you are certainly not "wrong." In fact, you just may be lucky because often wines that get the super-scores are more expensive, and harder to find.

So how do you know whether a highly-rated wine in this book will match your palate? Well, you can simply go to my Web site and answer a few questions to find out which "Palate Matchers" fit best with you and your palate might fit with all of them. Pretty cool huh? See How the Guide is Organized for a listing of the different "palate profiles." I've also included them in the Symbols key on the front cover flap, for easy reference when you are looking up wines in the book.

Kitchen Survivor™ Grades

"How long will a wine keep after it's opened?" Having heard this question more than any other from my restaurant customers and wine students, I decided several years ago that it was time to find out, so I started putting wines to the "kitchen survivor test." The resulting report card should help you make the most of the leftovers, by simply recorking and storing them in the fridge (even the reds), for enjoying later. Refer How the Guide is Organized for a breakdown of how the grading works.

Your Notes

There's space in each listing for your notes so you can keep track of the wines you try, and you can also enter your ratings and reviews at my Website, Andreawine. com. Set up a free profile, and then you can search by wine name, and add your review.

Other Helpful Buying Tools in the Guide

Throughout the *Guide,* I've included simple tools to address just about every major wine buying question I've ever been asked. They are:

Top Ten Lists—A quick reference to the wines I and my Web tasters think are the best in each grape or style category. It is important to note that depending on the wines' availability and other factors, each gets assessed by anywhere from a handful to several hundred tasters, and so the number of opinions reflected in each score varies. For example, pro tasters and and expert amateurs are often more likely than the broad population to review some of the less well-known wines. My rankings reflect this, showing a combination of very popular labels and some that may be new to you, but that I and other experienced palates think are really worth trying.

Food & Wine Pairing Basics—The core techniques sommeliers use to expertly match wine and food.

Andrea's Best Bets—These are my top, quick-reference recommendations for every common wine occasion and buying dilemma, from Thanksgiving wines to restaurant wine list best bets, party-crowd pleasers, blue chip bottles to impress the client, and more.

Affordable Agers—My short-list of wines that will age well for ten years or longer in your cellar, while not costing an arm and a leg. Cheers to that!

Entertaining with Wine—Everyone loves a wine party, and serving the right wine can make even a casual gathering memorable. These are my tips on choosing, buying the right amount, serving and highlighting wine when you're having company.

Wine List Decoder—This handy cross-reference chart will help you crack the code of different wine list terms, so you can quickly and easily find the styles you like.

Andrea's Complete Wine Course - **Mini-Course**— Mini-lessons covering wine styles, label terms, glassware, buying wine in stores and restaurants, and other housekeeping details to simplify buying and serving wine, so you can focus on enjoying it.

I had been in the restaurant wine business for more than a decade before I wrote my first book, *Great Wine Made Simple*. Having studied like crazy to pass the Master Sommelier exam (the hardest wine test you can imagine), I knew there were lots of great books out there. So why another? Because as I worked training waiters and budding sommeliers, I began to see that in practice those books weren't much help. Wine, like food, golf, the saxophone, and so many other sensory pursuits, is something you learn not by studying but by doing. So my books and my *Complete Wine Course* DVD teach wine not through memorization but the way I learned it—through tasting. It works, and it's fun, whether you are just a dabbler or a committed wine geek.

Similarly, I intend this guide to fill a gap. Most people around the country buy wine based on price and convenience. And whether it's people taking my wine classes, visitors to Copia, or visitors to my Web site, www.andreawine.com, they all have the same questions: What are the good, inexpensive wines? And if I'm going to splurge, which wines are really worth it? This buying guide is the first to answer those questions realistically, featuring wines in the broad marketplace, along with plenty of shrewd pro advice to help you make the most of every wine purchase.

What's New in This Year's Guide

Up-to-date prices - For this *Guide* I have reviewed the most recent vintage available as of the book's publication date, and included the national average suggested retail prices for each wine. Although prices for the same wine vary a lot by market (due to differences in local taxes and retailer discount practices), the national average retail price will give you an idea of what to expect when you are shopping.

Up-to-date vintages - This guide deals with the top-selling wines in the market, and so, for the most part, the year available in stores and restaurants will be the vintage covered in the guide. But if you find a different vintage, don't worry. Part of the quality promise of the wineries included in the *Guide* is that they have reasonable consistency from one year to the next. That said, prices can vary based on vintage, and there are certain wine categories for which vintage is a bigger consideration. If you find a different vintage from the one listed in the guide, here is a guideline:

White wines and reds under $20 - 1 year older or younger than the vintage in the *Guide* is a safe buy.

Reds over $20 - 2 years older or 1 year younger than the year in the *Guide* is safe to buy, but the price may differ if the vintage quality differed from the year reviewed.

Champagne/sparkling - most are non-vintage; for vintage-dated bottlings, the wine can be up to 5 years older or 1 year younger than the year in the *Guide*.

HOW THE GUIDE IS ORGANIZED

There are two ways to look up wines:

1. By Grape, Region, or Type

The wine reviews are grouped by major grape variety, region, or type, from white to red, and lightest to heaviest, as follows:

Within each section the wines are in alphabetical order by winery name.

2. By winery name

To find a specific winery's reviews, use the Winery Index at the back of the book.

Key to the Ratings and Symbols

This sample entry identifies the components of each wine listing.

1. **The Facts** -Name, vintage & where it is from
2. **The Price** - the national average retail price; Prices can vary a lot by market based on taxes and discount policies, but this will give you an idea of what to expect
3. **The Score** - on a 100-point scale; as with your grades in school, a 100 is perfect
4. **The Symbols** - There are two different kinds of symbols, as follows:

   Andrea's favorites
   ♗ Indicates an Andrea personal favorite wine

   Palate matchers
   🍴 A food-friendly wine that pairs well with diverse dishes and food flavors.
   🍎 A fruit-forward, "new world" style wine.
   ⚱ An "old world" style wine, with an earthy or mineral scent and flavor and subtle fruit
   ☺ A "crowd-pleaser" wine that will satisfy a lot of palates; generally big, lush wines
   👍 A wine-geek favorite - perfect for your connoisseur or wine aficionado friends.

5. **The Reviews** - My review and description of the wine, along with my Web site tasters' comments (in quotes) for some of the wines
6. **My Kitchen Survivor™** Grade
7. **Your notes** - Space for your wine notes.

---

❶ **Chateau Andrea Rose 2008**	❷ $	❸ Pts
New York	22	88

❹❺ 🍴 Tasters marvel at its "amazing quality for a bag-in-the-box." Pro buyers (including me) find it "every bit as good as the finest Cold Duck ... and sometimes better!"

❻ *Kitchen Survivor™ Grade: A*

❼ Your notes: _____

Kitchen Survivor™ *Grades*

Since "How long will it keep after I open it?" is one of the most common wine questions I'm asked, I decided it was time to give some solid answers.

And thus were born the Kitchen Survivor™ experiments. To test wines' open-bottle longevity, I handle them as follows:

Whites—Recorked with the original cork (whether natural or synthetic). Placed in the fridge.

Reds—Recorked with the original cork. Placed on the kitchen counter.

Sparkling wines—Opened carefully without popping (popping depletes carbonation faster). Closed with a "clamshell" stopper designed for sparkling wines—sold in housewares departments and sometimes wine stores. Placed in the fridge.

The same process is repeated after each daily retaste, until the wine's taste declines noticeably.

I do this for every wine I taste that's a candidate for inclusion in the guide. The great news is that far more often than you'd think, the good wines stay that way for days. Even more interesting, some wines that seem initially underwhelming actually come around and start tasting better after being open for a while (in the same way that some cheeses need to sit out at room temperature to show their best flavor or a pot of chili can taste better after a day or two in the fridge). Based on these taste tests, I grade each wine as follows:

C = a "one-day wine," which tastes noticeably less fresh the next day. This doesn't mean the wine is less worthy, just less sturdy—so plan to finish it with tonight's dinner.

B = holds its freshness for 2–3 days after opening

B+ = holds *and gets better* over 2–3 days after opening

A = has a 3- to 4-day "freshness window"

A+ = holds *and gets better* over 3–4 days

I hope these grades will give you the confidence to enjoy wine more often with your everyday meals, knowing that in most cases the bottle won't go "bad" if you don't finish it right away.

Your Notes

Would you add your voice to my wine rating engine on andreawine.com? I would love for you to log on and share your wine impressions with me and others for the next edition of the *Guide*. But even if you are not the survey type, keep notes for yourself. Whether you're at home or in a restaurant, the *Guide* is a handy place to keep track of what you drank, what you paid, what food you had with it, and what you thought. Don't you hate it when you've enjoyed a wine, then can't remember the name when you want to buy it again?

A Few Questions (and Answers) about the Wine Entries

How Were Wines Chosen for Inclusion in the Book?

As mentioned, most of the wines represented are top sellers in stores and restaurants nationally, from the following industry-defined tiers: premium, super-premium, ultra-premium and luxury ($20+). I also have also included in each category some bottlings that are "worth the search" - my new discoveries - although in some cases their availability may be skewed heavily to restaurants and fine wine shops rather than warehouse clubs or supermarkets. Why, you ask? Simply put, wineries with a limited supply often concentrate on restaurant lists and upscale shops because of the image enhancement and more expert handling they can offer. I promise these wines are worth seeking out. In many cases, fine wine shops will special-order a wine if you ask. Don't see one of your favorite wines? Keep in mind that both popularity and availability of specific wines can vary a lot regionally, so a big brand in your area may not have the same sales and presence in other markets. This is especially true with local wines—for example, the Texas Chenin Blanc or New York Riesling that's on every table in your neck of the woods may not even be distributed in the next state.

Can You Really Define "Outstanding" Wine?

Indeed I can. We all can. Broadly, it is a wine that captures your attention. It could be the scent, the taste, the texture, or all three that make you say first, "Mmm. . . ," and then, "Wow" as your impressions register in the moment, in the context of all your prior experience and the price you paid. If it all sounds very personal and subjective, you're exactly right—it is. That is why I felt a guide like this, showcasing the impressions of real-world buyers, was so important. The fact that the wines herein are big sellers is already an endorsement. The details put each wine in context—of price, similar-style wines, occasion, and whatever else buyers feel is important. No other wine buying guide does that.

Who Are the Tasters? You

Continuing with the tradition begun with my old Web site, I collect tasting data 24/7 on my new site, www. Andreawine.com, from thousands of American wine buyers. Part of the group includes trade colleagues (retail and restaurant buyers, sommeliers, hoteliers, chefs, waiters, importers, and distributors). I also recruit consumer tasters through my wine club; my wine students; and of course, the friends and family network. I originally thought consumers would be less keen than trade to share their wine opinions, but I was wrong. Consumers account for more than 70% of the total responses. Although I don't purposely exclude anyone, I do review the data for signs of ballot stuffing from winery companies and adjust for any suspicious responses (they are rare).

Why Do These Tasters' Opinions Matter?

Clearly, this *Guide for Everyone* takes a populist perspective that's different from every other wine publication on the market—and that is exactly what I intend. I think the honest assessments and perspective of consumers who have to pay their own money for wine (while wine journalists rarely do), and the restaurateurs and retailers who serve them, are extremely important and helpful—because they're the real world.

I am not dismissing the value of and expertise behind the leading critics' scoring reports. (After all, if expert opinions were not important in wine, I'd be out of job!) But I do think the views of the dominant critics often further the notion that there are haves and have-nots in the wine world: the 90+–rated "good stuff" that none of us can afford; and the rest—the wines we see every day whose lower scores seem bad by comparison. That perspective is perhaps valuable to a tiny, elite group of luxury wine buyers. But for what I call the OTC (other than collectors) market, which makes up the bulk of the nation's buyers (including just about everyone I know), this dichotomy leaves us feeling utterly insecure about our own taste and budget, skeptical about the quality of the selection at the stores and restaurants we frequent, and self-conscious about our (legitimate) desire for value for the money—in the vernacular: good, cheap wine. If I've achieved my goal, this *Guide*'s real-world information will give you a renewed sense of confidence in your own taste and some great word-of-mouth guidance on new wines to try that are actually available where you shop and dine.

And as the ratings engine on Andreawine.com begins to include new voices - yours and mine, as well as other pros whose experienced opinion you can trust - it will also validate diverse, real-world wine tastes. Not everyone loves the currently-popular "big, alcoholic, oaky and pricey" styles promoted by the big-name critics. Nor should they. Part of the excitement of wines is that they *don't* all taste the same, and that the good ones aren't all expensive. This *Guide* and the ratings on Andreawine.com celebrate that very fact. Come join the party!

ANDREA'S TOP WINES *

Best of the Big Six Grapes

Name	Score	Price
Top 10 Rieslings		
Eroica, Columbia Valley 2007	90	22
Saint M, Pfalz, Germany 2006	89	12
Gunderloch Estate, Germany 2007	89	17
Darting Kabinett, Germany 2007	89	17
Strub Niersteiner Paterberg Spatlese, Germany 2007	88	18
Dr. Konstantin Frank Dry, Finger Lakes, New York 2007	88	18
Bonny Doon Pacific Rim, Germany/California 2007	88	8
Trefethen Estate Dry, Napa 2007	87	22
Kendall-Jackson Vintner's Reserve, California 2006	86	10
Pierre Sparr Selection, Alsace, France	86	14
Top 10 Sauvignon/Fume Blancs		
Robert Mondavi Fume Blanc, Napa 2007	91	20
Matanzas Creek, Sonoma 2007	91	24
Grgich Hills Fume Blanc, Napa 2007	91	28
Flora Springs Soliloquy, Napa 2007	91	25
St. Supery, Napa 2006	90	23
Robert Mondavi To-Ka-Lon Reserve, Napa 2006	90	40
Chalk Hill, Chalk Hill-Sonoma 2006	90	28
Kim Crawford, New Zealand 2008	89	19
Duckhorn, Napa 2007	89	23
Girard, Napa 2007	89	15

*The wine ranking in each style category reflects the wine's numerical taste score, its relative value for the money, and the number of raters. Among multiple wines with the same rating, the less expensive wines, or wines rated by more tasters, are pushed higher in the ranking. To find the complete tasting notes for each wine, refer to the Winery Index in the back of the book. Also visit Andreaine.com for tasting videos and more information on each wine.

Top 10 Chardonnays

Chalk Hill Estate,		
Chalk Hill-Sonoma 2005	93	40
Chateau St. Jean Robert Young Vyd,		
Alexander Valley 2006	92	25
Grgich Hills Estate, Napa 2006	92	42
Wakefield Estate, Australia 2007	91	17
Chalone Estate, Monterey 2006	91	25
Kim Crawford Unoaked,		
New Zealand 2007	90	17
Souverain, Sonoma 2006	90	17
Stuhlmuller, Alexander Valley 2006	90	23
Kendall-Jackson Vintner's Reserve,		
California 2006	89	14
Catena, Mendoza 2006	89	18

Top 10 Pinot Noirs

Williams-Selyem, Sonoma Coast, 2006	93	45
Domaine Drouhin, Willamette Valley 2006	93	60
Rochioli, Russian River 2006	92	55
Cristom Mt. Jefferson Cuvee,		
Willamette Valley 2006	92	30
Chalone Vineyard Estate,		
Chalone California 2006	91	40
Sanford, Santa Rita Hills 2006	90	24
Truchard, Carneros 2005	90	35
Etude, Carneros 2006	90	40
Willamette Valley Vineyards Reserve,		
Oregon 2005	89	25
Acacia, Carneros 2007	89	26

Top 10 Merlots

Grgich Hills Estate, Napa 2004	92	40
Falesco Montiano, Latium Italy 2005	92	45
Sebastiani, Sonoma 2005	90	17
Arboleda, Aconcagua Chile 2005	90	19
Frog's Leap, Napa 2005	90	34
Matanzas Creek,		
Bennett Valley Sonoma 2005	90	35
Duckhorn, Napa 2005	90	52
Souverain, Alexander Valley 2006	89	19
Shafer, Napa 2005	89	46
Franciscan Oakville Estate, Napa 2005	88	25

Top 10 Cabernet Sauvignons and Blends

Joseph Phelps Insignia, California 2005	96	200
Robert Mondavi Reserve, Napa 2005	94	135
Sequoia Grove Rutherford Bench Reserve, Napa 2004	93	60
Mt. Veeder, Napa 2005	92	40
Grgich Hills Estate, Napa 2004	92	60
Louis Martini Napa Valley Reserve, Napa 2005	91	25
Penfolds Bin 389, Australia 2005	91	37
Provenance Vineyards, Rutherford 2005	91	42
Beaulieu Vineyard (BV) George de Latour Private Reserve, Napa 2005	91	115
Frog's Leap, Napa 2005	90	38

Top 10 Shiraz/Syrahs and Rhone-Style Reds

E & M Guigal Cote-Rotie Brune et Blonde, France 2003	93	75
Chateau de Beaucastel, Chateauneuf-du-Pape 2005	93	100
Chalone Vineyard Estate Syrah, Chalone 2005	91	30
Jade Mountain Napa Syrah, California 2004	92	28
Wakefield Promised Land Shiraz, Cabernet, South Australia 2005	90	13
Wolf Blass Yellow Label, Australia 2006	89	13
E & M Guigal, Cotes-du-Rhone 2004	89	15
Andrew Murray Syrah Tous Les Jours, Central Coast 2006	89	16
D'Arenberg The Footbolt Shiraz, Australia 2005	89	20
Penfolds Kalimna Bin 28 Shiraz, Australia 2005	89	26

Best of the Rest

Name	Score	Price
Top 10 Champagnes and Sparkling Wines		
Taittinger Comtes de Champagne 1998	91	270
Bollinger Brut Special Cuvee Champagne NV	90	60
Schramsberg Blanc de Noirs, Napa 2005	90	37
Gosset Brut Rose Champagne NV	90	45
Piper-Heidseick Brut, Champagne 2000	90	65
Veuve Clicquot La Grande Dame, Champagne 1998	90	165
Charles Heidseick Brut, Champagne NV	90	45
Dom Perignon, Champagne 2001	90	175
Roederer Estate, Anderson Valley NV	89	22
Perrier-Jouet Fleur de Champagne 1999	89	139
Top 10 Pinot Gris/Grigios		
Pighin Friuli Grave, Italy 2007	90	15
Bollini Trentino, Italy 2007	89	15
Lageder, Italy 2007	88	18
Trimbach Reserve, Alsace, France 2004	88	22
Willamette Valley Vineyards, Oregon 2006	88	15
Erath, Oregon 2007	87	14
Flora Springs, Napa 2006	87	14
MacMurray Ranch, Russian River 2006	87	14
Maso Canali, Italy 2006	87	16
Ponzi, Oregon 2007	87	17
Top 10 Italian and Spanish Reds		
Marchesi di Gresy Barbaresco Martinenga, Piedmont 2005	96	60
Alvaro Palacios Les Terrasses, Priorat 2005	91	33
Pesquera Crianza, Ribera del Duero 2005	91	35
Luce Super Tuscan, Tuscany 2004	91	60
Abadia Retuerta Seleccion Especial, Sardon de Duero, Spain 2005	90	22
Muga Rioja Reserva, Spain 2004	90	24
Tenuta Sette Ponti Crognolo, Tuscany 2006	90	35
Castello di Gabbiano Alleanza, Tuscany, Italy 2005	90	35
Badia a Coltibuono Sangioveto, Tuscany 2003	90	60
Palacios Remondo La Montesa Rioja Crianza, Spain 2004	89	20

Top 10 Red Zinfandels

Ridge Geyserville, Sonoma 2005	92	32
Francis Ford Coppola Director's Cut, California 2006	91	20
Grgich Hills Estate, California 2003	91	28
Frog's Leap, Napa 2006	90	28
Deloach Vneyards, Russian River 2006	89	18
Renwood, Shenandoah Valley 2005	89	20
Quivira, Dry Creek Valley 2006	89	20
Girard Old Vine, California 2006	89	24
C G Di Arie, Shenandoah Valley 2006	89	25
Rancho Zabaco, Russian River 2005	89	28

THE REVIEWS

WHITE WINES
Sparkling/Champagne

Style Profile: Although all the world's bubblies are modeled on Champagne, only the genuine article from the Champagne *region* of France is properly called *Champagne. Sparkling wine* is the proper term for the other bubblies, some of which can be just as good as the real thing. Limited supply and high demand—plus a labor-intensive production process—make Champagne expensive compared to other sparklers but still an affordable luxury in comparison to other world-class wine categories, like top French Burgundy or California Cabernet estates. The other sparklers, especially Cava from Spain and Italian Prosecco, are affordable for everyday drinking. *Brut* (rhymes with *root*) on the label means the wine is utterly dry, with no perceptible sweetness. But that *doesn't* mean they all taste the same. In fact, each French Champagne house is known for a signature style, which can range from delicate and elegant to rich, full, and toasty—meaning there's something for every taste and food partner.

Serve: Well chilled; young and fresh (only the rare luxury French Champagnes improve with age). Open with utmost care: flying corks can be dangerous.

When: Anytime! Bubbly not just for special occasions, and it's great with meals.

With: Anything and anyone, but especially sushi, shellfish, fried foods and popcorn.

In: A narrow tulip- or flute-type glass; the narrow opening preserves the bubbles.

Kitchen Survivor™ Tip for Bubbly Wine: Kitchen-ware shops and wine stores often sell "clamshell" stoppers specially designed to close Champagnes and sparkling wines if you don't finish the bottle. I've found that if you open the bottle carefully in the first place (avoid "popping" the cork, which is also the safest technique), a stoppered sparkling wine will keep its fizz for at least three days in the fridge, often longer. Having a hard time thinking of something else to toast? How about, "Here's to [insert day of week]." That's usually good enough for me!

Argyle Brut Sparkling, Oregon NV	$ 19	Pts 86

The Asian pear scent and flavor are delicious for just sipping and with subtle foods like shellfish.
Kitchen Survivor™ Grade: A
Your notes: _____

Bollinger (*BOLL-en-jur*) Brut Special Cuvee Champagne, France NV	$ 60	Pts 90

"Expensive" relative to other major brut NV brands, but the baked apple and croissant flavors and long finish make this wine a breed apart.
Kitchen Survivor™ Grade: A
Your notes: _____

Bouvet (*boo-VAY*) Brut Sparkling, Loire Valley, France NV	$ 16	Pts 84

☺ Classy and affordable, with a complex scent of wilted blossoms and sweet hay, a crisp apple-quince flavor, and creamy texture.
Kitchen Survivor™ Grade: B+
Your notes: _____

Charles Heidsieck (*HIDE-sick*) Brut Reserve Champagne, France NV	$ 55	Pts 89

☗ This "well rounded and luxurious" bubbly is full and seductive, with scents of toasted hazelnut and baking pastry, and luxuriant apricot fruit flavor.
Kitchen Survivor™ Grade: A
Your notes: _____

Codorniu Cava Rose,   **$**   **Pts**
Spain NV   **14**   **85**

☺ As good as many French Roses for a fraction of the price. Creamy bubble, dried cherry fruit, soft spicy finish that pairs perfectly with BBQ chicken.

Kitchen Survivor™ Grade: A

Your notes: _____

Domaine Carneros Brut Sparkling,   **$**   **Pts**
California 2003   **25**   **89**

One of my favorite California sparklers, for its biscuity, floral elegance. It is sublime with smoked salmon on a potato chip with a little pouf of sour cream.

Kitchen Survivor™ Grade: B

Your notes: _____

Domaine Carneros Le Reve Blanc de   **$**   **Pts**
Blancs Sparkling, California 2001   **75**   **88**

👍 This is one of California's best bubblies, with a firm core of fresh pear fruit, floral and fresh-bread scent, and long finish. Pair with baked brie.

Kitchen Survivor™ Grade: A+

Your notes: _____

Domaine Chandon (*shahn-DOHN*) Brut   **$**   **Pts**
Rose Sparkling, California NV   **18**   **88**

🍴 One of the best California roses on the market right now, with delicious spiced cherry fruit and a long finish. Pair it with blackened chicken.

Kitchen Survivor™ Grade: B

Your notes: _____

Domaine Chandon Brut   **$**   **Pts**
Classic Sparkling, California NV   **16**   **87**

☺ This "classy but affordable" American bubbly is in top form, with baked apple, crisp pear and granola flavors. Great for just sipping, and with sushi.

Kitchen Survivor™ Grade: B+

Your notes: _____

Domaine Chandon Riche (Reesh),   **$**   **Pts**
Sparkling, California NV   **20**   **86**

What makes it "riche" is a hint of sweetness—not at all cloying. A great accompaniment to Chinese Orange Flavor Chicken and other spicy dishes.

Kitchen Survivor™ Grade: A

Your notes: _____

Domaine Ste. Michelle Brut   **$**   **Pts**
Sparkling, Washington NV   12   84

☺ My tasters note, "you can't beat the price" of this nicely balanced, crisp, and appley sparkler.
Kitchen Survivor™ Grade: B

Your notes: _____

Dom Perignon Champagne Brut,   **$**   **Pts**
France 2001   165   90

"Shop around for the best deal," because you can't beat it "when you want to impress," and the "good fruit flavor" and "yeasty" scent are "always reliable."
Kitchen Survivor™ Grade: B

Your notes: _____

Duval-Leroy Brut Champagne.   **$**   **Pts**
France NV   40   88

This Champagne begins scents of fresh, cinnamon-sprinkled Fuji apple slices. On the palate are flavors of toasted almonds, lemon and apple tart. A special treat with runny cheeses like Camembert or Brie.
Kitchen Survivor™ Grade: B

Your notes: _____

Freixenet (*fresh-uh-NETT*) Brut   **$**   **Pts**
de Noirs, Cava Rose, Spain NV   10   86

"Yum's the word" for this wine. The mouthwatering taste of tangy strawberries is great with fried foods, spicy foods . . . any foods. And it held up for weeks in the fridge. An amazing deal that's worth the search.
Kitchen Survivor™ Grade: A+

Your notes: _____

G.H. Mumm Cordon Rouge Brut,   **$**   **Pts**
Champagne, France NV   35   85

Medium-bodied, with a pretty scent floral and hay scent and a crusty bread-granola quality. A deal!
Kitchen Survivor™ Grade: A

Your notes: _____

Gloria Ferrer Sonoma Brut,   **$**   **Pts**
California NV   20   86

Crisp Anjou pear with a touch of earthiness and nice finesse. Great acidity that refreshes with spicy dishes and briny shellfish such as chilled oysters & clams.
Kitchen Survivor™ Grade: A

Your notes: _____

Gosset (*go-SAY*) Brut Rose Champagne, France NV — $ 45 — Pts 88

This is one of my favorite rose Champagnes. The scent and flavors of dried cherries, exotic spices, and toasted nuts would please any serious wine drinker. Forget toasting and serve it with salmon, tuna, duck, or pork.

Kitchen Survivor™ Grade: A

Your notes: ______________________________

Gruet (*groo-AY*) Brut St. Vincent Sparkling, New Mexico NV — $ 16 — Pts 83

New Mexico? Gruet's "great bubblies, which are tasty and of good value," prove "all that prickles in the desert isn't cactus!" It's a natural "pardner" for Tex Mex.

Kitchen Survivor™ Grade: B+

Your notes: ______________________________

Iron Horse Wedding Cuvee Brut Sparkling, California NV — $ 30 — Pts 87

☺ Romantics love the name; and it is my choice for receptions, having inspired more "What was the name of that wine?" reactions than any other in the history of my wine career. The great acidity and crisp tangerine and green apple flavors pair easily with app's and light fish and chicken dishes.

Kitchen Survivor™ Grade: B

Your notes: ______________________________

J Cuvee 20 Brut Sparkling, Sonoma, California NV — $ 32 — Pts 88

This wine seems to get better every year, and the package is gorgeous. Rich and yeasty, with baked apple fruit and a lush finish. Pair with crabcakes.

Kitchen Survivor™ Grade: A

Your notes: ______________________________

Krug Grande Cuvee Multivintage Champagne, France — $ 165 — Pts 89

🎖 👍 I love this wine, and the Web tasters agree with me that it "really is worth the splurge." Krug's truly unique, full, nutty, baked-brioche style is big enough to pair with roasted meats and game birds.

Kitchen Survivor™ Grade: A

Your notes: ______________________________

Laurent-Perrier Brut LP,	$	Pts
Champagne, France NV	42	86

🍴 This wine's known for its elegance and racy acidity, which makes it a great food partner *and* a great Kitchen Survivor. A nice pairing with briny oysters & clams.
Kitchen Survivor™ Grade: A+

Your notes: _____

Mionetto (*me-oh-NETT-oh*) DOC	$	Pts
Prosecco (*pro-SECK-oh*) Brut,	16	88
Veneto, Italy NV		

☺ This Prosecco is dry, refreshing, and sophisticated but also affordable. Prosecco is the grape name. Add peach puree to make the Bellini cocktail. Great with savory antipasti (sausage, cheese, olives).
Kitchen Survivor™ Grade: B

Your notes: _____

Moët & Chandon (*MWETT eh*	$	Pts
shahn-DOHN) Brut Imperial	40	87
Champagne, France NV		

This is one of the best Brut NVs on the market at the moment, with with "medium body and more fruit flavor and acidity" than its sister bottling, Moët & Chandon White Star
Kitchen Survivor™ Grade: B

Your notes: _____

Moët & Chandon White Star	$	Pts
Champagne, France NV	40	86

☺ 🍴 My trade and consumer tasters alike tout this as "fantastic Champagne," and I agree. Its "reliable, crowd-pleasing style," with just a whisper of sweetness, is great with spicy foods and sushi.
Kitchen Survivor™ Grade: A

Your notes: _____

Mumm Napa Brut Cuvee	$	Pts
Sparkling, California NV	18	87

☺ The best it's ever been! A recent bottle got me on board with my Web tasters' "French style, for a great price" enthusiasm. The toasty baked apple flavor would be great with wild mushroom pasta.
Kitchen Survivor™ Grade: B

Your notes: _____

Perrier-Jouët (*PEAR-ee-ay JHWETT*)   **$**   **Pts**
Fleur de Champagne Brut, France 1999   **139**   **89**

The wine is as beautiful as the bottle, with elegant scents of biscuits, white flowers, and baked apples.
Kitchen Survivor™ Grade: A

Your notes: _____

Perrier-Jouët Grand Brut   **$**   **Pts**
Champagne, France NV   **45**   **86**

The Web tasters give this one gives it high marks, and for the price it remains a solid bet, with yeasty dried-apple flavors and medium body.
Kitchen Survivor™ Grade: B

Your notes: _____

Piper-Heidsieck (*HIDE-sick*) Cuvee   **$**   **Pts**
Brut Champagne, France NV   **42**   **88**

This "really dry brut style" comes on with major toastiness in the scent, followed by a frisky acidity and white pepper spiciness that makes it great with salty and fatty flavors and "an absolute joy to drink."
Kitchen Survivor™ Grade: A

Your notes: _____

Piper-Heidsieck (*HIDE-sick*) Cuvee Brut   **$**   **Pts**
2000 Champagne, France NV   **65**   **90**

A fantastic example of a vintage Champagne, showing gorgeous brioche and almond croissant scents and flavors. Pair it with trout (or other fish) almondine, or aged Gouda cheese on walnut bread.
Kitchen Survivor™ Grade: A

Your notes: _____

Piper-Sonoma Brut Sparkling, Sonoma,   **$**   **Pts**
California NV   **16**   **87**

This California outpost of the French Champagne Piper-Heidsieck yields one of California's best bubblies - especially for the price. It's got a toastiness that makes it rich enough to pair with pork or even duck.
Kitchen Survivor™ Grade: A+

Your notes: _____

Pol Roger Brut Reserve   **$**   **Pts**
Champagne, France NV   **45**   **88**

👍 "Wonderful producer. Great product at this price point," noted my tasters. It is one of the top brut Champagnes in the delicate, elegant, appley style.

Kitchen Survivor™ Grade: A+

Your notes: _____

Pommery (*POMM-er-ee*) Brut   **$**   **Pts**
Royal Champagne, France NV   **40**   **87**

Pommery, a French classic, emerged on the US scene with its trendy "Pops" mini-bottles - and never looked back. It's an elegant style with a creamy scent and subtle pear flavor that's delicious for solo sipping.

Kitchen Survivor™ Grade: A

Your notes: _____

Roederer Estate Brut Sparkling,   **$**   **Pts**
California NV   **22**   **89**

😊 "About as close to Champagne as you can get without buying French." The full, toasty style is the best of both worlds: "reasonably priced," with the taste of "a special occasion wine."

Kitchen Survivor™ Grade: A

Your notes: _____

Scharffenberger Brut,   **$**   **Pts**
California NV   **19**   **88**

🎺 In my blind tasting this rich but balanced bottling beat out many of the more expensive bubblies. Delicious with salads, light fish dishes and hard cheeses.

Kitchen Survivor™ Grade: A

Your notes: _____

Schramsberg Blanc de Noirs,   **$**   **Pts**
California 2005   **37**   **91**

🏆 At less than half the price of the Schramsberg Reserve (my favorite from this winery), this bottling mimics the toasty, nutty style that would seduce French Champagne lovers. Great to pair with salmon, pork, duck, or wild mushroom risotto

Kitchen Survivor™ Grade: A

Your notes: _____

Segura Viudas (*seh-GUHR-uh vee-YOU-duss*) Aria Estate Cava Brut, Spain NV — $ 12 — Pts 85

🍴 ☺ For the money, one of the most delicious sparklers on the market, with ripe, vibrant pear fruit and a creamy texture. Perfect with a Cobb salad lunch!

Kitchen Survivor™ Grade: A

Your notes: _____

Segura Viudas Reserva Heredad Estate Cava Brut, Spain NV — $ 20 — Pts 87

👍 Both the handsome metal-clad bottle and the earthy, mushroomy scent and flavor are quite commanding. Definitely a bubbly for a meal of seafood stew laced with fennel and Pernod.

Kitchen Survivor™ Grade: A

Your notes: _____

Taittinger (*TAIT-in-jur*) Brut La Française Champagne, France NV — $ 55 — Pts 88

🍴 🥂 One of my favorites among the subtle, elegant house-style Champagnes, with finesse and delicacy that "simply dance across the tongue."

Kitchen Survivor™ Grade: A

Your notes: _____

Taittinger Comtes de Champagne Blanc de Blancs Champagne, France 1998 — $ 270 — Pts 90

👍 🥂 Although "slightly under the radar" this is the luxury Champagne I'd buy before all others (if I could afford it). It is incredibly elegant, toasty, and long. Although I never can wait, the wine does cellar beautifully. Blow out the decadence and pair it with truffle risotto. You can tighten your belt tomorrow!

Kitchen Survivor™ Grade: A

Your notes: _____

Veuve Clicquot (*voov klee-COH*) La Grande Dame Champagne, France 1998 — $ 155 — Pts 90

"Pricey but worth it" is the consensus for this big, beautiful wine with floral, biscuity, nutty/pear/cream/sherry notes, and an endlessly long finish.

Kitchen Survivor™ Grade: A

Your notes: _____

Pinot Gris/Pinot Grigio

Grape Profile: Pinot Gris (*pee-no GREE*) is the French and Grigio (*GREE-jee-oh*) the Italian spelling for this crisp, delicate white wine grape whose sales under the "Grigio" label continue to see scorching growth. The French and American versions tend toward the luscious style; the Italians are more tangy and crisp. In France, Pinot Gris is a signature in the Alsace region, and Oregon vintners have made this style a calling card as well. The California bottlings tend to be labeled according to the style they are mimicking - Pinot Gris if it's the exotic French style, Pinot Grigio if it's the crisp and minerally Italian style. To many of my trade tasters it's "the quintessential quaffing wine" and "a real winner by the glass" in restaurants. Happily, many of the cheapest Pinot Grigios remain among the best. I couldn't put it better than the taster who wrote, "If it doesn't *taste* a lot better, why should I *pay* a lot more?" As the Italians would say, *Ecco!*

Serve: Well chilled; young and fresh (as one of my wine buying buddies says to the waiters *she* teaches: "The best vintage for Pinot Grigio? As close to yesterday as possible!").

When: Anytime, but ideal with cocktails, outdoor occasions, lunch, big gatherings (a crowd pleaser).

With: Very versatile, but perfect with hors d'oeuvres, salads, salty foods, and fried foods.

In: An all-purpose wine stem is fine.

A to Z Pinot Gris,	$	Pts
Oregon 2006	13	82

🍎 Super-peachy and lush - a tasty quaff on its own, but also ideally priced and styled for summer BBQ. *Kitchen Survivor™ Grade: C*

Your notes: _____

Adelshiem Vineyard Pinot Gris,   **$**   **Pts**
Willamette Valley, Oregon 2006   **18**   **85**

👍 🏆 This Oregon classic winery goes for - and achieves - elegance. The minerally, gingery scents and pear fruit are incredibly subtle and refined.

Kitchen Survivor™ Grade: B

Your notes: _____

Alois Lageder (ah-lo-EEZ *la-GAY-der*)   **$**   **Pts**
Pinot Grigio, Alto Adige, Italy 2007   **18**   **88**

👍 💨 One of the benchmark PGs, with pear fruit, floral scent, and smoky finish add up to complexity that few expect from Pinot Grigio. Pair with clam pasta.

Kitchen Survivor™ Grade: B

Your notes: _____

Banfi San Angelo Pinot Grigio,   **$**   **Pts**
Italy 2007   **18**   **86**

☺ This "fresh, frisky," citrusy, made-for-food wine is perfect for salads, antipasti and tomato-y pastas.

Kitchen Survivor™ Grade: B

Your notes: _____

Bethel Heights Pinot Gris,   **$**   **Pts**
Willamette Valley, Oregon 2006   **18**   **84**

Textbook Oregon Pinot Gris in the restrained style, with hay and floral scents, and honeyed pear flavors.

Kitchen Survivor™ Grade: B

Your notes: _____

Big House Pinot Grigio,   **$**   **Pts**
California 2007   **14**   **83**

☺ A fun, easy-priced, easy-open (screwtop) wine with juicy pineapple fruit flavor. Can you say "party"?

Kitchen Survivor™ Grade: B

Your notes: _____

Bollini Pinot Grigio Trentino,   **$**   **Pts**
Italy 2005   **18**   **89**

🍺 👍 🏆 This is Pinot Grigio on a whole different level: marzipan, honey, Fuji apple flavors, chalky texture, amazing length.

Kitchen Survivor™ Grade: A+

Your notes: _____

Cavit (*CAV-it;* rhymes with $ Pts
"have it") Pinot Grigio, Italy 2007   8   82

☺ "A nice sipper" or for big parties because it's light, crisp, and bargain priced.

Kitchen Survivor™ Grade: B

Your notes: _____

Chehalem Pinot Gris, $ Pts
Willamette valley, Oregon   19   85

🍴 🍷 "Ruby red grapefruit" flavor with a hint of earthiness that adds complexity. Pair with sweet crab or scallops.

Kitchen Survivor™ Grade: B

Your notes: _____

Clos du Bois Pinot Grigio, $ Pts
California 2006   14   85

☺ A top California Pinot Grigio; ripe pear fruit, a hint of mineral. A great pairing with summer salads.

Kitchen Survivor™ Grade: A

Your notes: _____

Conte di Lucca Pinot Grigio, $ Pts
Italy 2007   14   88

🍴 Much more than your typical PG, with plush pear fruit with a whisper of almond and tarragon perfume. Tasty with fennel-scented sausages.

Kitchen Survivor™ Grade: A

Your notes: _____

Danzante Pinot Grigio, $ Pts
Italy 2007   8   85

🍴 Compared to a lot of the better-known Italian PGs this is "twice the wine at half the price." It's subtle, with crisp green apple-mineral flavors that pair with anything salty or fatty - can you say fried chicken?

Kitchen Survivor™ Grade: B

Your notes: _____

Ecco Domani (*ECK-oh dough-* $ Pts
***MAH-nee*) Pinot Grigio, Italy 2007**   10   82

☺ "Tastes clean and refreshing," say fans of Gallo's Italian offspring that tastes crisp and lemony. Pros point out that it's "a great value for the money."

Kitchen Survivor™ Grade: B

Your notes: _____

Erath Pinot Gris,   **$**   **Pts**
Oregon 2007   **14**   **87**

👆 Search this one out - for the price it's one of Oregon's best PGs, succulent with honeyed pear flavor.
Kitchen Survivor™ Grade: B

Your notes: _____

Estancia Pinot Grigio,   **$**   **Pts**
California 2007   **12**   **85**

🔑 This wine's subtle chalkiness and snappy grapefruit flavors scream for a goat cheese salad.
Kitchen Survivor™ Grade: B

Your notes: _____

Firesteed Pinot Grigio,   **$**   **Pts**
Oregon 2006   **13**   **86**

☺ A top value in Oregon Pinot Gris, balancing tropical fruit and floral scents with nice acidity.
Kitchen Survivor™ Grade: B

Your notes: _____

Flora Springs Pinot Grigio,   **$**   **Pts**
California 2006   **14**   **87**

👆 I think this is the best California Pinot Grigio on the market, and agree with my tasters that it offers "delicious" pineapple fruit, long finish, and "good value."
Kitchen Survivor™ Grade: B

Your notes: _____

Folonari (*foe-luh-NAH-ree*)   **$**   **Pts**
Pinot Grigio, Italy 2007   **10**   **83**

☺ Trade buyers say this "underrated overachiever" is ideal when you're seeking a crisp, sippable, value-priced white.
Kitchen Survivor™ Grade: C

Your notes: _____

Gallo Family Vineyards Sonoma Reserve   **$**   **Pts**
Pinot Gris, California 2007   **15**   **88**

As winemaker Gina Gallo says, this wine is "all about the fruit: peach, fig, and mandarin orange." Yum!
Kitchen Survivor™ Grade: C

Your notes: _____

J Pinot Gris, Russian River Valley,   **$**   **Pts**
Sonoma, California 2007   **20**   **86**

A class act, balancing hay, floral and mineral scents with ripe melon and tangerine fruit, and fresh acidity.
Kitchen Survivor™ Grade: B

Your notes: _____

King Estate Pinot Gris,   **$**   **Pts**
Oregon 2007   **17**   **87**

This winery's best Pinot Gris yet, with bright tutti-frutti, pineapple, quince and Asian pear flavors.
Kitchen Survivor™ Grade: B

Your notes: _____

Livio Felluga (*LIV-ee-oh fuh-LOO-*   **$**   **Pts**
***guh*) Map Label Pinot Grigio, Italy 2007**   **18**   **86**

♆ 👍 *Lean, stylish,* and *exciting* are words pros use to describe this standout Pinot Grigio. I like the pretty floral nose, white pepper, and ripe apricot flavors.
Kitchen Survivor™ Grade: B

Your notes: _____

MacMurray Ranch Pinot Gris,   **$**   **Pts**
California 2007   **20**   **87**

Subtle honeyed pear and apricot, ginger scent, mineral finish; one of California's best Pinot Gris.
Kitchen Survivor™ Grade: B

Your notes: _____

Maso Canali Pinot Grigio,   **$**   **Pts**
Italy 2006   **23**   **87**

🍃 ♆ Expensive for PG, but it also delivers much more than you expect, It is sleek, minerally, citrusy, appley, layered and long. Pair it with shellfish pasta.
Kitchen Survivor™ Grade: A

Your notes: _____

Morgan R&D Franscioni Vineyard,   **$**   **Pts**
Pinot Gris, California 2007   **17**   **86**

🍎 I love the stylish mango and melon vibrance of this wine. Great on its own, or with spicy sushi.
Kitchen Survivor™ Grade: B

Your notes: _____

Pighin Pinot Grigio Grave,   **$**   **Pts**
Italy 2006   **16**   **90**

♆ 🍃 I was blown away by the savor and complex-

ity of this Grigio: white pepper, citrus zest, mineral grip, crisp apple. So zippy, lively and long - really cries out for some garlicky clams or a seafood stew.
Kitchen Survivor™ Grade: A

Your notes: _____

	$	Pts
Ponzi Pinot Gris, **Oregon 2007**	17	87

♟ This wine's mineral and ripe pear character is like classic Alsace Pinot Gris, but without the heaviness. Delicious with seafood salads.
Kitchen Survivor™ Grade: A

Your notes: _____

	$	Pts
Robert Mondavi Private Selection **Pinot Grigio, California 2006**	10	85

☺ One of the best budget Pinot Grigios from California! Easy-drinking, with lots of lively apricot and peach flavors. A great pick for parties.
Kitchen Survivor™ Grade: B+

Your notes: _____

	$	Pts
Ruffino Lumina Pinot Grigio, Venezia- **Giulia, Italy 2006**	13	83

♟ More to it than the usual Italian Pinot Grigio; pear flavor and mineral with scents of flowers and hay. Great with tomato-sauced pastas or sausages.
Kitchen Survivor™ Grade: C

Your notes: _____

	$	Pts
Santa Margherita Pinot Grigio, **Italy 2007**	18	82

Although some consumers and most trade tasters appraise Santa Margherita as "way overpriced," many still say it's a "favorite" that will "impress your friends." In my book, the exploding PG category offers so many better and cheaper alternatives.
Kitchen Survivor™ Grade: C

Your notes: _____

	$	Pts
Trimbach Pinot Gris Reserve, **Alsace, France 2004**	22	88

Subtle pear, with a "wow!" finish of almond croissant.
Kitchen Survivor™ Grade: B

Your notes: _____

Twin Fin Pinot Grigio,   **$**   **Pts**
California 2006   **8**   **84**

☺ Juicy-crisp pear and ripe cantaloupe flavors; one of the best price/value California Grigios, period.

Kitchen Survivor™ Grade: C

Your notes: _____

WillaKenzie Pinot Gris,   **$**   **Pts**
Oregon 2006   **17**   **85**

🍎 Juicily sippable canned pears and vanilla. Yummy on its own, but also a great bet to pear with spicy Thai or Indian fare.

Kitchen Survivor™ Grade: C

Your notes: _____

Willamette Valley Vineyard Pinot   **$**   **Pts**
Gris, Oregon 2007   **15**   **87**

🍴 "Great with food," thanks to the "crisp tartness" and "loads of flavor"—apricot, ginger and grapefruit.

Kitchen Survivor™ Grade: C

Your notes: _____

Woodbridge (Robert Mondavi)   **$**   **Pts**
Pinot Grigio, California 2007   **7.99**   **85**

☺ A favorite Woodbridge wine with my tasters, with "lively" lemon flavor that's "lipsmacking as a sipping wine," but also a nice pairing garlicky shrimp scampi.

Kitchen Survivor™ Grade: B

Your notes: _____

Riesling

Grape Profile: I am thrilled to say that after many years of steering clear, consumers have finally embraced Riesling, one of my very favorite grapes. There's lots to love, including the price/quality ratio, and high Kitchen Survivor™ survivor grades - thanks to their tangy, crisp acidity, Riesling wines really hold up in the fridge. That makes them ideal for lots of everyday dining situations, e.g., you want a glass of white with your takeout sushi, but your dinner mate wants red with the beef teriyaki. Or maybe you want to start with a glass of white wine while you're cooking dinner and then switch to red with the meal. It's nice to know that with many Rieslings you can go back to the wine over several days, and every glass will taste as good as the first one.

Germany, the traditional source of great Rieslings, continues to grow its presence in the *Guide*. And that's great, because no other region offers so many *world class* wines for under $25. Look for German Rieslings from the Mosel, Rheingau, Pfalz, and Nahe regions. Other go-to Riesling regions are Washington State, Australia, New Zealand, and Alsace, France.

Prepare to be impressed. Rieslings are light bodied but loaded with stunning fruit flavor, balanced with tangy acidity.

Serve: Lightly chilled is fine (the aromas really shine when it's not ice cold); it's good young and fresh, but the French and German versions can evolve nicely for up to 5 years.

When: Every day (okay, my personal taste there); classy enough for "important" meals and occasions.

With: Outstanding with shellfish and ethnic foods with a "kick" (think Asian, Thai, Indian, Mexican). There's also an awesome rule-breaker match: braised meats!

In: An all-purpose wineglass.

	$	Pts
Annie's Lane Clare Valley Riesling, Australia 2007	14	85

♟ The totally dry, zippy, juicy-peach and mineral flavor is perfect for "it's gonna be too sweet" Riesling-phobes. A perfect pairing with sole in lemon butter.
Kitchen Survivor™ Grade: A
Your notes: _____

	$	Pts
Beringer Napa Valley Dry Riesling, California 2006	14	85

A truly delicious offering that replaces their slightly sweet Johannisberg Riesling. Dense Fuji apple fruit, white flowers on the scent, light minerals in the finish.
Kitchen Survivor™ Grade: A
Your notes: _____

Blue Fish Sweet Riesling, Pfalz, Germany 2007

	$	Pts
	11	83

The popularity of this sweet, screwtop wine tells you: wine buyers are no longer afraid of either! It's soft for sipping, and can handle Tex-Mex and other foods with a kick.

Kitchen Survivor™ Grade: B

Your notes: _____

Bonny Doon Pacific Rim Dry Riesling, USA/Germany 2007

	$	Pts
	14	89

☺ ⚸ This endures as one of the most popular wines with my tasters—with raves about the "yummy, juicy-fruity yet dry" flavor. *Pacific Rim* is the winery's shorthand for "drink this with Asian foods."

Kitchen Survivor™ Grade: A

Your notes: _____

Chateau Ste. Michelle Columbia Valley Dry Riesling, Washington 2007

	$	Pts
	12	84

☺ Peach and apricot flavor and soft acidity underpin the apricot fruit of this crowd-pleaser Riesling. Nice with Indian, Thai or Chinese food.

Kitchen Survivor™ Grade: A+

Your notes: _____

Clean Slate Riesling, Germany 2007

	$	Pts
	11	85

♟ What's not to love? EZ open screwtop, delicious peaches 'n' cream/petrol/apple scents and flavors, great price.

Kitchen Survivor™ Grade: A

Your notes: _____

Columbia Crest Two Vines Riesling, Washington 2007

	$	Pts
	8	83

☺ This honeysuckle-peachy wine is "lip-smacking with spicy foods," and "a super value." A touch of sweetness balanced by zingy acidity, so it's not heavy.

Kitchen Survivor™ Grade: B

Your notes: _____

Columbia Winery Cellarmaster's	$	Pts
Reserve Riesling, Washington 2007	12	84

☺ Lush with ripe peach, apricot, and honey flavors, spiked with crisp acidity, and a touch of sweetness.
Kitchen Survivor™ Grade: A

Your notes: _____

Darting Durkhiemer Riesling Kabinett,	$	Pts
Pfalz, Germany 2007	17	89

👌 🏆 🌶 I'm always thrilled when I find this on wine lists. Its bewitching floral aromas and spicy-tangy core are just glorious—with food or without.
Kitchen Survivor™ Grade: A+

Your notes: _____

Dr. Konstantin Frank Dry Riesling,	$	Pts
New York 2007	18	88

🏆 What an impressive fan base for this wine; the "best dry Riesling in the United States" (I concur), which "comes close to German quality," with incredible peachy fruit density and zingy acidity.
Kitchen Survivor™ Grade: A

Your notes: _____

Dr. Loosen Riesling Kabinett	$	Pts
Estate, Germany 2006	20	85

🌶 🏆 "Perfect with Asian meals," say my tasters, because the mineral/petrol scents and steely acidity set off spicy and pungent flavors beautifully.
Kitchen Survivor™ Grade: A

Your notes: _____

Eroica (*ee-ROY-cuh*) Riesling,	$	Pts
Washington 2007	22	90

🍴 🌶 "The best Riesling made in America . . ."? It's a contender. The dense core of apple and peach fruit and mineral complexity make it "as good as top-notch German Riesling." Pairs beautifully with crab & lobster.
Kitchen Survivor™ Grade: A+

Your notes: _____

Fetzer Valley Oaks Johannisberg Riesling, California 2006

$ 12 Pts 83

🍷 They've lightened up on the sweetness of this wine, and the character is more delicate and floral - very nice. A delicious match with Chinese food.

Kitchen Survivor™ Grade: B+

Your notes: _____

Firestone Vineyard Riesling, California 2006

$ 12 Pts 83

☺ Riesling is Firestone's signature wine, and always a peachy, juicy, easy quaffer.

Kitchen Survivor™ Grade: C

Your notes: _____

Gunderloch Riesling Estate, Germany 2006

$ 17 Pts 89

👍 This wine exemplifies great German Riesling—so approachable, yet with amazing complexity: flowers, chamomile tea, fresh cream, white peach.

Kitchen Survivor™ Grade: A

Your notes: _____

Hogue Johannisberg Riesling, Washington 2007

$ 10 Pts 83

☺ Attention all white Zin fans: Here's a great alternative that's a little on the sweet side, with ripe, peachy fruit flavor and a candied orange finish.

Kitchen Survivor™ Grade: B

Your notes: _____

Jekel Riesling, California 2006

$ 11 Pts 84

Nice floral nose and juicy peach flavor. The touch of sweetness makes it a perfect partner for spicy foods.

Kitchen Survivor™ Grade: B+

Your notes: _____

J.J. Prum Riesling Kabinett Wehlener Sonnenuhr, Germany 2007

$ 22 Pts 85

👍 🏆 🍷 This is textbook Mosel Riesling—peaches-and-cream and petrol character, packed with concentration.

Kitchen Survivor™ Grade: A+

Your notes: _____

J. Lohr Bay Mist Riesling,   **$**   **Pts**
California 2007   **8.50**   **82**

What you expect for the price: a light and traightfor-ward Riesling with nice apple fruit and soft acidity.
Kitchen Survivor™ Grade: B

Your notes: _____

Johannishof Charta Riesling,   **$**   **Pts**
Rheingau, Germany, 2007   **17**   **85**

♟ For sweet-phobes, "charta" tells you "dry." This one tingles with Meyer lemon flavors and lingering minerals in the finish. Pair with sausages & Gruyere.
Kitchen Survivor™ Grade: A+

Your notes: _____

Kendall-Jackson Vintner's Reserve   **$**   **Pts**
Riesling, California 2006   **10**   **86**

☺ For tasters new to Riesling, I often suggest this one: a blue chip brand name & great varietal charac-ter - lush peach and tangerine fruit - for a great price.
Kitchen Survivor™ Grade: A

Your notes: _____

Kesselstatt RK Riesling,   **$**   **Pts**
Mosel, Germany 2007   **16**   **85**

❧ The light body, honeysuckle and petrol scent, soft peach-apple flavors, and creamy finish are textbook Mosel Riesling. An ideal match for crab or scallops.
Kitchen Survivor™ Grade: A

Your notes: _____

Leitz Dragonstone Riesling,   **$**   **Pts**
Rheingau, Germany 2007   **16**   **85**

"Excellent" lively, citrus zest and tangerine flavors. A great "intro" German Riesling to pair with spicy fare.
Kitchen Survivor™ Grade: A

Your notes: _____

Maximin Grunhauser Abtsberg   **$**   **Pts**
Riesling Spatelese, Mosel, Germay 2007   **31**   **88**

♟ ✤ Behold classic Mosel Riesling: slate-y, peach, honeysuckle & cream scents, a hint of sweetness and a bewitching honeyed-mineral quality in the finish.
Kitchen Survivor™ Grade: A

Your notes: _____

Mirassou Riesling,   **$**   **Pts**
California 2007   **12**   **84**

Not super complex, but a tasty bargain, with a touch of petrol in the scent and ripe apple-citrus fruit.
Kitchen Survivor™ Grade: B

Your notes: _____

Pierre Sparr Selection Riesling,   **$**   **Pts**
Alsace, France 2006   **14**   **87**

"When you're sick of oak, take this for the cure," say my tasters of this sleek, tangy, mouthwatering Riesling with the scent of honey and Asian pears. Yum!
Kitchen Survivor™ Grade: A+

Your notes: _____

Robert Mondavi Private Selection   **$**   **Pts**
Riesling, California 2007   **12**   **86**

☺ ⚡ How do they do it? The petrol and peach are classic Riesling, but the yum factor and great price are "house wine" material. Bravo!
Kitchen Survivor™ Grade: B+

Your notes: _____

Saint M Pfalz Riesling,   **$**   **Pts**
Germany 2006   **12**   **89**

🏆 Absolutely outstanding, and a gift at this price. Loaded with peaches and cream, mandarin orange and minerally-slatiness that just goes on and on.
Kitchen Survivor™ Grade: A+

Your notes: _____

Strub Niersteiner Paterberg   **$**   **Pts**
Riesling Spatlese, Germany 2007   **18**   **88**

☺ ⚡ "One of the best" Rieslings under $20. The lemon custard creaminess and lively acidity are a great match for steamed clams or summer salads.
Kitchen Survivor™ Grade: A+

Your notes: _____

Tim Adams "The Benefit" Riesling,   **$**   **Pts**
Australia 2007   **15**   **88**

⚡ Completely dry, with tangy starfruit, Granny Smith apple and lemon peel notes that linger in the finish. Pair it with Chinese, Thai or sushi.
Kitchen Survivor™ Grade: A

Your notes: _____

Trefethen Estate Dry Riesling, $ Pts
Napa 2007 22 87

♟ 👍🍷 Trefethen's decades of commitment to this grape shows in the petrol-y, green apple and mineral complexity. The bone dry racy style screams for a sophisticated seafood dish like Oysters Rockefeller.

Kitchen Survivor™ Grade: A

Your notes: _____

Trimbach Riesling, $ Pts
Alsace, France 2005 18 85

🍷 ♟ The fan club grows and grows for this Alsace classic. It's bone dry, with an amazing acidity and deep lemon–green apple flavor. World class.

Kitchen Survivor™ Grade: A+

Your notes: _____

Two Princes Riesling, $ Pts
Nahe, Germany 2007 13 84

🍎 Delicate and soft, with creamy peach-yogurt flavors; great with spicy fare or hard cheeses & sausages.

Kitchen Survivor™ Grade: A+

Your notes: _____

Wakefield Promised Land Riesling, $ Pts
Australia 2005 13 84

🍎 A lot of complexity for this price: classical petrol note overlaying rich but laser-pure flavors and scents of mandarin orange and honeysuckle, with good acid to balance the touch of sweetness.

Kitchen Survivor™ Grade: A+

Your notes: _____

Wolf-Blass Yellow Label Riesling, $ Pts
Australia 2006 10 85

🍷 What a treat to find a Riesling at this price with not only citrus peel and juicy peach character, but the classic "petrol" note of its French and German brethren. Bravo!

Kitchen Survivor™ Grade: A+

Your notes: _____

Sauvignon Blanc/Fume Blanc

Grape Profile: Sauvignon Blanc (*soh-veen-yoan BLAHNK*), one of my favorite white wine grapes, is on the rise, and for good reason: Truly great ones are still available for under $15—something you can't say about many wine categories these days. Depending on where it's grown (cool, moderate, or warm zones), the exotically pungent scent and taste range from zesty and herbal to tangy lime-grapefruit to juicy peach and melon, with vibrant acidity. The grape's home base is France's Loire Valley and Bordeaux regions. The Loire Valley versions are usually minerally, with elegance and great acidity; the Bordeaux versions are most often barrel-fermented and blended with the local Semillon grape, giving them a waxy, creamy richness. California and Washington State make excellent versions, oftened labeled Fume Blanc (*FOO-may BLAHNK*) - a tip-off that the wine is barrel-fermented and barrel-aged, and thus fuller in body. In the Southern Hemisphere, New Zealand Sauvignon Blancs continue to earn pro and consumer raves, South Africa produces some smokin' examples, and now Chile is coming on strong with great bottlings that scream character for a bargain price. Another of Sauvignon Blanc's major virtues is its food versatility: It goes so well with the foods many people eat regularly (especially those following a less-red-meat regimen), like chicken and turkey, salads, sushi, Mexican, and vegetarian.

THANKS, KIWIS! Most New Zealand Sauvignon Blancs are now bottled with a screw cap for your convenience and to ensure you get fresh wine without "corkiness" (see "Buying Lingo" for a definition). Hooray!

Serve: Chilled but not ice cold.

When: An amazing food partner, but the tasting notes also spotlight styles that are good on their own, as an aperitif.

With: As noted, great with most everyday eats as well as popular ethnic tastes like Mexican food.

In: An all-purpose wineglass.

Arboleda Sauvignon Blanc,   **$**   **Pts**
California 2007   **17**   **86**

🌿 A super example of how Chile is making it happen with the SB grape. Buys like a bargain, but tastes truly impressive, with grassy and herbaceous, vivid green apple, pineapple and lime sorbet notes.

Kitchen Survivor™ Grade: A

Your notes: _____

Babich Sauvignon Blanc, Marlborough   **$**   **Pts**
New Zealand 2007   **12**   **85**

🌿 This "zingy, appley" bottling always delivers value and classic NZ character. It's "a great food wine."

Kitchen Survivor™ Grade: A

Your notes: _____

Benziger Sauvignon Blanc,   **$**   **Pts**
Sonoma, California 2007   **15**   **86**

A "great wine list buy," say fans, citing the bright citrus, apple, and melon aromas and crisp acidity that make it great with a wide range of foods.

Kitchen Survivor™ Grade: B

Your notes: _____

Beringer Sauvignon Blanc, Napa,   **$**   **Pts**
California 2007   **15**   **87**

🍎 A lush potion of Granny Smith apple, lime, kiwi, melon. It's both juicy and crisp, to drink solo or pair with grilled shrimp, Tex Mex, fried chicken, life itself.

Kitchen Survivor™ Grade: A

Your notes: _____

Bonterra Sauvignon Blanc,   **$**   **Pts**
Mendocino, California 2007   **14**   **88**

🍎 Bonterra is one of the largest wineries using all organically-grown grapes, and also one of the best. This SB drips with juicy melon and kiwi flavors.

Kitchen Survivor™ Grade: A

Your notes: _____

Brampton Sauvignon Blanc, Rustenberg   **$**   **Pts**
South Africa 2007   **14**   **90**

🌿 As good as it gets from S. Africa. A juiced-up palate of key lime, kiwi and gooseberry. Pair it with coconut milk curries, or risotto with shrimp & herbs.

Kitchen Survivor™ Grade: A

Your notes: _____

Brancott Reserve Sauvignon Blanc,   **$**   **Pts**
Marlborough, New Zealand 2007   **17** **87**
👍 "One of New Zealand's best" SBs, with "lavish" herb and passion fruit flavors and a light smokiness in the finish. Pair it with smoked salmon eggs Benedict.
Kitchen Survivor™ Grade: A+
Your notes: _____

Brancott Sauvignon Blanc,   **$**   **Pts**
Marlborough, New Zealand 2007   **11** **87**
☺ One of my panel's perennial favorites: "Like summertime on the front porch," said one taster. You can smell the cut grass along with gooseberry, grapefruit and kaffir lime leaves. Bring on the guacamole!
Kitchen Survivor™ Grade: A
Your notes: _____

Cakebread Cellars Sauvignon Blanc,   **$**   **Pts**
Napa, California 2007   **30** **87**
🍎 👍 Fans of Cakebread's Chardonnay try this. The vibrant grapefruit aromas with a hint of fig and vanilla give fantastic bang for the buck.
Kitchen Survivor™ Grade: A
Your notes: _____

Casa Lapostolle (*lah-poh-STOLE*)   **$**   **Pts**
Sauvignon Blanc, Casablanca, Chile 2007 **10** **87**
☺ This bottling has so much more than I expect at this price: vivid honeydew, kiwi flavors, and a long finish. Pair it with ceviche or guacamole.
Kitchen Survivor™ Grade: A
Your notes: _____

Chalk Hill Winery Sauvignon Blanc,   **$**   **Pts**
Chalk Hill-Sonoma, California 2006   **28** **90**
🍷 🍎 Like all of Chalk Hill's wines, this SB is sumptuous without being over-the-top. The honeyed fig and melon flavors, and vanilla oakiness, are just what the doctor ordered for any fish in a *beurre blanc* sauce.
Kitchen Survivor™ Grade: B
Your notes: _____

Chateau Coucheroy Bordeaux Blanc,   **$**   **Pts**
Graves, France 2005   **17**   **88**

♟ Tasted blind, this rivaled classified Bordeaux whites at 3x the price. Creamy, minerally, waxy lemon and almond flavors, with a really long finish.
Kitchen Survivor™ Grade: B+
Your notes: _____

Chateau Ste. Michelle Columbia Valley   **$**   **Pts**
Sauvignon Blanc, Washington 2007   **10**   **88**

☺ Three cheers: tasty, affordable, consistent. Okay, four—exotic: grapefruit and lemongrass scent, ginger flavor, creamy texture. Irresistible with sushi or crab.
Kitchen Survivor™ Grade: B
Your notes: _____

Chateau St. Jean Fume Blanc,   **$**   **Pts**
Sonoma, California 2006   **12**   **87**

A touch of barrel aging gives this wine a creamy scent, balanced by fruit flavors of grapefruit, melon, and fig, plus tangy acidity. Smokin' for the price.
Kitchen Survivor™ Grade: B+
Your notes: _____

Chimney Rock Fume Blanc,   **$**   **Pts**
Napa, California 2007   **19**   **88**

This wine leaps out of the glass with lively melon, cucumber, lime and floral notes. A great partner for sushi, avocado-crab salad, or goat cheese.
Kitchen Survivor™ Grade: A
Your notes: _____

Cloudy Bay Sauvignon Blanc,   **$**   **Pts**
Marlborough, New Zealand 2007   **28**   **85**

👍 This wine put the now-famous "grassy gooseberry" style of NZ SBs on the map in the 1980s. The consensus is that it's "hard to find" and "expensive" but "still yummy," especially "with Thai shrimp."
Kitchen Survivor™ Grade: A
Your notes: _____

Dancing Bull Sauvignon Blanc,   **$**   **Pts**
California 2007   **12**   **84**

Tasty peach fruit with a twist of lime; great price!
Kitchen Survivor™ Grade: B
Your notes: _____

Domaine Vincent Delaporte   **$**   **Pts**
Sancerre, Loire, France 2006   24   87

🔧 ⚚ "Classic" Sancerre with lime, talc, and grape-fruit notes that are a classic match for fresh goat cheese.

Kitchen Survivor™ Grade: A+

Your notes: _____

Dry Creek Vineyard Fume Blanc,   **$**   **Pts**
Sonoma, California 2007   12   85

☺ The vivid tangerine and peach flavors, and the nice price, are great for porch-sippin' and picnics.

Kitchen Survivor™ Grade: A

Your notes: _____

Drylands Marlborough Sauvignon Blanc,   **$**   **Pts**
New Zealand 2007   15   87

The yin of crushed herbs and the yang of passion fruit cry out for shellfish ceviche or dilled salmon.

Kitchen Survivor™ Grade: A

Your notes: _____

Duckhorn Sauvignon Blanc, Napa   **$**   **Pts**
California 2007   23   89

🔧 👋 The "high price" reflects a premium for the famous Duckhorn name, but the tangerine fruit, nice balance, and awesome length are worth it when you want to impress. Pair with sundried tomato pasta.

Kitchen Survivor™ Grade: A

Your notes: _____

Edna Valley Vineyard Paragon Sauvignon   **$**   **Pts**
Blanc, Edna Valley, California 2007   12   85

This Chardonnay house makes a fine SB, too, with layers of lemon, green apple and mineral and a clean, snappy finish. Toss up a goat cheese salad and enjoy!

Kitchen Survivor™ Grade: B

Your notes: _____

Emmolo Sauvignon Blanc,   **$**   **Pts**
Napa, California 2005   15   86

🔧 👋 A mouthwatering explosion of exotic, pure peach and mango fruit that lingers in the finish.

Kitchen Survivor™ Grade: A

Your notes: _____

Ferrari-Carano Fume Blanc, Sonoma, California 2007 **$** 17 **Pts** 86

☺ This is one of California's benchmark Fumes, balancing grapefruit and subtle herbaceousness with richness from the touch of oak and the exotic tropical-guava-mango fruit. Delish!

Kitchen Survivor™ Grade: B+

Your notes: _____

Flora Springs Soliloquy, Napa, California 2007 **$** 25 **Pts** 91

☖ ♟ I love the laser-pure key lime and kiwi fruit, steely minerality and tingly acidity of this vibrant wine that's tailor-made for mussels or sushi.

Kitchen Survivor™ Grade: A+

Your notes: _____

Frei Brothers Reserve Sauvignon Blanc Russian River Valley, California 2007 **$** 20 **Pts** 87

🍎 The price is edging up, but the fresh, vivid cling peach and passion fruit flavors and incredibly long finish really impress. Match it with coconut milk curries, or scallops in a tarragon cream sauce.

Kitchen Survivor™ Grade: A

Your notes: _____

Frog's Leap Sauvignon Blanc, Rutherford, Napa, California 2007 **$** 18 **Pts** 89

👍 ♟ A wine list regular worth looking for. The 100% SB character of gooseberries and flinty, penetrating citrus is always utterly delicious (not just leap years!).

Kitchen Survivor™ Grade: A

Your notes: _____

Geyser Peak Sauvignon Blanc, Alexander Valley, California 2006 **$** 14 **Pts** 85

This is a tasty, classic California Sauvignon Blanc, combining the crisp tang of citrus with the juicier taste of kiwi. Match it with bacon-arugula salad.

Kitchen Survivor™ Grade: B+

Your notes: _____

Girard Sauvignon Blanc, Napa, California 2007 $ 15 Pts 89

♀ Honeydew & Asian pear flavor that always tastes like twice the price. Pair with goat cheese crostini.

Kitchen Survivor™ Grade: A+

Your notes: _____

Grgich (*GER-gich;* both are hard *g* as in *girl*) Hills Fume Blanc, Napa, California 2007 $ 28 Pts 91

♀ ✋ Grgich's signature style is crisp, with scents of fresh herbs and citrus and flavors of grapefruit and melon. Pair with Cioppino or chowder.

Kitchen Survivor™ Grade: B+

Your notes: _____

Groth Sauvignon Blanc, Napa, California 2007 $ 18 Pts 88

🍎 Barrel aging gives this wine a signature fig and cream richness, perfectly balanced with citrusy acidity. Pair it with tomato-mozzarella-basil salad.

Kitchen Survivor™ Grade: A

Your notes: _____

Gunn Estate Sauvignon Blanc, Marlborough, New Zealand 2007 $ 15 Pts 88

This is classic NZ SB on steroids. Intense key lime, passion fruit and crushed herb notes, with a touch of green pepper in the finish, make it a perfect partner for cilantro-laced dishes, goat cheese, shellfish.

Kitchen Survivor™ Grade: B

Your notes: _____

Hall Sauvignon Blanc, Napa, California 2007 $ 20 Pts 84

A solid offering in the clean, citrusy-grapefruit style that's a perfet match for raw oysters or spicy wings.

Kitchen Survivor™ Grade: B

Your notes: _____

Hanna Sauvignon Blanc, Russian River Valley, California 2007 $ 18 Pts 85

🍎 The lively passion fruit, grass and grapefruit notes are classic for Russian River SB. A great match for spinach and feta crostini, or fennel foccacia.

Kitchen Survivor™ Grade: ?

Your notes: _____

Hogue Fume Blanc, Columbia Valley, Washington 2007
   $ 10   **Pts** 84

☺ "A very good wine at a very good price," with fresh apple, herbs, and citrus peel plus a juicy mouthfeel.

Kitchen Survivor™ Grade: A+

Your notes: _____

Honig Sauvignon Blanc, Napa, California 2007
   $ 16   **Pts** 87

⚡ "Excellent!" SB that balances mango and passion fruit with steely, grapefruity subtlety. A great match for oysters & clams, or fresh goat cheese.

Kitchen Survivor™ Grade: B+

Your notes: _____

Joel Gott Sauvignon Blanc, California 2007
   $ 12   **Pts** 86

☺ A super price for such a scrumptious Sauvignon Blanc dripping with honeydew, kiwi, and lime flavors.

Kitchen Survivor™ Grade: A+

Your notes:: _____

Jolivet (Pascal) Sancerre (*jhoe-lee-VAY sahn-SAIR*), France 2005
   $ 23   **Pts** 88

🏆 ⚡ A perennial favorite with my tasters, this wine's well balanced and utterly "alive" taste and scent (lemongrass, lime cream, and honey) are great for the price. Mathc with a goat cheese-herb omelet.

Kitchen Survivor™ Grade: A+

Your notes: _____

Joseph Phelps Sauvignon Blanc, Napa, California 2006
   $ 32   **Pts** 87

👍 "You pay for" the French barrel aging and the pedigree, but the wine is quite luscious and complex, with layers of grapefruit, fennel, lemon oil and minerals.

Kitchen Survivor™ Grade: B+

Your notes: _____

Kendall Jackson Vintner's Rerserve Sauvignon Blanc, California 2007
   $ 12   **Pts** 87

🍎 ☺ "Lipsmacking" is the word for this "best value" Sauvignon Blanc with great lime and grapefruit top notes fattened up by melon and fig. Yum!

Kitchen Survivor™ Grade: A

Your notes: _____

Kenwood Sauvignon Blanc, Sonoma, California 2006   **$** 12   **Pts** 84

☺ The taste of this lovely Sauvignon Blanc reminds me of a melon salad with lime, honey, and mint.

Kitchen Survivor™ Grade: A

Your notes: _____

Kim Crawford Sauvignon Blanc, Marlborough, New Zealand 2008   **$** 19   **Pts** 89

♟ The superb price-quality makes this a "major favorite" with my panel. It's got laser-pure SB fruit—key lime, passion fruit, and honeydew with a hint of grassiness—and an incredibly long finish.

Kitchen Survivor™ Grade: A+

Your notes: _____

Kunde Magnolia Lane Sauvignon Blanc, Sonoma, California 2006   **$** 16   **Pts** 85

Tasty and refreshing, with lively grapefruit and tangerine flavors and scents. Nice on its own, but also great with a Greek salad (feta, tomatoes, olives).

Kitchen Survivor™ Grade: C

Your notes: _____

Lucien Crochet (*loo-SYEN crow-SHAY*) Sancerre, France 2005   **$** 23   **Pts** 88

♟ ⚗ ⚑ ☞ "Definitive Sauvignon Blanc" is the consensus on this top-scoring wine. The floral-herbaceous nose, creamy-but-not-heavy texture, crisp citrus flavor, and finesse are "a huge relief for the oak-weary."

Kitchen Survivor™ Grade: B+

Your notes: _____

Markham Vineyards Sauvignon Blanc, Napa, California 2006   **$** 15   **Pts** 85

☺ A nice go-to SB that's "on lots of wine lists." The grilled pineapple and lemon pie flavors make for tasty solo sipping, but also pair well with Caesar salad.

Kitchen Survivor™ Grade: B

Your notes: _____

Mason Sauvignon Blanc, Napa, California 2006   **$** 16   **Pts** 87

🍎 I love this kiwi and passion fruit–scented wine

that's "like New Zealand Sauvignon Blanc without the grassiness." Great for spicy food, and awesome value.

Kitchen Survivor™ Grade: B+

Your notes: _____

Matanzas Creek Sauvignon Blanc,   **$**   **Pts**
Sonoma, California 2007   **24**   **91**

I have put this classy, blue chip SB on wine lists for years, and it always delivers great fruit lushness and palate weight - like a Chardonnay with better acidity for fine cuisine such as lobster or scallops.

Kitchen Survivor™ Grade: A+

Your notes: _____

Merryvale Starmont Sauvignon Blanc,   **$**   **Pts**
Napa, California 2007   **17**   **85**

One of the best wines in Merryvale's lineup, with lush and lively kiwi, melon, and grapefruit flavors.

Kitchen Survivor™ Grade: B

Your notes: _____

Monkey Bay Sauvignon Blanc,   **$**   **Pts**
New Zealand 2007   **11**   **87**

☺ Amazing—this wine bested benchmark Cloudy Bay *twice* in blind tastings with pro palates. Cut grass, lime, grapefruit, long finish—cool label, too!

Kitchen Survivor™ Grade: A

Your notes: _____

Morgan Sauvignon Blanc, Monterey,   **$**   **Pts**
California 2007   **16**   **87**

Another of my go-to wine list picks, because it's so luscious —cling peach, pineapple and lime —and yet pairs so well with anything from garlic to wasabi.

Kitchen Survivor™ Grade: A+

Your notes: _____

Murphy-Goode Fume Blanc,   **$**   **Pts**
California 2006   **12**   **83**

The oaky & tropical "Chardonnay-like" style is a good intro to the tangy SB grape.

Kitchen Survivor™ Grade: C

Your notes: _____

Nobilo Sauvignon Blanc, Marlborough   **$**   **Pts**
New Zealand 2008   **13**   **85**

☺ This NZ SB took the market by storm, offering the classic grapefruit/herbal style the region is known for, at a "great price." Pair it with smoked salmon.

Kitchen Survivor™ Grade: A+

Your notes: _____

Provenance Vineyards Rutherford   **$**   **Pts**
Sauvignon Blanc, California 2007   **20**   **88**

🍎 Irresistible, lipsmacking flavors of honeydew, peach compote and vanilla cream. One of the most decadent and delicious Sauvignon Blancs, period.

Kitchen Survivor™ Grade: A+

Your notes: _____

Rancho Zabaco Sauvignon Blanc,   **$**   **Pts**
Russian River Valley, California 2007   **18**   **87**

Succulent kiwi and honeydew flavors with a whisper of tarragon that carries into the finish. Pair it with scallops with tarragon cream sauce, or grilled shrimp.

Kitchen Survivor™ Grade: B

Your notes: _____

Redwood Creek Sauvignon Blanc,   **$**   **Pts**
California 2007   **8**   **83**

Lively, "tropical" fruit flavor for a "good price."

Kitchen Survivor™ Grade: C

Your notes: _____

Robert Mondavi Napa Fume Blanc,   **$**   **Pts**
Napa, California 2007   **20**   **91**

♀ ☺ Perennially one of Mondavi's best wines, this always wines my blind tastings. It's got fruit, spice, and lemongrass; vivid citrus; and a rich texture.

Kitchen Survivor™ Grade: B+

Your notes: _____

Robert Mondavi To-Ka-Lon Reserve   **$**   **Pts**
Fume Blanc, Napa, California 2006   **40**   **90**

♀ 👍 Waxy, honeyed, rich and layered, with plenty of lemon pie acidity to balance. A Gruyere gratin, or a Hollandaise dish, are blow-you-away pairings.

Kitchen Survivor™ Grade: B+

Your notes: _____

Rodney Strong Charlotte's Home   **$**   **Pts**
Sauvignon Blanc, Sonoma, California 2007   **14**   **86**

🍎 The SB grassiness plays background to the sumptuous spiced pear, mango and pineapple fruit.

Kitchen Survivor™ Grade: B

Your notes: _____

Sauvignon Republic Russian River Valley   **$**   **Pts**
Sauvignon Blanc, California 2007   **18**   **87**

🍎 Totally thrilling and lipsmacking, with green apple Jolly Rancher, kiwi and passion fruit flavors.

Kitchen Survivor™ Grade: B

Your notes: _____

Souverain Sauvignon Blanc, Alexander   **$**   **Pts**
Valley, Sonoma, California 2007   **15**   **88**

Souverain's quality across the board is exceptional for the price. There's lots of juicy melon, peach and citrus fruit with a whisper of herbaceousness that makes this a great match for seafood salads & sushi.

Kitchen Survivor™ Grade: A

Your notes: _____

St. Supery Sauvignon Blanc, Napa,   **$**   **Pts**
California 2006   **23**   **90**

🏺 Perennially one of the best" California Sauvignon Blancs, with a "bright, crisp and amazingly complex" flavor—"peach and lime," as well as a lingering creaminess that pairs beautifully with cream sauces.

Kitchen Survivor™ Grade: A+

Your notes: _____

Silverado Miller Ranch Sauvignon Blanc,   **$**   **Pts**
Napa, California 2006   **17**   **89**

🏆 Free of oak, and chock-full of laser-pure fruit: melon, apple, grapefruit and passion fruit.

Kitchen Survivor™ Grade: B

Your notes: _____

Simi Sauvignon Blanc, Sonoma,   **$**   **Pts**
California 2007   **15**   **85**

This wine's got a creamy roundness from oak, balanced with a clean melony tang. Great with ceviche.

Kitchen Survivor™ Grade: B+

Your notes: _____

Spy Valley Sauvignon Blanc,   **$**   **Pts**
Marlborough, New Zealand 2007   **14**   **87**

"Tart apples with a nice grassy finish" make this "wonderful" wine a NZ classic, and one of the best on the market for the money. Pair it with briny seafood.

Kitchen Survivor™ Grade: A

Your notes: _____

Sterling Vineyards Napa County   **$**   **Pts**
Sauvignon Blanc, California 2007   **15**   **87**

This "go-to brand" has grapefruit, nectarine, and key lime flavors and scents. Amazing value!

Kitchen Survivor™ Grade: B+

Your notes: _____

Trinchero Family Sauvignon Blanc,   **$**   **Pts**
Santa Barbara, California 2007   **10**   **85**

This wine really delivers for the bargain price, with zingy acidity and citrus-melon flavors that are tailor-made for smoked salmon & dill, or garlicky shrimp.

Kitchen Survivor™ Grade: B

Your notes: _____

Veramonte Sauvignon Blanc,   **$**   **Pts**
Chile 2007   **12**   **88**

Another superb bargain offering in Chilean SB, with exotic kiwi, honeydew, and passion fruit flavors.

Kitchen Survivor™ Grade: B+

Your notes: _____

Villa Maria Private Bin Sauvignon   **$**   **Pts**
Blanc, New Zealand 2006   **14**   **85**

This New Zealand Sauvignon Blanc offers a nice balance between the grassy/herbal scent, and the tangy passion fruit-melon taste. Pair it with an herb omelet.

Kitchen Survivor™ Grade: B+

Your notes: _____

Voss Sauvignon Blanc,   **$**   **Pts**
California 2007   **16**   **87**

A super-lively Sauvignon Blanc—juicy with lips-macking kiwi, white peach, and grapefruit flavors.

Kitchen Survivor™ Grade: B+

Your notes: _____

Wairau River Sauvignon Blanc, **$** **Pts**
Marlborough, New Zealand 2007 **17** **88**

Textbook NZ SB style. Think the "3Gs": grapefruit, grass and gooseberry. Pair it with another "g," goat cheese, and the fruit comes bursting forth.

Kitchen Survivor™ Grade: A+

Your notes: _____

Waterbrook Sauvignon Blanc, Columbia **$** **Pts**
Valley, Washington 2006 **12** **86**

Across the board, this brand offers something rare at this price - complexity! This wine's layers of apricot and melon, and nice palate weight, make it great to sip on its own, or to pair with crab or curried shrimp.

Kitchen Survivor™ Grade: B

Your notes: _____

Chardonnay

Grape Profile: Chardonnay is the top-selling white varietal wine in this country and the fullest-bodied of the major white grapes. That rich body, along with Chardonnay's signature fruit intensity, could explain its extraordinary popularity with Americans, although in truth this grape's style is pretty chameleonlike. It can yield wines of legendary quality, ranging from crisp and austere to soft and juicy to utterly lush and exotic (and very often oaky), depending on whether it's grown in a cool, moderate, or warm climate. I am pleased to say that, as these notes indicate, buyers find all of these styles worthy, perhaps offering some hope to pros who bemoan a noticeable "sameness" to many of the brand names. All Chardonnays are modeled on white Burgundy wines from France. The world-class versions are known for complexity, and often oakiness; the very best are age worthy. The rest, in the $ and $$ price categories, are pleasant styles meant for current drinking. California Chardonnays by far dominate store and restaurant sales, but the quality and value of both Washington State's and Australia's are just as good. Although no Oregon offerings made the survey due to limited production, they're worth sampling. And while Sauvignon Blanc is New Zealand's calling card, check out their unoaked Chardonnays, too.

Serve: Chilled; however, extreme cold mutes the complexity of the top bottlings. Pull them off the ice if they get too cold.

When: There's no occasion where Chardonnay *isn't* welcomed by the majority of wine lovers; the grape's abundant fruit makes it great on its own, as an aperitif or a cocktail alternative.

With: Some sommeliers carp that Chardonnay "doesn't go well with food," but I don't think most consumers agree. Maybe they have a point that it "overpowers" some delicate culinary creations in luxury restaurants, but for those of us doing most of our eating and drinking in less-rarefied circumstances, it's a great partner for all kinds of food. The decadent, oaky/buttery styles that are California's calling card can even handle steak. And my personal favorite matches are lobster when I'm splurging, and buttered popcorn when I'm not.

In: An all-purpose wineglass.

A by Acacia Chardonnay,	**$**	**Pts**
California 2007	**11**	**84**

A value bottling from a Chardonnay specialist (they make nice Pinot, too). Delicate and crisp apple flavors make it a CA Chard that compliments rather than overtakes food.

Kitchen Survivor™ Grade: B

Your notes: _____

Acacia Chardonnay Carneros, Napa	**$**	**Pts**
California 2006	**22**	**89**

🍷 An elegant Chardonnay with apple-vanilla subtlety and a long mineral finish that warrants a delicate meal such as sole with lemon butter.

Kitchen Survivor™ Grade: B

Your notes: _____

Alexander Valley Vyds Estate Chardonnay,	**$**	**Pts**
Alexander Valley, California 2006	**15**	**88**

🍷 This Chard bursts with crisp Fuji apple and pear flavors, with lots of juicy acidity that makes it super with food – particularly shellfish and Caesar salad.

Kitchen Survivor™ Grade: B

Your notes: _____

Alice White Chardonnay,	$	Pts
Australia 2007	9	85

☺ A lot of lip-smacking Golden Delicious apple fruit for not a lot of money. Great price & taste for parties.

Kitchen Survivor™ Grade: B+

Your notes: _____

Arrowood Chardonnay, Sonoma,	$	Pts
California 2007	30	85

A Sonoma classic Chardonnay that strikes a subtle balance of toasty oak and plump peach and apple fruit.

Kitchen Survivor™ Grade: B+

Your notes: _____

Au Bon Climat Santa Barbara	$	Pts
Chardonnay, California 2006	20	89

🍃 The "elegant tropical fruit" makes this "twice the wine at half the price" compared to many big-name California Chardonnays. Fabulous with crab salad.

Kitchen Survivor™ Grade: A

Your notes: _____

Beaulieu Vineyard (BV) Coastal	$	Pts
Estates Chardonnay, California 2006	9	84

This Chardonnay is a solid performer with my tasters, with textbook apple-pear flavors and a not-too-heavy style that pairs nicely with chicken salad or Caesar.

Kitchen Survivor™ Grade: C

Your notes: _____

Beaulieu Vineyard (BV) Carneros	$	Pts
Chardonnay, California 2006	19	86

Elegant and subtly creamy, the wine fills out with honeyed apple compote fruit in the mid-palate and a lingering talcum and cream finish.

Kitchen Survivor™ Grade: C

Your notes: _____

Benziger Family Chardonnay Los Carneros,	$	Pts
Sonoma, California 2007	18	87

Cool-climate Carneros fruit gives this crisp apple-flavored Chard juicy acidity and subtlety.

Kitchen Survivor™ Grade: C

Your notes: _____

Beringer Founders' Estate   **$**   **Pts**
Chardonnay, California 2006   **11**   **84**

For the money, a "clean and soft," "consistent" value Chard with easy-drinking apple fruit.

Kitchen Survivor™ Grade: C

Your notes: _____

Beringer Napa Chardonnay,   **$**   **Pts**
California 2006   **16**   **86**

☺ A benchmark Napa Valley Chardonnay with ripe fruit and soft but toasty oak, for a great price.

Kitchen Survivor™ Grade: C

Your notes: _____

Beringer Private Reserve Chardonnay,   **$**   **Pts**
California 2006   **35**   **89**

One of the best releases yet of this wine, with subtle layers of apple, pear and pineapple fruit kissed by soft vanilla and allspice flavors and scents. Classic Napa.

Kitchen Survivor™ Grade: C

Your notes: _____

Blackstone Monterey Chardonnay,   **$**   **Pts**
California 2007   **12**   **84**

"Fruity" and buttery, with great roundness in the mouth.

Kitchen Survivor™ Grade: C

Your notes: _____

Bonterra Chardonnay, Mendocino,   **$**   **Pts**
California 2006   **14**   **86**

Cheers to the tropical fruit juiciness that impresses for the price, and to the grape farming - all organic.

Kitchen Survivor™ Grade: B

Your notes: _____

Buena Vista Carneros Chardonnay,   **$**   **Pts**
California 2006   **19**   **85**

Lots of lush Cali Chard character for the money, with buttery grilled pineapple flavors and a long finish.

Kitchen Survivor™ Grade: B+

Your notes: _____

Cakebread Cellars Napa Chardonnay,   **$**   **Pts**
California 2007   **45**   **88**

✋ This is a Napa classic in style - toasty oak, rich baked apple fruit - and pedigree (everybody loves the blue chip name). Big enough to even pair with steak.

Kitchen Survivor™ Grade: B

Your notes: _____

Cambria Katherine's Vineyard   **$**   **Pts**
Chardonnay, California 2006   **19**   **86**

🍎 A "big seller" in the buttery, oaky style, with rich tropical fruit for the price. Great with corn chowder.

Kitchen Survivor™ Grade: C

Your notes: _____

Casa Lapostolle Cuvee Alexandre   **$**   **Pts**
Chardonnay, Casablanca, Chile 2006   **14**   **86**

🍎 A benchmark "oaky" Chardonnay with toasty, cinnamon-spice, vanilla, and rich tropical fruit.

Kitchen Survivor™ Grade: B

Your notes: _____

Catena Chardonnay, Mendoza,   **$**   **Pts**
Argentina 2006   **18**   **89**

🍺 🏆 👍 A "rarity" among New World Chards with "the ideal balance" of ripe fruit and oak, along with subtle, almost Burgundian, floral and mineral notes.

Kitchen Survivor™ Grade: B

Your notes: _____

Chalk Hill Chardonnay,   **$**   **Pts**
California 2005   **40**   **93**

🍺 🍎 The toasty oak and luscious mango-grilled pineapple fruit are big enough to pair even with steak. The price is reasonable, and the quality often better, compared to other luxury California Chards. It ages really well, too. Pair with truffled scrambled eggs.

Kitchen Survivor™ Grade: B

Your notes: _____

Chalone Chardonnay Estate, Chalone,   **$**   **Pts**
California 2006   **25**   **91**

🍺 🏆 👍 For decades, a favorite of wine lovers for its "unique mineral quality," elegance, and "beautiful stone fruit" flavor. Pairs with grilled fish and chicken, or mushroom pasta, beautifully. Ages great, too.

Kitchen Survivor™ Grade: B+

Your notes: _____

Chateau Montelena Chardonnay, $ Pts
Napa, California 2006 42 89

♟ ☝"Worth every penny," say tasters of Montelena's understated elegance, featuring flinty-spicy aromas; crisp apple fruit; and a subtle, long finish.

Kitchen Survivor™ Grade: A

Your notes: _____

Chateau Ste. Michelle Columbia $ Pts
Valley Chardonnay, Washington 2006 13 87

"A lot of yum for the money": tasty pear-citrus fruit and a buttery scent in perfect balance for solo sipping, and for pairing with fish or chicken on the grill.

Kitchen Survivor™ Grade: B

Your notes: _____

Chateau St. Jean Robert Young $ Pts
Chardonnay, Alexander Vly, California 2006 25 92

♟ ♟ A "California classic" with "amazing balance" of "subtle" oak framing the Asian pear fruit. I also find impressive mineral depth and Burgundy-like nuttiness that would pair perfectly with trout almondine.

Kitchen Survivor™ Grade: B

Your notes: _____

Chateau St. Jean Chardonnay, $ Pts
Sonoma, California 2007 15 86

☺ A classic, offering great "quality for the price," rich tropical and pear fruit, and restrained oak.

Kitchen Survivor™ Grade: B

Your notes: _____

Clos du Bois Chardonnay, Sonoma, $ Pts
California 2006 14 84

☺ A huge seller, for good reason: lots of citrus and melon fruit with subtle oak—at a good price.

Kitchen Survivor™ Grade: B

Your notes: _____

Columbia Crest Grand Estates $ Pts
Chardonnay, Washington 2007 11 86

☺ "Great value" thanks to the sweet spices, baked-apple fruit, and a hint of butter, at an easy price.

Kitchen Survivor™ Grade: B+

Your notes: _____

Cuvaison (*KOO-veh-sahn*) Carneros   **$**   **Pts**
Chardonnay, California 2006   **22**   **89**

🍎 This is a "wow" for the price, with a luscious tropical richness and lavish-but-balanced oak. Delish with grilled corn on the cob and steamed clams.

Fridge Survivor Grade: B

Your notes: _____

Dynamite Vineyards Chardonnay,   **$**   **Pts**
North Coast, California 2007   **11**   **84**

A good party wine because clean and juicy, with crowd-pleasing flavors of peach and tangerine.

Kitchen Survivor™ Grade: C

Your notes: _____

Edna Valley Vineyard Paragon   **$**   **Pts**
Chardonnay, California 2007   **12**   **86**

Medium-bodied and elegant, with lots of layers for the price - tangerine, nectarine, only a whisper of oak.

Kitchen Survivor™ Grade: B

Your notes: _____

Estancia Pinnacles Ranches Chardonnay,   **$**   **Pts**
Monterey, California 2007   **12**   **85**

This popular Chard is lively and balanced, with lemony acidity and soft apple fruit. Great with polenta.

Kitchen Survivor™ Grade: B

Your notes: _____

Far Niente Estate Bottled Chardonnay,   **$**   **Pts**
California 2006   **56**   **85**

♟ ☕ California ripeness, French-style subtlety. With concentrated pineapple fruit and a toasty mineral scent, it is delicious young but ages well for 7+ years.

Kitchen Survivor™ Grade: A

Your notes: _____

Ferrari-Carano Alexander Valley   **$**   **Pts**
Chardonnay, California 2006   **28**   **88**

🍎 "A value if you can afford it" sums up the fact that of the luxury Chards, this is relatively affordable. Nice spicy fruit, rich oak, and luscious tropical fruit.

Kitchen Survivor™ Grade: B

Your notes: _____

Fetzer Valley Oaks Chardonnay,   **$**   **Pts**
California 2007   **9**   **84**

☺ Three cheers for the sustainable farming, consistent style—fruity, with toasty oak—and great price.

Kitchen Survivor™ Grade: B

Your notes: _____

Flora Springs Barrel Fermented   **$**   **Pts**
Chardonnay, Napa, California 2007   **26**   **89**

♗ 🍎 This wine is decadence, with balance: lush tropical fruit, crème brûlée and buttered popcorn flavors and scents. Pair with risotto scented with truffle oil and parmesan. Or just pair with popcorn & a movie.

Kitchen Survivor™ Grade: B+

Your notes: _____

Franciscan Oakville Chardonnay, Napa,   **$**   **Pts**
California 2007   **18**   **88**

With toasty oak and ripe baked apple fruit that's "not overblown;" this wine "lets you (affordably) impress."

Kitchen Survivor™ Grade: C

Your notes: _____

Frei Brothers Chardonnay   **$**   **Pts**
Russian River Valley, California 2007   **20**   **86**

🍎 Nice RRV Chardonnay character for the price, with lush and juicy stone fruit flavors balanced with bright acidity, and kissed with soft vanilla oak.

Kitchen Survivor™ Grade: B

Your notes: _____

Gallo Family Vineyards Sonoma Reserve   **$**   **Pts**
Chardonnay, California 2007   **15**   **88**

♗ Year after year, this "outstanding for the price" Chard offers ripe, succulent flavors of pineapples, pears, and crisp apples, and nice balance.

Kitchen Survivor™ Grade: A

Your notes: _____

Geyser Peak Chardonnay, Alexander   **$**   **Pts**
Valley, California 2006   **14**   **84**

This wine offers pleasant apple, pear, and melon fruit and nuances of buttery oak, without being too heavy.

Kitchen Survivor™ Grade: B

Your notes: _____

Gloria Ferrer Chardonnay, Carneros,   **$**   **Pts**
California 2006   **16**   **88**

Cool-climate crisp apple flavors, with a soft hint of vanilla in the long finish. Pair with crab salad.

Kitchen Survivor™ Grade: B

Your notes: _____

Grgich (*GER-gich;* both are hard *g*, as in *girl*) Hills
Estate Chardonnay, Napa,   **$**   **Pts**   **Cali-**
California 2006   **42**   **92**

🏅 🏆 👌 The name has for decades meant blue-chip Napa Chard that's packed with rich fruit, yet elegant, subtle and with an endless finish. It always wins our blind tastings against wines twice as expensive.

Kitchen Survivor™ Grade: A

Your notes: _____

Hess Select Chardonnay,   **$**   **Pts**
California 2006   **10**   **86**

☺ A "great value for the money" favorite with my panel thanks to the incredible fruit: pineapple, mango, pear, and lemon. Delicious on its own, and with Caribbean dishes such as jerk chicken or pork.

Kitchen Survivor™ Grade: B

Your notes: _____

Jacob's Creek Chardonnay,   **$**   **Pts**
Australia 2007   **10**   **84**

Both trade and consumers rate this a value star. I give it extra credit for consistency and for the lively, bright citrus and peach flavor not weighed down with oak.

Kitchen Survivor™ Grade: C

Your notes: _____

J. Lohr Estates Riverstone Chardonnay,   **$**   **Pts**
Paso Robles, California 2006   **14**   **85**

This Chard's value for the price is always solid. The pineapple, peach and toasty oak style is great with grilled corn on the cob.

Kitchen Survivor™ Grade: B

Your notes: _____

Joseph Drouhin Pouilly-Fuisse   **$**   **Pts**
(*poo-YEE fwee-SAY*), France 2006   **24**   **86**

♟ Classic Pouilly-Fuisse, with creamy apple and fresh almond scents, steely dryness, and a long finish.

Kitchen Survivor™ Grade: A

Your notes: _____

Kendall-Jackson Vintner's Reserve   **$**   **Pts**
Chardonnay, California 2006   **14**   **89**

☺ It's "impossible to beat the price/quality" that this wine achieves every year. Its lively tangerine and melon fruit and soft oak are a triumph of balance and juiciness that keeps you coming back to the glass.

Kitchen Survivor™ Grade: A

Your notes: _____

Kim Crawford Unoaked   **$**   **Pts**
Chardonnay, New Zealand 2007   **17**   **90**

♟ ⚡ My tasters and I love the "pure fruit"—apple, pineapple, and peach—uncluttered by oak, and so will you. It's sophisticated, with a long, mineral finish. Keeps fresh for days after opening.

Kitchen Survivor™ Grade: A+

Your notes: _____

La Crema Chardonnay, Russian River   **$**   **Pts**
Valley, Sonoma, California 2006   **27**   **88**

🍎 "Balanced and yummy" and classically California: ripe baked apple/tropical fruit; toasty-sweet oak, soft cinnamon spice. Delicious with lobster pasta.

Kitchen Survivor™ Grade: B

Your notes: _____

Landmark Vineyards Overlook   **$**   **Pts**
Chardonnay, Sonoma, California 2006   **27**   **85**

🍎 This "California tropical" Chard has "huge body, heavy-duty oak, and smooooth" texture.

Kitchen Survivor™ Grade: C

Your notes: _____

Lindemans Bin 65 Chardonnay,   **$**   **Pts**
Australia 2006   **8**   **85**

☺ My tasters love the easy-drinking, fragrant tropical fruit and bright acidity, "for a great price."

Kitchen Survivor™ Grade: B+

Your notes: _____

Louis Jadot Macon-Villages   **$**   **Pts**
(LOO-ee jhah-DOUGH mah-COHN   20   84
vill-AHJH) Chardonnay, France 2007

♟ The Euro-dollar exchange rate is making this pricey, but the quality and classical style remain: no oak heaviness - just clean, refreshing green apple and citrus fruit, sparked with vivid acidity.

Kitchen Survivor™ Grade: B+

Your notes: _____

Louis Jadot Meursault (mur-SOW),   **$**   **Pts**
Burgundy, France 2007   45   85

♟ In the expensive world of Burgundy, a relatively affordable real-deal Meursault, with stony, nutty-toastiness and cinnamon-baked apple flavor.

Kitchen Survivor™ Grade: B

Your notes: _____

Louis Jadot Pouilly-Fuisse,   **$**   **Pts**
France 2007   30   84

🦪 ♟ Fresh, unoaked green apple fruit with a touch of mineral chalkiness in the finish. An ideal match for oysters, quiche, or a goat cheese salad.

Kitchen Survivor™ Grade: A

Your notes: _____

Matanzas Creek Chardonnay, Sonoma,   **$**   **Pts**
California 2006   29   89

🏅 👌 A "wine list stalwart" that deserves its fan club because it always delivers on intense pear and tropical fruit, toasty oak, good acidity and deft balance.

Kitchen Survivor™ Grade: B

Your notes: _____

McWilliam's Hanwood Estate   **$**   **Pts**
Chardonnay, Australia 2006   12   87

🏅 "Great Value!" with a "fruity, melons and vanilla taste" and nice subtlety for pairing with shellfish. I'd splurge on scallops or lobster since the wine's a deal.

Kitchen Survivor™ Grade: C

Your notes: _____

Merryvale Starmont Chardonnay,   **$**   **Pts**
Napa, California 2006   **20**   **84**

Always a solid offering with peach and baked apple flavors kissed by a touch of cinnamon and vanilla from the oak barrel aging. Nice with corn chowder.

Kitchen Survivor™ *Grade: B*

Your notes: _____

Mer Soleil (mare sew-*LAY*) Chardonnay,   **$**   **Pts**
Santa Lucia Highlands, California 2005   **42**   **85**

🍎 The oak is subtle on this dripping-with-banana/mango fruit Chard. You can also try their "Silver" bottling, which is completely unoaked.

Kitchen Survivor™ *Grade: B+*

Your notes: _____

Michel Laroche Chablis   **$**   **Pts**
St. Martin, Burgundy, France 2005   **25**   **85**

🍷 True French Chablis that's relatively available and affordable, with piercingly pure apple and citrus and a bit of wet-gravel mineral scent. Excellent with raw clams and oysters, and triple-creme cheeses.

Kitchen Survivor™ *Grade: A+*

Your notes: _____

Mirassou Monterey County   **$**   **Pts**
Chardonnay, California 2005   **12**   **84**

The pineapple and lemon flavors make this at once lush and lively; nice quality for the price.

Kitchen Survivor™ *Grade: B+*

Your notes: _____

Penfolds Koonunga Hill   **$**   **Pts**
Chardonnay, Australia 2007   **12**   **86**

Real character bang for the buk, with tropical fruit, butterscotch, and toastiness, all in balance.

Kitchen Survivor™ *Grade: B*

Your notes: _____

R.H. Phillips Dunnigan Hills   **$**   **Pts**
Chardonnay, California 2006   **8**   **84**

This wine's always a solid value, with vivid citrus and nectarine fruit and a nice kiss of not-too-heavy oak.

Kitchen Survivor™ *Grade: A*

Your notes: _____

Robert Mondavi Napa Chardonnay,   **$**   **Pts**
California 2006   **20**   **84**

This blue-chip brand delivers the baked-apple and toasty-spice flavor of benchmark Napa Chardonnay.

Kitchen Survivor™ Grade: C

Your notes: _____

Rodney Strong Sonoma   **$**   **Pts**
Chardonnay, California 2007   **15**   **86**

🍎 This huge seller is classic Sonoma: a coconut-sweet scent from oak and ripe peach-pineapple fruit.

Kitchen Survivor™ Grade: C

Your notes: _____

Rombauer Chardonnay Carneros,   **$**   **Pts**
California 2007   **32**   **88**

A consistent favorite for its "buttery and lightly toasty" richness and baked-apple fruit, balanced by vivid cool-climate acidity. A great match for creamy pastas.

Kitchen Survivor™ Grade: B

Your notes: _____

Rosemount Diamond Label   **$**   **Pts**
Chardonnay, Australia 2006   **10**   **83**

This Aussie's "still solid," with peach and tangerine fruit, the barest hint of oak, and a clean finish.

Kitchen Survivor™ Grade: B+

Your notes: _____

St. Francis Chardonnay, Sonoma,   **$**   **Pts**
California 2006   **17**   **87**

🍎 A constant in my wine classes due to the crowd-pleasing, textbook Sonoma Chardonnay character - ripe pear and tropical fruit, soft vanilla oak, buttery scent, nice balance - for a great price.

Kitchen Survivor™ Grade: A+

Your notes: _____

Salentein Chardonnay, Mendoza,   **$**   **Pts**
Argentina 2005   **18**   **88**

🍷 🏆 This one rivals Catena for best Argentinian Chardonnay, with an almost Meursault-like stony minerality that combines with hazelnut and baked apple-cinnamon on the scent. A real gem.

Kitchen Survivor™ Grade: A+

Your notes: _____

Sebastiani Sonoma Chardonnay,   **$**   **Pts**
California 2006   **13**   **89**

🍎 An absolutely stunning value for the price, with full-blown exotic mango-pineapple fruit, creamy butterscotch oak, and snappy acidity that gives balance and food-worthiness. Enjoy it with mushroom pasta.

Kitchen Survivor™ Grade: A

Your notes: _____

Silverado Napa Valley Chardonnay,   **$**   **Pts**
California 2006   **23**   **88**

🍃 Lots of crisp apple flavor in balance with soft oak, excellent structure and mineral notes on the long finish. A great match for subtle fish dishes and risottos.

Kitchen Survivor™ Grade: A

Your notes: _____

Simi Chardonnay, Sonoma,   **$**   **Pts**
California 2007   **18**   **82**

A Sonoma stalwart, with soft apple fruit playing backup to the prominent vanilla oakiness.

Kitchen Survivor™ Grade: C

Your notes: _____

Sonoma-Cutrer Russian River   **$**   **Pts**
Ranches Chardonnay, California 2006   **23**   **88**

🏆 In contrast to the "monster Chardonnay genre," this perennial favorite holds out for elegance and complexity. The oak's in the background so the softly floral-mineral scent and juicy pear flavor can shine.

Kitchen Survivor™ Grade: B+

Your notes: _____

Souverain Chardonnnay,   **$**   **Pts**
Alexander Valley, California 2007   **17**   **90**

🍾🍎 This brand delivers top quality and character for the price, with luxuriant mango and Fuji apple fruit, soft and spicy oak and a long finish.

Kitchen Survivor™ Grade: A

Your notes: _____

Sterling Vineyards Napa   **$**   **Pts**
Chardonnay, California 2006   **15**   **85**

A California classic with a vanilla scent and soft, lips-macking apple-quince fruit. Pair with cheesy polenta.

Kitchen Survivor™ Grade: A

Your notes: _____

Sterling Vintner's Collection Chardonnay,   **$**   **Pts**
Central Coast, California 2007   **13**   **85**

The trifecta: appley-crisp, easy-drinking, great value.

Kitchen Survivor™ Grade: B

Your notes: _____

Stuhlmuller Chardonnay, Alexander   **$**   **Pts**
Valley, California 2006   **23**   **90**

Really worth seeking out, for its layers and complexity: subtle cinnamon, brioche and baked apple, with a Burgundy-like nuttiness in the finish.

Kitchen Survivor™ Grade: C

Your notes: _____

Talbott (Robert) Sleepy Hollow   **$**   **Pts**
Chardonnay, California 2005   **43**   **88**

Every guest I've ever served adored the exotic marzipan, toasted nut, and honeyed pear flavors of this "restaurant wine" (rarely found in stores).

Kitchen Survivor™ Grade: B

Your notes: _____

Toasted Head Chardonnay,   **$**   **Pts**
California 2006   **14**   **84**

"Toasted Head" means more oakiness—they toast not only the sides of the barrels but the "head" (end piece) too, yielding a very toasty, rich, butterscotch scent. Nice on its own or with parmesan-laced risotto.

Kitchen Survivor™ Grade: C

Your notes: _____

Trefethen Estate Chardonnay,   **$**   **Pts**
California 2006   **30**   **87**

Trefethen's signature, with classy and subtle oak, pear, and pineapple fruit; with a touch of mineral in the finish. Perfect with trout in browned butter.

Kitchen Survivor™ Grade: B

Your notes: _____

Twin Fin Chardonnay, **$** **Pts**
California 2005 **10** **84**

🍎 A "hip label" wine that also tastes great—tangerine and apple fruit, soft oak, lively take-another-sip finish. A good style and price bet for parties.

Kitchen Survivor™ Grade: B

Your notes: _____

Wakefield Estate Chardonnay, Clare **$** **Pts**
Valley, Australia 2007 **17** **91**

⑂ Incredible layers for the price: lovely buttered popcorn toastiness in the scent and finish, balanced by round and juicy golden apple and pineapple fruit and a long finish. A bargain,, so you can splurge on the food match: lobster, or wild mushroom pasta.

Kitchen Survivor™ Grade: A+

Your notes: _____

William Hill Estate Chardonnay, **$** **Pts**
California 2006 **22** **88**

⑂ 🏆 Tastes like 3x the price, with Burgundy-like baked apple, spice and nutty qualities, but California-style juicy ripeness. If you want, the trade-up to the Reserve ($35) is worth it, too.

Kitchen Survivor™ Grade: A

Your notes: _____

Wolf Blass Yellow Label **$** **Pts**
Chardonnay, Australia 2006 **13** **88**

I'm always impressed with the value in this wine - such a cut above all the other big-brand Aussie Chards at a similar price. It's got lively apple-peach-melon fruit and just a touch of oak.

Kitchen Survivor™ Grade: B

Your notes: _____

Woodbridge Chardonnay, **$** **Pts**
California 2007 **8** **83**

☺ A "solid value" Chard with soft spiced apple fruit and a touch of vanilla from the oak aging. Perfect with Caesar salad, grilled chicken, even popcorn.

Kitchen Survivor™ Grade: C

Your notes: _____

Yellowtail Chardonnay,   **$**   **Pts**
Australia 2007   **8**   **84**

☺ The "delicious, easy-drinking" appley Chardonnay fruit makes this "hugely popular" wine "a value."
Kitchen Survivor™ Grade: B

Your notes: _____

Uncommon White Grapes and Blends

Category Profile: Welcome to one of the funnest sections of the book! A label of "other" for wines that don't fit neatly into a major category means some may not get the respect they deserve. But trust me, here is where you will find the gems in terms of deliciousness and uniqueness for the price. The group includes a diverse collection of wine types, including uncommon regions, grapes, or blends. Here is some background on each:

Uncommon Grapes and Regions—This category includes the grapes Albarino (from Spain), Pinot Blanc, Gewurztraminer, Gruner-Veltliner (from Austria), Moscophilero (from Greece), and Viognier, all meriting high marks from tasters and definitely worth your attention. The other-than-Pinot-Grigio Italian whites are also here, along with Spanish regional whites. (See the "Wine List Decoder" for more on these.)

Unique Blends—Blends of the white grapes Semillon and Chardonnay are common in Australia, and France's Alsace wineries sometimes blend the local grapes of the region - Riesling, Gewurztraminer, Pinot Gris and Pinot Blanc. This category also includes a growing crop of specialty multi-grape blends well worth trying—a sign consumers are continuing to branch out—yay!

Serve: Well chilled.

When: The uncommon grapes (like Gewurztraminer) and unique blends are wonderful when you want to surprise guests with a different flavor experience.

With: In my opinion, Gewurztraminer, Albarino, and the unusual grape blends are some of the most exciting food partners out there. They are especially suited to spicy ethnic fare such as Chinese, Thai and Indian. They are also great go-to choices for barbecue and the Thanksgiving feast.

In: An all-purpose wineglass.

Alice White Lexia,	$	Pts
Australia 2007	8	83

🍎 Bring on the dim sum! This "nice tasting," "nice price" wine based on the Muscat grape has honey-suckle-apricot flavors that are the perfect match for Chinese food. You could also pair it with spicy wings.

Kitchen Survivor™ Grade: B
Your notes: _____

Anne Boecklin Pinot Blanc Reserve,	$	Pts
Alsace, France 2006	16	89

🍴 🍷 A super-sophisticated fragrance of flowers, talc and marzipan. Subtle palate with honeyed pear, almond and mineral that begs to be matched with a classy dish such as lobster bisque or saffron risotto.

Kitchen Survivor™ Grade: B
Your notes: _____

Antinori Orvieto Campogrande,	$	Pts
Umbria, Italy 2006	11	83

☺ "Refreshing" with crisp pear fruit for a "good price." Pair it with cured meats or garlicky pastas.

Kitchen Survivor™ Grade: B
Your notes: _____

Ayama Chenin Blanc, Paarl, South	$	Pts
Africa 2007	12	89

🍴 Fragrant with dried blossoms, hay, beeswax and honey notes. Juicy Golden Delicious apple on the palate. Pair with smoked salmon or spicy sausages.

Kitchen Survivor™ Grade: B
Your notes: _____

Becker Viognier,	$	Pts
Texas 2007	15	86

🍸 One of the best Viogniers made in America, so it's worth the search. Gorgeous white peach and floral scents and tangerine-mango flavors Great with spicy boiled shrimp or Thai curry-steamed mussels.

Kitchen Survivor™ Grade: B
Your notes: _____

Big House White,   **$**   **Pts**
California 2006   **14**   **84**

🍎 ☺ This "great blend of ABCs" (anything but Chardonnay grapes) offers "totally refreshing" flavors of peach and kiwi that make it a delicious sipper.

Kitchen Survivor™ Grade: B

Your notes: _____

Boutari Moschofilero, Mantinia,   **$**   **Pts**
Greece 2007   **17**   **86**

Mo-sko-FEEL-er-o is the grape, a local specialty of the Mantinia district in Greece. The piercingly floral, roses and jasmine scent, and the bright apricot and grapefruit flavors, are like the Greek sunshine itself.

Kitchen Survivor™ Grade: B

Your notes: _____

Burgans Albarino (*boor-GAHNS***   **$**   **Pts**
all-buh-REEN-yoh), **Bodegas**   **14**   **85**
Vilarino-Cambados, Spain 2007

👍 "A wonderful alternative to Chardonnay; great with shellfish," say my tasters. The peachy scent and crisp mineral finish are "great bargain Albarino."

Kitchen Survivor™ Grade: B+

Your notes: _____

Chateau St. Jean Gewurztraminer,,   **$**   **Pts**
Sonoma, California 2007   **15**   **85**

My tasters "adore" and the floral scent and apricot fruit flavor that makes this wine "great with spicy tuna rolls" and, I'd say, Asian food in general.

Kitchen Survivor™ Grade: B

Your notes: _____

Chateau Ste. Michelle   **$**   **Pts**
Gewurztraminer, Washington 2007   **10**   **87**

Fragrant and fantastic. The spiced apricot-fruit cocktail flavor is clean and scrumptious on its own or with Chinese food, especially sesame chicken.

Kitchen Survivor™ Grade: B

Your notes: _____

Columbia Crest Two Vines   **$**   **Pts**
Gewurztraminer, Washington 2007   **8**   **84**

This wine's sweet spice and ginger-mandarin orange flavors make it "great with spicy and ethnic foods."
Kitchen Survivor™ Grade: B+

Your notes: _____

Conundrum White Blend,   **$**   **Pts**
California 2006   **22**   **86**

🍎 This "interesting combo" of grapes (Chard, Sauvignon Blanc, Chenin Blanc, and more) has a rich, exotic tropical style and a very devoted following.
Kitchen Survivor™ Grade: B

Your notes: _____

Dry Creek Vineyard Dry Chenin Blanc,   **$**   **Pts**
Clarksburg, California 2007   **11**   **86**

♀ "Like biting a Golden Delicious apple"—juicy, with snappy acidity and a creamy finish. De-lish.
Kitchen Survivor™ Grade: B

Your notes: _____

Fall Creek Chenin Blanc,   **$**   **Pts**
Texas 2006   **7**   **85**

Crisp, appley, and slightly sweet; a picnic in a bottle that would go great with spicy boiled shrimp.
Kitchen Survivor™ Grade: C

Your notes: _____

Fetzer Valley Oaks Gewurztraminer,   **$**   **Pts**
California 2006   **9**   **84**

Here's a "favorite" of my tasters for its luscious floral and apricot flavors; "just made for Chinese takeout."
Kitchen Survivor™ Grade: B

Your notes: _____

Folie a Deux Menage a Trois White   **$**   **Pts**
Blend, California 2007   **12**   **83**

🍎 The trois (three) grapes -Chard, Sauvignon Blanc, and Chenin Blanc - yield a juicy tutti-fruiti flavor.
Kitchen Survivor™ Grade: C

Your notes: _____

Hermanos Lurton Rueda,   **$**   **Pts**
Spain 2006   **14**   **88**

Crisp and crackling-fresh, with chalky, citrus peel and quince notes. Tailor-made for briny seafood, garlicky pastas and fried foods.

Kitchen Survivor™ Grade: A

Your notes: _____

Hidalgo La Gitana (*ee-DAHL-go*   **$**   **Pts**
***la hee-TAH-nuh*) Manzanilla**   **16**   **89**
Sherry, Spain NV

This sherry's "nutty," "clean" flavor and bracing tanginess are super with salty or fried foods, Manchego cheese, and Spanish Marcona almonds.

Kitchen Survivor™ Grade: A

Your notes: _____

Hirsch Gruner Veltliner #1, Kamptal,   **$**   **Pts**
Austria 2007   **16**   **88**

A great food wine, with "delicious" grapefruit and pineapple flavors, and a hint of white pepper and ginger in the finish. Bring on the oysters mignonette!

Kitchen Survivor™ Grade: B+

Your notes: _____

Hogue Gewurztraminer,   **$**   **Pts**
Washington 2006   **8**   **85**

This apricot-gingery Gewurz is "del-ish for sipping" and with "Chinese food." I also like it with sausages.

Kitchen Survivor™ Grade: B

Your notes: _____

Hugel (*hew-GELL*) Gewurztraminer,   **$**   **Pts**
France 2005   **18**   **85**

A fave of my tasters for the floral and sweet spice scent and lychee-nut/apricot flavor.

Kitchen Survivor™ Grade: A

Your notes: _____

Hugel Pinot Blanc Cuvee Les Amours,   **$**   **Pts**
France 2005   **14**   **85**

The apple-pear flavor, mineral complexity, and liveliness of this Pinot Blanc are great for the price.

Kitchen Survivor™ Grade: B

Your notes: _____

Inama "Vin Soave," Soave Classico, $ 17   Pts 88
Veneto, Italy 2007

♟ Not your grandmother's Soave. This one is fantastic, with scents of hay, rose hips, citrus peel and talcum powder that echo on the palate and into the long finish. A great match fried foods and even tough-to-pair artichoke and asparagus dishes.

Kitchen Survivor™ Grade: B

Your notes: _____

Ken Forrester Petit Chenin Blanc, $ 10   Pts 89
Stellenbosch, South Africa 2007

♟ ♟ A stunning value, with great complexity for the price. Explosive scents of tropical blossoms and starfruit; on the palate, piercing acidity with flavors of tangerine, peach and kiwi. A great wine for sushi.

Kitchen Survivor™ Grade: A+

Your notes: _____

Marques de Riscal Rueda (*mar-KESS $ 9   Pts 85
***deh ree-SCAHL roo-AY-duh*), Spain 2006**

♟ ♟ This wine is fresh, sleek, and vibrant, tasting of key lime and kiwi, without oak flavor, great with food. In my book, a value star.

Kitchen Survivor™ Grade: B+

Your notes: _____

Martin Codax Albarino, Rias Baixas $ 15   Pts 87
(*all-buh-REEN-yo*), Spain 2006

♟ This "magic-with-food" wine's got floral, citrus, lime and pear, all oak free. Great with seafood salad.

Kitchen Survivor™ Grade: B+

Your notes: _____

Martinsancho Verdejo, Rueda, $ 20   Pts 85
Spain 2007

♟ There's no oak to mask the citrus and crisp apple with lively acidity, elegance and minerality. Beautiful.

Kitchen Survivor™ Grade: A

Your notes: _____

Paul Blanck Gewurztraminer $ 20   Pts 85
Classique, France 2005

I think this is one of Alsace's best Gewurztraminers for the money: lychee, rose petal, peach, minerals, *balance*.

Kitchen Survivor™ Grade: B+

Your notes: _____

Pierre Sparr Alsace-One,
France 2006

$	Pts
14	85

This Riesling, Pinot Blanc, Muscat, Gewurztraminer, and Pinot Gris mix, with lots of peach and pear fruit, is "great with food; great price."

Kitchen Survivor™ Grade: B

Your notes: _____

Pierre Sparr Pinot Blanc Reserve,
Alsace, France 2005

$	Pts
14	86

No oak or high alcohol to distract from the lip-smacking pear and quince fruit. Yum.

Kitchen Survivor™ Grade: B

Your notes: _____

Rocca delle Macie Occhio a Vento,
Vermentino, Tuscany, Italy 2006

$	Pts
17	89

The bewitching scents and flavors of wild fennel, marzipan and Asian pear are perfect to pair with fennel salad, caramelized onion pizza, or sausage pasta.

Kitchen Survivor™ Grade: A

Your notes: _____

Ruffino Orvieto Classico,
Umbria, Italy 2007

$	Pts
7	85

☺ This wine's crisp acidity, clean pear fruit, and nutty qualities are what everyday Italian white wine should be. A great match for antipasti and fried foods.

Kitchen Survivor™ Grade: B

Your notes: _____

Santa Ana Reserva Torrontes,
Mendoza, Argentina 2007

$	Pts
14	88

Drink more Torrontes! Argentina's signature white grape has irresistible floral, tutti-frutti and tangerine character that is great with BBQ, Chinese food, sushi, party hors d'oeuvres, or just for sipping.

Kitchen Survivor™ Grade: A+

Your notes: _____

Sella & Mosca La Cala Vermentino,
Sardinia, Italy 2007

$	Pts
14	86

Lots of yum for the price with lively pear fruit and a hint of mineral that screams for clam-sauced pasta.

Kitchen Survivor™ Grade: A+

Your notes: _____

Sokol Blosser Evolution, | **$** | **Pts**
Oregon NV | **15** | **85**

🍎 ☺ Like an aromatherapy treatment—honey-suckle, peach, apricot, pear—but a lot cheaper!
Kitchen Survivor™ Grade: B

Your notes: _____

Walter Glatzer Gruner-Veltliner | **$** | **Pts**
Kabinett, Austria 2006 | **12** | **85**

👌 This sommelier favorite's "tangy, mouthwatering lemongrass and spice" are an exotic, affordable treat.
Kitchen Survivor™ Grade: A

Your notes: _____

BLUSH/PINK/ROSE WINES

Category Profile: Although many buyers are snobby about the blush category, the truth is that for most of us white Zinfandel was probably the first wine we drank that had a cork. It's a juicy, uncomplicated style that makes a lot of buyers, and their wallets, very happy. Now for the gear switch—rose. The only thing true roses have in common with the blush category is appearance. Rose wines are classic to many world-class European wine regions. They are absolutely dry, tangy, crisp, and amazingly interesting wines for the money. I often say that with their spice and complexity they have red wine flavor, but the lightness of body and chillability gives them white wine style. They are *great* food wines. Don't miss the chance to try my recommendations or those of your favorite shop or restaurant. You will love them.

Serve: The colder the better.

When: The refreshing touch of sweetness in blush styles makes them great as an aperitif. Roses are great for both sipping and meals.

With: A touch of sweetness in wine can tone down heat, so spicy foods are an especially good partner for blush wine. Dry roses go with everything.

In: An all-purpose wineglass.

Beckmen Vineyards Grenache Rose,   **$**   **Pts**
Santa Barbara, California 2007   **18**   **84**

Totally dry, with mouthwatering pomegranate and pink grapefruit flavors that pair great with pizza.

Kitchen Survivor™ Grade: B

Your notes: _____

Beringer White Zinfandel,   **$**   **Pts**
California 2007   **7**   **85**

The standard-bearer White Zin, with fresh strawberry and raspberry flavors, and a juicy texture. The touch of sweetness is nice with foods that have a kick.

Kitchen Survivor™ Grade: B

Your notes: _____

Big House Pink,   **$**   **Pts**
California 2007   **12**   **85**

A fun sipper with juicy strawberry-watermelon flavor.

Kitchen Survivor™ Grade: B

Your notes: _____

Bodegas Ochoa (oh-*CHOH*-uh)   **$**   **Pts**
Garnacha Rosado, Spain 2006   **9**   **85**

This "wonderful summer rosé," completely dry with scents of "strawberry" and a "beautiful color," is "further proof that Spain is coming on strong."

Kitchen Survivor™ Grade: B+

Your notes: _____

Bonny Doon Vin Gris de Cigare   **$**   **Pts**
Pink Wine, California 2007   **12**   **85**

A bone-dry, tangy, spicy refresher that's great with food.

Kitchen Survivor™ Grade: B

Your notes: _____

Chateau d'Aqueria Tavel Rose,   **$**   **Pts**
Provence, France 2006   **17**   **85**

To visit the south of France, just pop this bottle, cook up a Provencale omelet, and enjoy the savory pomegranate and white pepper, and refreshing acidity.

Kitchen Survivor™ Grade: B

Your notes: _____

Domaine Ott Bandol Rose,   **$**   **Pts**
Provence, France 2006   **25**   **85**

The dollar-euro exchange rate makes this pricey now, but it's still "one of the best" classically styled French roses. It is totally bone dry, spicy-meaty, pomegranate-fruity, and great with herbed goat cheese crostini.

Kitchen Survivor™ Grade: B

Your notes: _____

Goats Do Roam Rose,   **$**   **Pts**
South Africa 2007   **8**   **85**

A "delicious" blend of Pinotage and Syrah, totally dry, with white pepper spice and tangy red currant fruit.

Kitchen Survivor™ Grade: B

Your notes: _____

La Vieille Ferme Cotes du Ventoux   **$**   **Pts**
Rose, France 2006   **9**   **85**

"Delicious" and "not sweet." The savory white pepper, pomegranate and strawberry notes are great with herbal dishes.

Kitchen Survivor™ Grade: B

Your notes: _____

Marques de Caceres Rioja Rosado,   **$**   **Pts**
Spain 2007   **8**   **85**

This wine's tangy strawberry-watermelon-spice flavor is de-lish! You can invite *any* food to this party.

Kitchen Survivor™ Grade: C

Your notes: _____

Solorosa Rose,   **$**   **Pts**
California 2007   **15**   **85**

 This not-at-all-sweet rose has lots of spice, savor, and juicy roundness. Fabulous with grill fare.

Kitchen Survivor™ Grade: B+

Your notes: _____

Sutter Home White Zinfandel,   **$**   **Pts**
California 2007   **7**   **85**

This trailblazing White Zinfandel is still juicy and pleasing and one of the best.

Kitchen Survivor™ Grade: B

Your notes: _____

RED WINES

Beaujolais/Gamay

Category Profile: Beaujolais (*bow-jhoe-LAY*) Nouveau, the new wine of the vintage that each year is shipped from France on the third Thursday in November (just in time for Thanksgiving), dominates sales in this category. (It also inspires scores of nouveau imitators riding its cash-cow coattails.) You can have fun with nouveau, but don't skip the real stuff—particularly Beaujolais-Villages (*vill-AHJH*) and Beaujolais Cru (named for the town where it is grown, for example, Morgon, Brouilly, and Moulin-à-Vent). These Beaujolais categories are a wine world rarity, in that they offer real character at a low price. The signature style of Beaujolais is a juicy, grapey fruit flavor and succulent texture with, in the crus, an added layer of earthy spiciness. All red Beaujolais is made from the Gamay grape.

Serve: Lightly chilled, to enhance the vibrant fruit.

When: Great as an aperitif and for alfresco occasions such as picnics and barbecues.

With: Many tasters said they swear by it for Thanksgiving. It's so soft, smooth, and juicy I think it goes with everything, from the simplest of sandwich meals to brunch, lunch, and beyond. It's often a great buy on restaurant wine lists and versatile for those really tough matching situations where you've ordered everything from oysters to osso bucco but you want one wine.

In: An all-purpose wineglass.

	$	Pts
Chateau de la Chaize Brouilly, France 2005	16	85

This is classic Beaujolais, with lots of soft berry fruit and a smoky, earthy scent like autumn leaves.
Kitchen Survivor™ Grade: B
Your notes: _____

	$	Pts
Duboeuf (Georges) Beaujolais-Villages, France 2007	11	85

It's "hard not to love" the plump berry flavor; good for those who don't normally drink red.
Kitchen Survivor™ Grade: B
Your notes: _____

Duboeuf (Georges) Moulin-A-Vent, $ Pts
France 2005   14   85

This is "great for the money" with lots of "spice, smooth berry fruit," and complexity.

Kitchen Survivor™ Grade: B

Your notes: _____

Louis Jadot Beaujolais-Villages, $ Pts
France 2007   14   82

☺ Earthier and less ripe than in past vintages - a change in style? I hope not because it's been such a consistent favorite of mine and the VOX-ers.

Kitchen Survivor™ Grade: B

Your notes: _____

Pinot Noir

Category Profile: Pinot Noir is my favorite of the major classic red grape varieties, because I love its smoky-ripe scent; pure fruit flavor; and, most of all, silken texture. When well made, it offers red wine intensity and complexity, without being heavy. Although Pinot Noir's home turf is the Burgundy region of France, few of those wines make the list of top sellers in the United States, because production is tiny. The coolest parts of coastal California (especially the Russian River Valley, Carneros, Monterey, Sonoma Coast, and Santa Barbara County) specialize in Pinot Noir, as does Oregon's Willamette (*will-AM-ett*) Valley. New Zealand is also growing in importance as a Pinot source. Pinot Noir from all the major regions is typically oak aged, but as with other grapes the amount of oakiness is matched to the intensity of the fruit. Generally the budget bottlings are the least oaky.

Serve: *Cool* room temperature; don't hesitate to chill the bottle briefly if needed.

When: Although the silky texture makes Pinot Noir quite bewitching on its own, it is also the ultimate "food wine." It is my choice to take to dinner parties and to order in restaurants, because I know it will probably delight both white and red wine drinkers and will go with most any food.

With: Pinot's versatility is legendary, but it is *the* wine for mushroom dishes, salmon, rare tuna, and any bird (especially duck). Smoked meats and fish, too.

In: An all-purpose wineglass. Or try a larger balloon stem; the extra air space enhances the wine's aroma.

A by Acacia Pinot Noir,	**$**	**Pts**
California 2007	**17**	**86**

A soft and silky bottling with vivid red cherry fruit and a hint of dried potpourri and tea leaf scent, with a long, smoky finish. Pair with seared pork tenderloin.
Kitchen Survivor™ Grade: B
Your notes: _____

Acacia Carneros Pinot Noir,	**$**	**Pts**
California 2007	**26**	**89**

Still seductive after all these years. As always, a sexy gaminess envelops the silky raspberry fruit. Long and earthy, and great with Gruyere or Manchego cheese.
Kitchen Survivor™ Grade: B
Your notes: _____

Adelsheim Pinot Noir,	**$**	**Pts**
Oregon 2006	**30**	**85**

☒ This Oregon classic's signature is subtlety - dried-cranberry fruit and a dusty-herbal-smoky scent.
Kitchen Survivor™ Grade: B
Your notes: _____

Argyle Pinot Noir, Willamette Valley,	**$**	**Pts**
Oregon 2006	**25**	**85**

🍎 One of Oregon's tastiest Pinots for lovers of the in-your-face fruity style, with a cherry-candy flavor.
Kitchen Survivor™ Grade: B
Your notes: _____

A to Z Pinot Noir,	**$**	**Pts**
Oregon 2006	**15**	**86**

This kind of value in Pinot Noir is all too rare. Strawßberry-rhubarb flavors, satiny texture and a hint of savory consomme in the finish. *The* match for grilled salmon. Great with caramelized roasted veggies, too.
Kitchen Survivor™ Grade: B
Your notes: _____

Au Bon Climat Santa Barbara   **$**   **Pts**
Pinot Noir, California 2006   **18**   **85**

🍴 🖐 *Oh-bohn-clee-MAHT* has a cult following and a nickname—"ABC" (for short) is among the truly great American Pinots, with layers of black cherry fruit, tea, and potpourri, a slightly "animal" earthiness, and perfect balance. The wines age nicely, too.
Kitchen Survivor™ Grade: B+
Your notes: _____

Beaulieu Vineyard (BV) Coastal   **$**   **Pts**
Estates Pinot Noir, Pay d'Oc, France 2006   **9**   **84**

✎ Formerly from California; the French-sourced fruit yields a subtler, more tangy style of Pinot with an earthy finish that pairs well with goat cheese salads.
Kitchen Survivor™ Grade: C
Your notes: _____

Beaulieu Vineyard (BV) Reserve Carneros   **$**   **Pts**
Pinot Noir, Napa, California 2006   **40**   **86**

Needs time to open up, then serves up flavors of Bing cherry tart with vanilla, cinnamon, and great length. A lovely match with red wine-braised duck.
Kitchen Survivor™ Grade: B+
Your notes: _____

Beringer Pinot Noir, Napa,   **$**   **Pts**
California 2007   **20**   **85**

A soft, fleshy, berry-flavored Pinot with a whiff of cardamom and vanilla scent. Pair with roasted veggies.
Kitchen Survivor™ Grade: C
Your notes: _____

Beringer Third Century Pinot Noir,   **$**   **Pts**
California 2006   **14**   **84**

Soft and fragrant with red cherry, allspice and tea flavors, and a silky-earthy finish.
Kitchen Survivor™ Grade: C
Your notes: _____

Benton Lane Pinot Noir,   **$**   **Pts**
Oregon 2006   **26**   **86**

🍎 Always " a fave from Oregon" for its voluptuous bing cherry fruit and ripe, slightly floral fragrance.
Kitchen Survivor™ Grade: C
Your notes: _____

Brancott Vineyards Marlborough   **$**   **Pts**
Reserve Pinot Noir, New Zealand 2007   **22**   **87**

This wine's cinnamon–black cherry flavors are laser pure and long, driven by firm acidity and framed with a tug of tea-like tannin. Pair with mushroom risotto.

Kitchen Survivor™ Grade: B

Your notes: _____

Brancott Vineyards South Island   **$**   **Pts**
Pinot Noir, New Zealand 2007   **14**   **85**

🍃 A solid value offering, which is hard to find in Pinot Noir. Soft red cherry with a savory sundried tomato & smoky quality that would be great with Chinese BBQ spareribs or chicken teriyaki.

Kitchen Survivor™ Grade: B

Your notes: _____

Buena Vista Carneros Pinot Noir,   **$**   **Pts**
California 2005   **26**   **84**

Classic Carneros, with aromas of potpourri and tea leaves and flavors of dried cherry and spice.

Kitchen Survivor™ Grade: B

Your notes: _____

Calera Central Coast Pinot Noir,   **$**   **Pts**
California 2006   **24**   **86**

🍃 Sweet sun-dried tomato and "dried cherry fruit" flavor, with a savory-meaty quality that begs for food such as a roasted game bird or wine-braised chicken.

Kitchen Survivor™ Grade: B+

Your notes: _____

Cambria (*CAME-bree-uh*) Julia's   **$**   **Pts**
Vineyard Pinot Noir, California 2006   **20**   **85**

This wine's savory gaminess and spice, lush plum flavor, and tug of tannin make it "memorable."

Kitchen Survivor™ Grade: B

Your notes: _____

Castle Rock Pinot Noir, Mendocino   **$**   **Pts**
California 2006   **14**   **88**

🍸 My Web tasters "love, love, love" the "soft," "lush" cherry fruit, spice, and and purity, especially for the price. A great match for rare grilled tuna.

Kitchen Survivor™ Grade: C

Your notes: _____

Chalone Vineyard Estate Pinot Noir,   **$**   **Pts**
Chalone, California 2006   **40**   **91**

   ♟ 👆 While the slightly musky, earthy raspberry fruit on this wine is beautiful from the start, aging for a few years brings it to a whole new level of truffly-gamy-berry seduction. Pair with wine-glazed pork.

Kitchen Survivor™ Grade: B

Your notes: _____

Chateau St. Jean Sonoma Pinot Noir,   **$**   **Pts**
California 2006   **19**   **86**

"A great beginner's Pinot Noir," with "yummy" "cherry jam" fruit and silky texture, with a juicy-tea finish.

Kitchen Survivor™ Grade: C

Your notes: _____

Clos du Bois Sonoma County   **$**   **Pts**
Pinot Noir, California 2006   **20**   **87**

The strawberry-rhubarb, smokiness, and "great Bing cherry flavors" are just delicious. My favorite from Clos du Bois, and a great match for grilled salmon.

Kitchen Survivor™ Grade: A

Your notes: _____

Cloudline Pinot Noir,   **$**   **Pts**
Oregon 2006   **22**   **85**

Smoky! With dried cranberry and a savory tomato paste-herbal character. Pair with fresh goat cheese.

Kitchen Survivor™ Grade: C

Your notes: _____

Coldstream Hills Pinot Noir, Yarra   **$**   **Pts**
Valley, Australia 2007   **33**   **87**

   ♟ 👍 I love this Aussie offering for its Burgundian smokiness, and sun-dried tomato flavor with lots of smoky, earthy exoticism; pair with wild mushrooms.

Kitchen Survivor™ Grade: C

Your notes: _____

Cristom Jefferson Cuvee Pinot Noir,   **$**   **Pts**
Willamette Valley, Oregon 2006   **30**   **92**

   ♟♟ This wine's signature smoky/cocoa scent, deep cherry fruit, and satiny texture are amazing. It cellars quite beautifully for up to 15 years in the best vintages. One of Oregon's crown jewels.

Kitchen Survivor™ Grade: B

Your notes: _____

David Bruce Santa Cruz Pinot   **$**   **Pts**
Noir, California 2005   **30**   **86**

This Pinot's gamy, savory spice, earth, and raspberry fruit are fleshy, dusky and truly distinctive.

Kitchen Survivor™ Grade: B

Your notes: _____

Deloach Russian River Pinot Noir,   **$**   **Pts**
California 2007   **18**   **88**

♀️ 🍎 A consistent bet for rich, cinnamon-spiced cherry flavor and silky texture, at an incredible price.

Kitchen Survivor™ Grade: B

Your notes: _____

Domaine Carneros Estate Pinot Noir,   **$**   **Pts**
California 2006   **40**   **88**

🏆 A "sophisticated" scent, subtle oakiness, and long finish "like *great* red Burgundy," with a new elegance compared to past bottlings. Perfect with duck.

Kitchen Survivor™ Grade: B

Your notes: _____

Domaine Drouhin (*droo-AHN*)   **$**   **Pts**
Willamette Valley Pinot Noir,   **60**   **93**
Oregon 2006

♀️ The "exuberant raspberry and cherry fruit" and soft vanilla oakiness make it among the most majestic wines from Oregon. It ages into a truffly jewel.

Kitchen Survivor™ Grade: B+

Your notes: _____

Duck Pond Pinot Noir,   **$**   **Pts**
Oregon 2006   **20**   **84**

A "light-on-the-wallet" Pinot with strawberry aromas, ripe raspberry flavors, and great food compatibility.

Kitchen Survivor™ Grade: B

Your notes: _____

Echelon Pinot Noir, Vin de Pays l'ill de   **$**   **Pts**
Beaute, France 2006   **9**   **83**

Historically a California wine; the French-sourced version is lighter, with fragrant red currant fruit and an earthy quality that pairs well with goat cheese.

Kitchen Survivor™ Grade: B+

Your notes: _____

Edna Valley Vineyard Paragon Vineyard   **$**   **Pts**
Pinot Noir, California 2007   **20**   **85**

"Light bodied" but pure cherry that's true to the grape, and belies a surprising ability to improve in bottle with a bit of cellaring. Pair with roast chicken.

Kitchen Survivor™ Grade: A

Your notes: _____

Erath Pinot Noir,   **$**   **Pts**
Oregon 2006   **16**   **87**

A real value star, with an elegant purity of red cherry and raspberry fruit kissed with a touch of sweet spice.

Kitchen Survivor™ Grade: B

Your notes: _____

Estancia Pinnacles Ranches Pinot Noir,   **$**   **Pts**
Monterey, California 2007   **15**   **85**

With its distinct herbal, strawberry rhubarb, and smoky character, this is nice for the money.

Kitchen Survivor™ Grade: B+

Your notes: _____

Etude Carneros Pinot Noir,   **$**   **Pts**
California 2006   **40**   **90**

👆 This wine's elegance, cherry-spice scent, juicy cherry-cranberry fruit, and long finish have been style signatures since the first vintage. Gorgeous, and it ages well, too.

Kitchen Survivor™ Grade: A

Your notes: _____

Fess Parker Santa Barbara Pinot   **$**   **Pts**
Noir, California 2006   **26**   **86**

🍗 "A find" with "chocolate, tobacco," and cherry-cola flavors that pair nicely with duck in red wine sauce.

Kitchen Survivor™ Grade: B+

Your notes: _____

Firesteed Pinot Noir,   **$**   **Pts**
Oregon 2006   **16**   **85**

☺ Delicious cranberry and dried cherry fruit, a nice kick of acid, and a "great price" make it "easy to love."

Kitchen Survivor™ Grade: C

Your notes: _____

Five Rivers Pinot Noir, Central Coast, California 2007

$	Pts
13	85

True Pinot Noir character at a super price: a touch of wet-clay earthiness and soft raspberry-strawberry fruit. A great match for seared scallops or fish.
Kitchen Survivor™ Grade: B
Your notes: _____

Frei Brothers Reserve Pinot Noir, Russian River Valley, California 2006

$	Pts
30	86

The price has continued to creep up, but the quality is there. Cherry cola and cinnamon on the nose, and a silky rich texture that's perfect with grilled salmon.
Kitchen Survivor™ Grade: B+
Your notes: _____

Gallo Family Vineyards Sonoma Reserve Pinot Noir, Sonoma, California 2007

$	Pts
15	88

Pure "raspberry and cherry" fruit, a cola scent, and supple-but-lively texture, at a nice price.
Kitchen Survivor™ Grade: B
Your notes: _____

Gloria Ferrer Pinot Noir, Carneros, California 2005

$	Pts
28	86

An elegant display of earthy-spiciness, pretty red fruits - pomegranate and cherry - and a silky texture.
Kitchen Survivor™ Grade: C
Your notes: _____

Iron Horse Estate Pinot Noir, Sonoma Green Valley, California 2006

$	Pts
40	89

🍎 A tea and sassafras fragrance, with "wow" black cherry and cola flavors. Pair with duck or, as the winery says, "bacon-cheddar macaroni and cheese."
Kitchen Survivor™ Grade: B
Your notes: _____

Irony Pinot Noir, Monterey, California 2006

$	Pts
16	86

Complexity at a nice price: tea leaves, potpourri and compoted cherries with a meaty richness that pairs nicely with bacon-roasted Brussels sprouts.
Kitchen Survivor™ Grade: B
Your notes: _____

J Wine Company Russian River   **$**   **Pts**
Pinot Noir, California 2006   38   88

🍎 "So incredibly jammy and rich," yet it maintains the balance and silkiness Pinot lovers look for with ripe cherry, raspberry and spiced tea notes.

Kitchen Survivor™ Grade: B

Your notes: _____

Kendall-Jackson Vintner's Reserve   **$**   **Pts**
Pinot Noir, California 2006   18   86

☺ This is a great intro to Pinot, with classic silky cherry and spice character at an affordable price.

Kitchen Survivor™ Grade: B

Your notes: _____

King Estate Pinot Noir,   **$**   **Pts**
Oregon 2006   27   85

There's nice soft cherry fruit and a rose-petal scent; the vivid acidity makes it a great match for slow-cooked pork or mild, hard cheeses such as Gruyere.

Kitchen Survivor™ Grade: B

Your notes: _____

La Crema Sonoma Coast Pinot Noir,   **$**   **Pts**
California 2006   22   88

This fuller-bodied style is a "favorite Pinot" choice for many, including me. It has deep cherry cola flavor and a silky spiciness. Pair with fennel-rubbed pork.

Kitchen Survivor™ Grade: C

Your notes: _____

MacMurray Ranch Central Coast   **$**   **Pts**
Pinot Noir, California 2006   20   86

Cola, red cherry, tea leaf, and a silky texture. In other words, texbook Central coast Pinot at a price that loves you back. Pair with rare-seared tuna.

Kitchen Survivor™ Grade: B

Your notes: _____

MacMurray Ranch Sonoma Coast   **$**   **Pts**
Pinot Noir, California 2006   28   88

♂ Fred's (as in *My Three Sons*) daughter Kate works with the Gallo family to make this de-lish Pinot with deep, black cherry–raspberry fruit and a vanilla scent.

Kitchen Survivor™ Grade: B+

Your notes: _____

Macrostie Pinot Noir, Carneros   **$**   **Pts**
California 2006   30   85

Satiny, elegant, and true to the dark cherry fruit of classic, with a soft vanilla-spiciness from oak aging.

Kitchen Survivor™ Grade: C

Your notes: _____

Mark West Central Coast Pinot   **$**   **Pts**
Noir, California 2006   14   88

"Very good value" with tangy cherry and cranberry flavors, plus soft spice and earthiness that pairs nicely with roast Thanksgiving turkey and all the trimmings.

Kitchen Survivor™ Grade: C

Your notes: _____

Meridian Pinot Noir,   **$**   **Pts**
California 2006   11   84

Perfect for every day, especially for the price. The juicy flavor "tastes like biting into fresh cherries."

Kitchen Survivor™ Grade: C

Your notes: _____

Merry Edwards Russian River   **$**   **Pts**
Valley Pinot Noir, California 2006   42   89

Elegance in a bottle, with perfumey layers of cola, red cherry, cinnamon and sassafras giving it depth. Pair with roast pork tenderloin and wild mushrooms.

Kitchen Survivor™ Grade: B

Your notes: _____

Miner Gary's Vineyard Pinot Noir,   **$**   **Pts**
California 2005   60   87

Many wineries produce an over-blown Garys' Vineyard-designate. Not here. While super-ripe, plummy and lushly oaked, this keeps the elegance that Pinot should have. Big enough to match lamb.

Kitchen Survivor™ Grade: B

Your notes: _____

Mirassou Pinot Noir,   **$**   **Pts**
California 2007   12   84

☺ A tangy, cherry-and-spice value Pinot. Perfect for every day, paired with simple chops or chicken.

Kitchen Survivor™ Grade: B

Your notes: _____

Morgan 12 Clones Pinot Noir,   **$**   **Pts**
California 2006   **31**   **85**

🍎 Although the price has gone up, the ripe dark berry fruit, plump texture and solid quality every year make this wine a consistent bet.

Kitchen Survivor™ Grade: B+

Your notes: ─────────────────────────

Panther Creek Shea Vineyard Pinot Noir   **$**   **Pts**
Willamette Valley, Oregon 2006   **40**   **86**

Lively and intense, with lots of layers; dark berry fruit and aromatics of incense, potpourri and orange peel.

Kitchen Survivor™ Grade: B

Your notes: ─────────────────────────

Ponzi Pinot Noir, Willamette Valley,   **$**   **Pts**
Oregon 2006   **35**   **89**

♟ In the classic charming Ponzi style: fragrant spice, floral and cherry aromas, sleek texture, bright cherry fruit and a coffee earthiness in the finish.

Kitchen Survivor™ Grade: C

Your notes: ─────────────────────────

Rex Hill Willamette Valley   **$**   **Pts**
Pinot Noir, Oregon 2006   **24**   **85**

The "cherry and earthy flavors" and hint of pomegranate are textbook Willamette Pinot.

Kitchen Survivor™ Grade: C

Your notes: ─────────────────────────

Robert Mondavi Pinot Noir,   **$**   **Pts**
Los Carneros, California 2006   **27**   **86**

The candied cherry character of Carneros, with oak-driven, rich notes of licorice and vanilla.

Kitchen Survivor™ Grade: B

Your notes: ─────────────────────────

Robert Mondavi Private Selection   **$**   **Pts**
Pinot Noir, California 2007   **11**   **86**

♟ A value star Pinot, with plump and silky raspberry-tea flavors that pair perfectly with grilled salmon.

Kitchen Survivor™ Grade: B+

Your notes: ─────────────────────────

Robert Sinskey Los Carneros   **$**   **Pts**
Pinot Noir, California 2006   **38**   **85**

The beloved-by-my-VOX-ers Sinskey style features sweet oak and cinnamon-spiced, supple, dark berry fruit with grace notes of orange peel and incense.

Kitchen Survivor™ Grade: B

Your notes: _____

Rochioli Russian River Pinot Noir,   **$**   **Pts**
California 2006   **55**   **92**

👍 In my opinion, one of the greatest California Pinot Noirs made, with a scent of cola and tea, pure cherry fruit, mineral finish, and *very* subtle smoky oak.

Kitchen Survivor™ Grade: A

Your notes: _____

Saintsbury Carneros Pinot Noir,   **$**   **Pts**
California 2006   **35**   **88**

👍 This "Carneros classic" is all elegance: cranberry, rhubarb, spice scents and flavors, sleek texture, and an "endless finish." Pair with duck confit salad.

Kitchen Survivor™ Grade: B+

Your notes: _____

Sanford Pinot Noir, Santa Rita   **$**   **Pts**
Hills, California 2006   **33**   **90**

🍷 A Santa Barbara classic, with exotic strawberry-rhubarb fruit, a meaty-smoky scent and, star anise spiciness. Pair with coriander-crusted rare tuna.

Kitchen Survivor™ Grade: B+

Your notes: _____

Sea Smoke Botella Pinot Noir,   **$**   **Pts**
Santa Rita Hills, California 2005   **40**   **85**

👍 The movie *Sideways* gave this wine a cult following that's deserved. The fruit intensity—spiced cherry, strawberry-rhubarb—and earthy-smoky complexity are exactly what Pinot Noir lovers are looking for. Pair with berry-sauced smoked pork loin.

Kitchen Survivor™ Grade: B+

Your notes: _____

Sebastiani Sonoma Coast Pinot Noir, California 2006 $ 18   Pts 88

♨ A price/value star, with sleek mineral-pomegranate-strawberry compote flavors and a spicy scent.

Kitchen Survivor™ Grade: B+

Your notes: _____

Sokol Blosser Willamette Pinot Noir, Oregon 2006 $ 22   Pts 88

♨ 🔥 My panel and I love this distinctive Pinot Noir style: pomegranate and rhubarb notes and a savory herbal-sundried tomato smokiness.

Kitchen Survivor™ Grade: B+

Your notes: _____

Sterling Vintner's Collection Pinot Noir, Central Coast, California 2007 $ 16   Pts 85

☺ Talk about value: real strawberry-red cherry fruit perfume and silkiness for a great price.

Kitchen Survivor™ Grade: C

Your notes: _____

Stoneleigh Pinot Noir, Marlborough, New Zealand 2007 $ 17   Pts 86

🔥 Silky and fragrant with rosepetals and fresh cherry in the scent, a soft, spicy cherry-cranberry flavor and long finish. Perfect with seared pork chops.

Kitchen Survivor™ Grade: A

Your notes: _____

Taz Pinot Noir, Santa Barbara, California 2006 $ 25   Pts 85

🍎 Classic Santa Barbara style: Bing cherry fruit and smokiness slaked with lively acidity that prolongs the licorice finish. Great with rare duck breast.

Kitchen Survivor™ Grade: ?

Your notes: _____

Truchard Carneros Pinot Noir, California 2005 $ 35   Pts 90

♨ The delicate side of Carneros, but still with great depth to the cranberry tea and smoky scents, and the satiny wild strawberries on the palate. Gorgeous.

Kitchen Survivor™ Grade: B

Your notes: _____

WillaKenzie Willamette Valley   **$**   **Pts**
Pinot Noir, Oregon 2006   **28**   **85**

🍎 A big-style wine for Oregon, with syrupy, "luscious black cherry fruit" and licorice flavors.

Kitchen Survivor™ Grade: B

Your notes: _____

Willamette Valley Vineyards Reserve   **$**   **Pts**
Pinot Noir, Oregon 2005   **25**   **89**

♟ "The best ever" from this winery, with deeply pure Bing cherry fruit and a mineral complexity that comes on as the wine opens up. Long, ripe cherry finish.

Kitchen Survivor™ Grade: B+

Your notes: _____

Willamette Valley Vineyards Whole   **$**   **Pts**
Cluster Pinot Noir, Oregon 2006   **19**   **84**

☺ The juicy cherry-grapey flavors and cherry-candy scent are great for just sipping. Great price, too.

Kitchen Survivor™ Grade: C

Your notes: _____

Williams-Selyem Pinot Noir,   **$**   **Pts**
Sonoma Coast, California 2006   **45**   **93**

♟ 👍"A benchmark," and yet they don't charge a stupid price. Like all the bottlings this will improve with age, if you aren't seduced by the layers it shows in youth: Ripe raspberry, cardamom, truffle and orange peel, with a terrifically lively and sleek texture.

Kitchen Survivor™ Grade: B+

Your notes: _____

Chianti, Sangiovese & Other Italian Reds

Category Profile: Remember the days when "Chianti" meant those kitschy straw-covered bottles? Tuscany's signature red has come a long way in quality since then, pulling much of the Italian wine world with it. But let me clear up some understandable confusion about the labels and styles. As quality has improved, Chianti has "morphed" into three tiers of wine—varietal Sangiovese (san-joe-VAY-zay), labeled with the grape name; traditional Chianti in a range of styles; and the luxury tier, which includes top regional wines like Brunello, and the so-called Super Tuscan reds (see below). Many of the major Tuscan wineries produce wines in all three categories. The basic Sangioveses largely populate the budget price tier, and some offer good value. (Most are, in my opinion, just "red wine" without a lot of character.) Chianti itself now spans the entire price and quality spectrum from budget quaff to boutique collectible, with the top-quality *classico* and *riserva* versions worthy of aging in the cellar. Finally, the Super Tuscans emerged because wineries wanted creative license to use international grapes outside the traditional Chianti "recipe" (and, I guess, with fantasy names like Summus, Sassicaia, and Luce, poetic license, too!). What they all have in common is that Italian "zest"—savory rustic spice in the scent, plus vibrant acidity—and international sophistication from the use of French oak barrels for aging and some French grapes (like Cab and Merlot) for blending. The wines are often cellar worthy and nearly always pricey—I've listed the deals in this section.

I have also included the rest of the world of Italian red wines, including the great wines of the Piedmont district, and many interesting emerging regional wines. These are often some of the best deals in red wine, period, and almost always very food-friendly, so check them out.

Serve: Cool room temperature (the budget-priced wines are generally nice with a light chill); the "bigger" wines—classicos, riservas, Super Tuscans, and Barolos—benefit from aeration (pour into the glass and swirl or decant into a pitcher or carafe with plenty of air space).

When: Any food occasion, from snack to supper to celebration.

With: Almost anything; truthfully, nearly every wine in this section warrants the "Food Friendly" symbol. Especially great wherever tomato sauce, cheese, olive oil, or savory herbs (rosemary, basil, oregano, sage) are present.

In: An all-purpose wineglass or larger-bowled red wine stem.

	$	Pts
Allegrini Valpolicella, Veneto		
Veneto, Italy 2005	13	87

Pros hail this bottling as "*the* classic Valpolicella," with almond liqueur scent, dried cherry flavor, vibrant acidity and soft tannins. Perfect with antipasti.

Kitchen Survivor™ Grade: B

Your notes: _____

	$	Pts
Antinori (Marchese) (*ahn-tee-*		
***NORE-ee mar-KAY-zee*)**	28	88
Chianti Classico Riserva, Tuscany, Italy 2005		

I used to think of this wine as overrated until I had a bottled-aged version. With a little cellaring, this wine's intensity, strawberry fruit, structure and peppery spice, gain incredible harmony.

Kitchen Survivor™ Grade: B+

Your notes: _____

	$	Pts
Avignonesi Vino Nobile di Montepulciano,	28	88
Tuscany, Italy 2005		

One of *the* names in the Vino Nobile region, and a great intro to the style: red cherry and red plum fruit, with notes of licorice, savory herbs and black olive.

Kitchen Survivor™ Grade: B+

Your notes: _____

	$	Pts
Badia a Coltibuono Chianti		
Cetamura, Tuscany, Italy 2005	10	86

☺ A tasty value bottling with lively cranberry-cherry flavor and soft spiciness. Bring on the pasta marinara!

Kitchen Survivor™ Grade: C

Your notes: _____

Badia a Coltibuono Chianti Classico, $ Pts
Tuscany, Italy 2005   25   87

Textbook Chianti Classico with lots of dried
strawberry and red licorice flavor hiding under a taut,
spicy, chalky cloak. Pair with grilled chicken skew-
ered with bacon and sage, or a cheesy tomato-y pasta.

Kitchen Survivor™ Grade: B+

Your notes: _____

Badia a Coltibuono Sangioveto, $ Pts
Tuscany, Italy 2003   60   90

A classical Sangiovese-based super Tuscan with
lots of leather and herb complexity, deep dark cherry
fruit and impressive ageability, for a good price.

Kitchen Survivor™ Grade: B

Your notes: _____

Belguardo Serrata, Maremma, $ Pts
Tuscany, Italy 2005   16   88

The Sangiovese gives savory brightness to the
cherry-raspberry fruit, while the Merlot and Cab in
the blend give a minty, cedary licorice note. Delish!

Kitchen Survivor™ Grade: B

Your notes: _____

Cantina Zaccagnini Montepulciano $ Pts
d'Abruzzo, Italy 2006   15   87

☺ My web tasters "fell in love" with the soft,
food-loving savory spice and sweet strawberry flavors
for a "value" price. Perfect for pizza and cured meats.

Kitchen Survivor™ Grade: B

Your notes: _____

Castelgiocondo Brunello di Montalcino, $ Pts
(Frescobaldi) Tuscany, Italy 2003   65   89

While intended for aging, this wine shows complex layers of cocoa, charred wood, dried cherries and
figs and coriander spice, even in youth. Decant it for
aeration and pair with a well-marbled steak.

Kitchen Survivor™ Grade: B+

Your notes: _____

Castello Banfi Brunello di Montalcino,   **$**   **Pts**
Tuscany, Italy 2003   **70**   **87**
♛ This wine needs some bottle age to soften the palate-coating tannin and dense fig and mocha flavors.
Kitchen Survivor™ Grade: B+
Your notes: _____

Castello Banfi Chianti Classico Riserva,   **$**   **Pts**
Tuscany, Italy 2004   **18**   **86**
♛ Classic Chianti with savory spice and dried herb notes, and mouthwatering strawberry fruit.
Kitchen Survivor™ Grade: A
Your notes: _____

Castello di Gabbiano Alleanza,   **$**   **Pts**
Tuscany, Italy 2005   **35**   **90**
♛ 🍎Old world chalkiness, new world fruit: this is an alliance (*alleanza* in Italian) of the talents of Beringer and Castello di Gabbiano. A blend of plummy Merlot, spicy-tangy Sangiovese and dusty-cocoa Cab, in ideal balance. Pair with cheesy pastas.
Kitchen Survivor™ Grade: A+
Your notes: _____

Castello di Gabbiano Chianti   **$**   **Pts**
Classico, Tuscany, Italy 2005   **13**   **88**
☺ A soft, light Chianti, with red cherry flavors and spicy notes that "can't be beat for the price." Bravo!
Kitchen Survivor™ Grade: B+
Your notes: _____

Castello di Gabbiano Chianti   **$**   **Pts**
Classico Riserva, Italy 2005   **23**   **89**
♛ You get a lot for the money with this "textbook Chianti Classico Riserva," with a cornucopia of red fruit, lively acidity, a tug of tannin and a savory finish.
Kitchen Survivor™ Grade: B+
Your notes: _____

Citra Montepulciano d'Abruzzo   **$**   **Pts**
(*CHEE-truh mon-teh-pool-CHAH-no*   **6**   **85**
***dah-BROOT-so*), Italy 2007**
🌶 ☺ A yummy little wine for the money, whose fruity earthy spice make almost any dish taste better.
Kitchen Survivor™ Grade: B
Your notes: _____

Col d'Orcia Brunello di Montalcino,   **$**   **Pts**
Tuscany, Italy 2003   **55**   **88**

♟ Aerate to soften the grip of firm tannin and unlock the layered rosemary, earth, pepper and strawberry. Pair with a rich beef stew or grilled sausages.

Kitchen Survivor™ Grade: B+

Your notes: _____

Falesco Vitiano (*fuh-LESS-co*   **$**   **Pts**
***vee-tee-AH-no*), Umbria, Italy 2006**   **12**   **88**

♟ ☺ "There's probably no better wine for the money," say my tasters. It's "spicy," "fruity," "smooth," "just delicious!" That's right, and as a full-blooded blend of Sangiovese, Merlot and Cab it bursts with dark jammy fruit: plums, cherries and blackberry. You could go pizza at this price, but it's good enough for serious gourmet food - the best risotto or pasta you can muster.

Kitchen Survivor™ Grade: B

Your notes: _____

Felsina Berardenga (*FELL-see-nuh*) Chianti   **$**   **Pts**
Classico, Tuscany, Italy 2006   **25**   **89**

👍 A "great" "ageable" Tuscan with bright strawberry-cherry fruit and savory-earthy tomato notes. Really shines with hearty food like spaghetti Bolognese or slow-braised beef or pork scented with rosemary.

Kitchen Survivor™ Grade: B+

Your notes: _____

Fonterutoli Chianti Classico,   **$**   **Pts**
Tuscany, Italy 2005   **25**   **87**

♟ Red fruits, lively acidity and a peppery note lead to a subtly chalky finish. Pair with some crusty bread dipped in great olive oil to let the flavors emerge.

Kitchen Survivor™ Grade: B

Your notes: _____

Frescobaldi Nipozzano Chianti   **$**   **Pts**
Rufina Riserva, Tuscany, Italy 2005   **25**   **89**

♟ Mmm...Chianti dressed in velvet, with plenty of ripe plum fruit, licorice, and black olive nuances, and a grip of tannin. Pair with fennel sausage on crostini.

Kitchen Survivor™ Grade: B+

Your notes: _____

Il Poggione Brunello di Montalcino,   **$**   **Pts**
Tuscany, Italy 2003   70   88

♟ Brooding and savory, with layers of sassafras, earth, leather, tar and dried fig. The chewy tannins will soften with air and fare, such as a fennel foccacia with roasted figs and shaved Pecorino cheese.

Kitchen Survivor™ Grade: B+

Your notes: _____

La Vite Lucente, Tuscany,   **$**   **Pts**
Italy 2006   25   89

♗ I wish more Super Tuscans were as affordable as this Merlot/Sangiovese/Cab blend. Unmistakably Tuscan with its brown spice, clay and dried cherry scents, lively acidity and chalky texture. Deep cherry on the palate, delivering both lushness and finesse.

Kitchen Survivor™ Grade: A+

Your notes: _____

Le Volte (Ornellaia), Tuscany,   **$**   **Pts**
Italy 2006   28   87

A nice "intro" Super Tuscan based on Sangiovese which gives it snappy cranberry and savory herb notes; plus Merlot and Cab that add a plummy, dusty quality. Like all good Italian wines, it's meant for food such as a tender pork roast with garlic and sage.

Kitchen Survivor™ Grade: B+

Your notes: _____

Luce Super Tuscan, Tuscany,   **$**   **Pts**
Italy 2004   60   91

"Complex and luxurious" with dark berries, nuts, minty-spice, and oak in the scent and palate. A good value among super Tuscans, blended from Merlot and Sangiovese. Pair with a top-quality grilled steak.

Kitchen Survivor™ Grade: A+

Your notes: _____

Marchesi di Barolo Barolo DOCG,   **$**   **Pts**
Piedmont, Italy 2003   55   88

♟ Barolo is meant for aging and for food. This is one that shows its alluring black plum fruit, mushroom, smoke and tarry quality in youth, if you decant and pair with a cheesy or buttery risotto or pasta.

Kitchen Survivor™ Grade: B+

Your notes: _____

Marchesi di Gresy Barbaresco Martinenga,   **$**   **Pts**
Piedmont, Italy 2005   **60**   **96**

♻ 🍎 ⚥ A bewitching wine that exhibits luxuriant fruit and old world character at the same time. The gorgeous dark cherry jam fruit is pumped up with coriander, clove and balsamic notes and a succulent mouthfeel. Yet there is fantastic tannic structure that will carry the wine for years in the cellar. A triumph at any price. For Barbaresco, this price is a deal.

Kitchen Survivor™ Grade: B+

Your notes: _____

Michele Chiarlo Barbera d'Asti   **$**   **Pts**
'Le Orme', Italy 2005   **15**   **87**

A lot of Italian character for the money! The lively acidity and flavor of dried cherries, sweet spice, and balsamic lingers into the finish and gets even better with aeration. Pair with a lusty sage-mushroom pasta.

Kitchen Survivor™ Grade: B+

Your notes: _____

Monte Antico (*MOHN-tay ann-*   **$**   **Pts**
***TEE-coh*), Tuscany, Italy 2005**   **12**   **85**

☺ Served "by the glass at in-the-know Italian restaurants," because the "plum fruit" and lively spice are "a tasty package" that's "robust but not overpowering" for food. Perfect with olive tapenade or pasta marinara.

Kitchen Survivor™ Grade: B

Your notes: _____

Nozzole (*NOTES-oh-lay*) Chianti   **$**   **Pts**
Classico Riserva, Italy 2005   **30**   **85**

💤 The "rich red berry fruit," "great acidity," and "savory spice" make it "ready to drink" and "great with food" such as lamb with rosemary and garlic.

Kitchen Survivor™ Grade: A

Your notes: _____

Poggio alla Badiola, Tuscany,   **$**   **Pts**
Italy 2006   **18**   **86**

🍎 This Sangiovese/Merlot blend is the perfect combo of soft and dark fruit, with that Italian savor you expect from Tuscany: licorice, spice, a hint of tar. Great with fresh mozzarella, basil and tomato salad.

Kitchen Survivor™ Grade: B

Your notes: _____

Poliziano Vino Nobile di Montepulciano,   **$**   **Pts**
Tuscany, Italy 2005   **25**   **86**

Of all the Tuscan reds, Vino Nobile shows the most dark ripe fruit when young - black plum and blackberry, with a dusty, forest floor note that's a great match for earthy dishes like wild mushroom ravioli.

Kitchen Survivor™ Grade: B+

Your notes: _____

Rocca delle Macie Chianti Classico,   **$**   **Pts**
Tuscany, Italy 2006   **18**   **86**

♟ A savory and chalky Chianti, with scents of green herbs, leather and licorice gracing the peppery strawberry palate. Perfect with garlicky, cheesy pastas.

Kitchen Survivor™ Grade: C

Your notes: _____

Ruffino Aziano Chianti Classico,   **$**   **Pts**
Tuscany, Italy 2006   **13**   **83**

"Good basic Chianti" for the price, with stewed tomato, spice and strawberry flavors.

Kitchen Survivor™ Grade: C

Your notes: _____

Ruffino Chianti Classico Riserva   **$**   **Pts**
Ducale (*doo-CALL-eh*) Oro (Gold   **40**   **89**
Label), Tuscany, Italy 2004

One of the most-tasted reds on my Web site. "Pricey" but "worth it," with "wow-level complexity and leather," and "roasted fig" fruit. Pair it with fresh figs with black pepper, balsamic and fresh mozzarella.

Kitchen Survivor™ Grade: A+

Your notes: _____

Ruffino Chianti Classico Riserva   **$**   **Pts**
Ducale (Tan Label), Italy 2005   **24**   **87**

🍴 "Worth the extra money" over a bargain Chianti because its "impresses." The leathery earth and spicy cherry fruit "pairs beautifully" with garlicky meats.

Kitchen Survivor™ Grade: B+

Your notes: _____

Santa Cristina Sangiovese,   **$**   **Pts**
Antinori, Tuscany, Italy 2006   13   83

This "easy to drink for everyday" wine is better than ever, with earthy cherry fruit and lively acidity.

Kitchen Survivor™ Grade: C

Your notes: _____

Straccali Chianti,   **$**   **Pts**
Italy 2007   10   83

☺ "I'd buy it again," say my Web tasters of this soft, juicy Chianti that's "a bargain for everyday drinking."

Kitchen Survivor™ Grade: C

Your notes: _____

Taurino Salice Salentino Rosso Riserva,   **$**   **Pts**
Apulia, Italy 2005   12   88

My Web tasters love the "rustic, mouth-watering bright berries" and the "great character for the price." It really is a top deal, and the ultimate pizza partner.

Kitchen Survivor™ Grade: B+

Your notes: _____

Tenuta del Terriccio Tassinaia,   **$**   **Pts**
Tuscany, Italy 2004   35   88

The cedary Cabernet shows in this Super Tuscan trio blend with Merlot and Sangiovese. The firm acidity and chalky tannin, and lively core of blackberry and cranberry fruit, are exemplary. Bottles in our cellar have aged well. Let it breath, and pair with a grilled steak, pesto pasta, or aged pecorino with olive oil.

Kitchen Survivor™ Grade: A

Your notes: _____

Tenuta Sette Ponti Crognolo,   **$**   **Pts**
Tuscany, Italy 2006   35   90

One of the "best for the price" Super Tuscans on the market. A savory balsamic-strawberry blend of Sangiovese and Merlot that serves up cumin and cardamom spices with aeration. An affordable ager, too.

Kitchen Survivor™ Grade: A

Your notes: _____

MERLOT'S KISSING COUSINS: If you are looking for something different but similar to Merlot,
check out two South American specialties. First,
there's Argentina's Malbec (*MAHL-beck*), a red grape
originally from Bordeaux. It's similar in body and
smoothness to Merlot, with lots of smoky aromatic
complexity. Some wineries to look for: Salentein,
Navarro Correas, Catena, and Chandon Terrazas.
Second, from Chile, try Carmenere (*car-muh-
NAIR-eh*), also a Bordeaux import that was originally misidentified as Merlot in many Chilean
vineyards. Its smooth texture and plum fruit are
complemented by an exotically meaty-smoky scent.
Look for Carmeneres from Concha y Toro, Mont-
Gras, Arboleda, and Veramonte Primus. Check out
"Other Reds" for more on these.

Merlot

Grape Profile: When early 1990s news reports linked
heart health and moderate red wine drinking, Merlot
joined the ranks of go-to wine grapes that inspire
instant customer recognition. As producers scrambled to meet the new demand, a lot of so-so Merlot
began to flood the market, making this a tricky category for finding quality and character. The selections
in this section are the worthy ones.

As with other market-leading varietals like Chardonnay and Cabernet Sauvignon, Merlot can range
both in price, from budget to boutique, and in complexity, from soft and simple to "serious." Across the
spectrum, Merlot is modeled on the wines from its
home region of Bordeaux, France. At the basic level,
that means medium body and soft texture, with nice
plum and berry fruit flavor.

The more ambitious versions have more body, tannin, and fruit concentration and usually a good bit of
oakiness in the scent and taste. Washington State,
California's Sonoma and Napa regions, and Chile are
my favorite growing regions for varietal Merlot. Most
Merlot producers follow the Bordeaux practice of
blending in some Cabernet Sauvignon (or another of

the classic Bordeaux red grapes) to complement and enhance the wines' taste and complexity.

Serve: *Cool* room temperature.

When: With meals, of course; and the basic bottlings are soft enough to enjoy on their own as a cocktail alternative.

With: Anything with which you enjoy red wine, especially cheeses, roasts, fuller-bodied fish, and grilled foods.

In: An all-purpose wineglass or larger-bowled red wine stem.

	$	**Pts**
Arboleda Merlot, Aconcagua, Chile 2005	**19**	**90**

♗ Another star performance from this brand, with more bewitching, meaty-smoky complexity than you ever expect from Merlot. Explosive violet, boysenberry, black licorice and hot tar on the nose; a juicy blueberry mid-palate and incredibly charred, peppery-herbal finish. Pair it with braised lamb shanks.
Kitchen Survivor™ Grade: B+
Your notes: _____

	$	**Pts**
Beaulieu Vineyard (BV) Coastal Estates Merlot, California 2005	**9**	**86**

🍎 ☺ What a deal—juicy plummy fruit, smoke, and spice. One of the best budget Merlots out there.
Kitchen Survivor™ Grade: C
Your notes: _____

	$	**Pts**
Beringer Napa Merlot, Napa California 2005	**20**	**86**

One of Beringer's nicest reds—velvety, dusty, cocoa, juicy-ripe dark cherries, vanilla, spice . . . Yum!
Kitchen Survivor™ Grade: B
Your notes: _____

	$	**Pts**
Beringer Third Century Merlot, North Coast, California 2005	**14**	**84**

🍎 A solid, fruit-forward Merlot with soft plum compote flavors, a smooth texture and delicate spice.
Kitchen Survivor™ Grade: C
Your notes: _____

Black Box Merlot,   **$**   **Pts**
California 2006 (3L box)   **22**   **84**

Juicy plum fruit and a slightly vegetal dustiness that my Web tasters say is "great for a box" and for the price. A great wine choice for casual parties.

Kitchen Survivor™ Grade: NA

Your notes: _____

Blackstone Merlot,   **$**   **Pts**
California 2005   **12**   **85**

☺ One of the most-tasted and "favorite value" wines in the survey. Folks "love the smooth-'n'-juicy plum" flavor. For many, a favorite "house red."

Kitchen Survivor™ Grade: C

Your notes: _____

Blackstone Sonoma Reserve Merlot,   **$**   **Pts**
Sonoma, California 2005   **16**   **88**

♟ For me, *this* is the Blackstone to buy. For a small trade-up you get classy wine that beats many a $25 bottle. Lots of cocoa, smoke and dark berry fruit.

Kitchen Survivor™ Grade: C

Your notes: _____

Bogle Merlot,   **$**   **Pts**
California 2006   **12**   **84**

♟ A popular brand that's huge with my Web tasters for the "soft cherry flavor" and "awesome value."

Kitchen Survivor™ Grade: C

Your notes: _____

Canoe Ridge Merlot, Columbia Valley,   **$**   **Pts**
Washington 2006   **26**   **85**

Although it's gotten pricey, it's a big seller for its classy mix of new world plummy fruit and and old world earth, tobacco and smoky notes.

Kitchen Survivor™ Grade: C

Your notes: _____

Casa Lapostolle Cuvee Alexandre   **$**   **Pts**
Merlot, California 2005   **20**   **87**

New World ripe-cherry fruit, Bordeaux-like mocha, earth, vanilla. Very classy. Pair with mushroom risotto.

Kitchen Survivor™ Grade: B

Your notes: _____

Chateau Ste. Michelle Columbia	$	Pts
Valley Merlot, Washington 2004	16	85

This wine's "Bordeaux-style elegance" and smooth plum flavor are reliable year in and year out.

Kitchen Survivor™ Grade: B

Your notes: _____

Chateau St. Jean Merlot,	$	Pts
Sonoma, California 2006	25	87

Although it's a little pricey, this wine shows St. Jean's deft hand with the Bordeaux red grapes. The dark berry, coffee and smoky notes are long and harmonious. An elegant partner for prime rib or cheeses.

Kitchen Survivor™ Grade: B

Your notes: _____

Clos du Bois Alexander Valley	$	Pts
Reserve Merlot, California 2005	23	87

Big velvety tannins, dark berry fruit, cocoa, and vanilla, with a long coconut-smoky finish.

Kitchen Survivor™ Grade: B

Your notes: _____

Clos du Bois Sonoma Merlot,	$	Pts
California 2004	18	84

Popular for sure, though I find the fruit light rather than succulent. I'm outnumbered by the many fans who say it's "yummy." The reserve (above) is my pick.

Kitchen Survivor™ Grade: C

Your notes: _____

Columbia Crest Grand Estates	$	Pts
Merlot, Washington 2005	11	86

☺ A top choice for the money, with lots of plum fruit, a vanilla-berry scent, and length you don't expect for this price. A great "house wine" pick.

Kitchen Survivor™ Grade: B

Your notes: _____

Columbia Crest Two Vines Merlot Cabernet,	$	Pts
Columbia Valley, Washington 2005	8	86

♟ A heck of a wine for the price (better than the straight Two Vines Merlot). The Merlot gives it juicy crushed berries, the Cab gives it velvetiness. Nice!

Kitchen Survivor™ Grade: C

Your notes: _____

Columbia Winery Merlot, Columbia Valley, Washington 2005 $ 16   Pts 87

"Amazing for the money," with blackberry and cedary oak, "great structure," and a long finish.

Kitchen Survivor™ Grade: B+

Your notes: _____

Duckhorn Napa Merlot, Napa, California 2005 $ 52   Pts 90

🍷 The full-throttle blackberry fruit, toasty oak, and lush texture are "for lovers of *big* Merlot." It's a benchmark that's "pricey but worth it." Pair with baked brie, seared duck or olive tapenade crostini.

Kitchen Survivor™ Grade: B+

Your notes: _____

Dynamite Vineyards Merlot, Mendocino, California 2006 $ 11   Pts 84

"Bang for the buck" berry fruit, with a touch of earth.

Kitchen Survivor™ Grade: C

Your notes: _____

Edna Valley Vineyard Merlot, San Luis Obispo, California 2006 $ 14   Pts 85

🍎 You get a lot for the money with this brand better known for whites. This Merlot's a juicy little number with crushed berries and a touch of vanilla flavor.

Kitchen Survivor™ Grade: C

Your notes: _____

Estancia Merlot, Central Coast, California 2005 $ 15   Pts 85

This "solid brand" delivers good Merlot quality for the money, with smooth, plum and licorice flavors.

Kitchen Survivor™ Grade: C

Your notes: _____

Falesco Montiano, Latium, Italy 2005 $ 45   Pts 92

🍷 🍎 "Merlot on steroids" with plush plum, blackberry, licorice and cocoa flavors. Few Merlots ever achieve this complexity. Pair with the best steak you can buy, truffle risotto, or some great cheeses.

Kitchen Survivor™ Grade: B

Your notes: _____

Ferrari-Carano Merlot, Sonoma,   **$**   **Pts**
California 2005   25   85

Although the spicy vanilla oak is ample, it's balanced by the depth of dark cherry and blackberry fruit. Give it some air: the wine actually tasted better the day after opening. Pair it with seared duck or tuna.

Kitchen Survivor™ Grade: B+

Your notes: _____

Fetzer Valley Oaks Merlot,   **$**   **Pts**
California 2006   9   85

☺ One of the best basic California Merlots out there, with "juicy" berry flavors and a good survivor grade that makes it a great "house wine."

Kitchen Survivor™ Grade: A

Your notes: _____

Franciscan Oakville Estate Merlot,   **$**   **Pts**
California 2005   22   88

The raves continue to rack up for this quintessential Napa Merlot with lush cherry fruit; plush tannins; and just enough light, toasty oak to give it "layers and layers."

Kitchen Survivor™ Grade: B

Your notes: _____

Francis Coppola Diamond Series   **$**   **Pts**
Blue Label Merlot, California 2006   17   87

This wine delivers a lot of yum for the price. The plum flavors, soft earthiness, vanilla-scented oak, and velvety-smooth tannins are what California Merlot should be. Pair it with char-grilled chicken or pork.

Kitchen Survivor™ Grade: C

Your notes: _____

Frei Brothers Reserve Merlot, Dry   **$**   **Pts**
Creek Valley, California 2006   20   88

Although the price has gone up, this wine delivers nice Merlot complexity: dark plum, dusty tobacco and red licorice. Pair it with fig-stuffed pork roast.

Kitchen Survivor™ Grade: B

Your notes: _____

Frog's Leap Merlot, Napa,   **$**   **Pts**
California 2005   **34**   **90**

⚱ The complex fig and cassis fruit, layers of licorice and roasting coffee, and long finish, make this one of the best Merlots in America. Pair it with osso bucco, cheesy risottos, or grilled steak.

Kitchen Survivor™ Grade: B+

Your notes: _____

Gallo Family Vineyards Sonoma   **$**   **Pts**
Reserve Merlot, California 2005   **16**   **88**

🍎 Just tasty wine. The "luscious" plum jam flavor thrills fans of big reds, without being over-the-top.

Kitchen Survivor™ Grade: C

Your notes: _____

Gloria Ferrer Carneros Merlot, Sonoma,   **$**   **Pts**
California 2005   **18**   **88**

Mmm. Merlot as it should be: plummy-cocoa character, soft texture, smoky finish. Pair with earthy dishes such as roasted mushrooms or aged cheeses.

Kitchen Survivor™ Grade: B

Your notes: _____

Grgich Hills Estate Merlot, Napa,   **$**   **Pts**
California 2004   **40**   **92**

⚱ 🏆 This wine shows the rarely-reached potential of the Merlot grape. There is old world earthiness - dust, truffle, espresso - along with new world depth of fig, plum and cassis fruit, with a lift of mintiness and long, earth-dusty finish. Really fantastic.

Kitchen Survivor™ Grade: B

Your notes: _____

J. Lohr Los Osos Merlot, Paso Robles,   **$**   **Pts**
California 2006   **15**   **85**

Blueberry and dark plum fruit underpinned by a nice smoky, cedary note from the soft oak.

Kitchen Survivor™ Grade: C

Your notes: _____

Kendall-Jackson Vintner's Reserve   **$**   **Pts**
Merlot, California 2005   **18**   **86**

🍎 This is Merlot in the luscious style—redolent with black cherry flavor and smooth texture.

Kitchen Survivor™ Grade: B+

Your notes: _____

Kenwood Merlot,   **$**   **Pts**
California   14   85

☺ Smooth and plummy, with a hint of smokiness. A "nice for the money" "everyday Merlot."

Kitchen Survivor™ Grade: C

Your notes: _____

L'Ecole No. 41 Walla Walla Valley   **$**   **Pts**
Merlot, Washington 2004   33   85

♟ "Not cheap," but there's "value" because you get so much chocolatey-dark cherry depth of fruit for the money. Rich and ripe enough to pair with chocolate.

Kitchen Survivor™ Grade: B

Your notes: _____

Lindemans Bin 40 Merlot, South Eastern   **$**   **Pts**
Australia 2007   7   84

☺ At this price, it's no wonder there's a huge fan club for this wine's "easy drinking" plump plum and berry fruit. Soft enough to pair with fish such as salmon.

Kitchen Survivor™ Grade: C

Your notes: _____

Marilyn Merlot, Napa,   **$**   **Pts**
California 2006   27   86

Although "you pay for the name," this is a pleasant bottle, with voluptuous plum and dark cherry fruit and vanilla oakiness.

Kitchen Survivor™ Grade: B

Your notes: _____

Markham Merlot, Napa,   **$**   **Pts**
California 2004   23   85

Still a value compared to other high-end California Merlots, with smooth raspberry flavors and soft oak.

Kitchen Survivor™ Grade: B

Your notes: _____

Matanzas Creek Merlot, Bennett Valley,   **$**   **Pts**
Sonoma, California 2005   35   90

☙ This wine has always had an impressive depth and "benchmark quality." A hint of green herbs in the scent accents the "very Sonoma" boysenberry fruit and sweet oak. Delicious with grilled squab or duck.

Kitchen Survivor™ Grade: B+

Your notes: _____

Merryvale Starmont Merlot, Napa   **$**   **Pts**
California 2005   24   85
Although it's better-known for Chardonnay, Merry-
vale makes a fine Merlot, with chocolatey-plummy
fruit with a whiff of fresh herbs and vanilla. Nice!
Kitchen Survivor™ Grade: B
Your notes: _____

Pine Ridge Crimson Creek Merlot,   **$**   **Pts**
Napa, California 2005   32   86
The lively red fruits (cherry, cranberry) and savory
herbal/peppery notes make this among the more food
friendly CA Merlots; it could handle the Thanksgiv-
ing spread, from spicy stuffing to tangy cranberries.
Kitchen Survivor™ Grade: B
Your notes: _____

Ravenswood Vintner's Blend   **$**   **Pts**
Merlot, California 2006   10   84
"Easy-drinking," "jammy, smooth" plum fruit and a
great brand for an "easy price."
Kitchen Survivor™ Grade: C
Your notes: _____

Robert Mondavi Winery Merlot, Napa,   **$**   **Pts**
California 2005   23   85
♟ A solid, subtle Merlot with red cherry, red licorice
and savory herb notes, with soft vanilla oak in the fin-
ish. Pair it with olive tapenade or tangy goat cheeses.
Kitchen Survivor™ Grade: C
Your notes: _____

Rodney Strong Sonoma Merlot,   **$**   **Pts**
California 2004   19   85
🍎 Beats "other Merlots at this price" say my Web
tasters, who love the "cedar, spice, blueberry and
coconut." Pair with pork roast with herbs and garlic.
Kitchen Survivor™ Grade: C
Your notes: _____

Rutherford Hill Merlot,   **$**   **Pts**
California   25   87
☺ Velvety-smooth, lush with plum and berry fruit
and a nice vanilla-cocoa finish. Bring on the burgers!
Kitchen Survivor™ Grade: C
Your notes: _____

St. Clement Merlot, Napa,   **$**   **Pts**
California 2005   **28**   **88**

♟ An "unsung hero" winery whose deft touch with reds shows here. Complex gravelly, herbal and tobacco scent, red cherry fruit on the palate and a lift of cedar in the finish. Pair it with rosemary lamb.

Kitchen Survivor™ Grade: B+

Your notes: _____

St. Francis Sonoma Merlot,   **$**   **Pts**
California 2005   **22**   **84**

Big and oaky, with palate-coating tannins, dark berry fruit and coconut-dill nuances. As my Web tasters say, "a big-steak wine."

Kitchen Survivor™ Grade: C

Your notes: _____

Sebastiani Sonoma County   **$**   **Pts**
Merlot, California 2005   **17**   **90**

♟ 🍎 More CA Merlot for the money than any other in the book. Loads of blueberry fruit layered with bay leaf, tobacco, coconut and dark chocolate notes that linger in the long finish. Where so many Merlots have become mundane, this one rocks. At this price, it's a gift. Delicious on its own, but St. Andre cheese is the perfect, decadent pairing.

Kitchen Survivor™ Grade: B

Your notes: _____

Shafer Napa Merlot,   **$**   **Pts**
California 2005   **46**   **89**

"Pricey but very tasty" sums it up for this rich, classy wine in the lush, powerful "cult" style (meaning huge dark-berry fruit, plush tannins and lavish vanilla-oak).

Kitchen Survivor™ Grade: B+

Your notes: _____

Simi Merlot, Sonoma   **$**   **Pts**
California 2005   **20**   **84**

Lavishly oaked, with big blackberry fruit; vanilla, clove, and coconut scents. A nice match for big and juicy grilled blue cheese burgers.

Kitchen Survivor™ Grade: C

Your notes: _____

Souverain Alexander   **$**   **Pts**
Valley Merlot, California 2006   19   89

"Exceptional quality for the price," with a deep, plummy scent and flavor plus a "wet leaves" earthiness, and a "very long finish." Really super.

Kitchen Survivor™ Grade: B

Your notes: _____

Stag's Leap Wine Cellars Napa   **$**   **Pts**
Merlot, California 2005   42   84

Although it's gotten pricey, this Merlot's still a big seller. Nice complexity in the layers of red cherry and red plum fruit, with a whiff of tea and tobacco.

Kitchen Survivor™ Grade: C

Your notes: _____

Sterling Vineyards Merlot, Napa   **$**   **Pts**
California 2005   22   86

Sterling's best Napa bottling in years, with velvety-co-cocoa tannins, black plum fruit and a smoky finish.

Kitchen Survivor™ Grade: B+

Your notes: _____

Sterling Vintner's Collection Merlot,   **$**   **Pts**
Central Coast, California 2005   15   86

☺ This wine really delivers for the price: lots of juicy and plump dark berry fruit, smooth texture and a soft kiss of oak. A great "house red" candidate.

Kitchen Survivor™ Grade: B

Your notes: _____

Stonestreet Merlot, Alexander Valley,   **$**   **Pts**
Sonoma, California 2005   32   84

A big-tannin, big-oak wine that's also a big seller. The palate delivers plum fruit and a dusty smokiness.

Kitchen Survivor™ Grade: C

Your notes: _____

Twin Fin Merlot,   **$**   **Pts**
California 2006   8   84

Juicy cherry Jell-O flavors and a touch of sweet oak flavor. Really pleasant for the price.

Kitchen Survivor™ Grade: C

Your notes: _____

William Hill Estate Merlot, Napa,	$	Pts
California 2005	25	86

Soft layers of red licorice and a tangy sassafras note, complimented by abundant raspberry and boysenberry fruit. Pair it with fig-stuffed pork roast.

Kitchen Survivor™ Grade: C

Your notes: _____

Cabernet Sauvignon and Blends

Grape Profile: Although Merlot ranks above it, Cabernet Sauvignon remains a top-selling red varietal wine. It grows well virtually all over the wine world and gives good to excellent quality and flavor at every price level, from steal to splurge. Its style can vary, based on the wine's quality level, from uncomplicated everyday styles to the superintense boutique bottlings. The most famous and plentiful sources of Cabernet are Bordeaux in France, California (especially Sonoma and Napa), Washington State, and Italy on the high end with its Super Tuscan versions; and I think Chile shines in the low- to mid-priced category. Classically, it has a scent and taste of dark berries (black cherry, blackberry), plus notes of spice, earth, cocoa, cedar, and even mint that can be very layered and complex in the best wines. It has medium to very full body and often more tannin—that bit of a tongue-gripping sensation that one of my waiters once described, perfectly I think, as "a slipcover for the tongue, ranging from terry cloth to suede to velvet," depending on the wine in question. Oakiness, either a little or a lot depending on the growing region and price category, is also a common Cabernet feature. Combined, these can make for a primo mouthful of wine, which surely explains why Cabernet is king of collectible wines.

A note about blends: As described previously for Merlot, Cabernet Sauvignon wines often follow the Bordeaux blending model, with one or more of the traditional Bordeaux red grapes—Merlot, Cabernet Franc, Petit Verdot, and Malbec—blended in for balance and complexity. Australia pioneered blending Cabernet Sauvignon with Shiraz—a delicious combination that the wine buying market has embraced. Those blends are listed either here or in the Shiraz section, according to which of the two grapes is dominant in the blend (it will be listed first on the label, too).

Serve: Cool room temperature; the fuller-bodied styles benefit from aeration—pour into the glass a bit ahead of time or decant into a carafe (but if you forget, don't sweat it; if you care to, swirling the glass does help).

When: With your favorite red wine meals, but the everyday bottlings are soft enough for cocktail-hour sipping.

With: Anything you'd serve alongside a red; especially complements beef, lamb, goat cheese and hard cheeses, pesto sauce, and dishes scented with basil, rosemary, sage, or oregano.

In: An all-purpose wineglass or larger-bowled red wine stem.

	$	Pts
Alexander Valley Vineyards Cabernet Sauvignon, California	20	85

A Merlot that drinks like a Cab, with blackberry fruit, velvety tannins, vanilla oak and a touch of cedar.

Kitchen Survivor™ Grade: C

Your notes: _____

	$	Pts
Alice White Cabernet Sauvignon, Australia 2007	7	82

Another solid offering from this value brand, with soft blackberry fruit and a hint of cedar and mint.

Kitchen Survivor™ Grade: C

Your notes: _____

	$	Pts
Alice White Cabernet Shiraz, Australia 2007	7	84

☺ This "yummy budget choice" has "nice plum fruit" and a touch of cedar in the scent.

Kitchen Survivor™ Grade: C

Your notes: _____

	$	Pts
Arboleda Cabernet Sauvignon Aconcagua Valley, Chile 2006	19	89

⚱ A "trade-up" Chilean that's worth it. Alluring black licorice and a juicy meatiness on the nose; the palate is dense with dusky blackberry fruit, a luxuriant suede texture and a long smoky, tarry finish.

Kitchen Survivor™ Grade: B

Your notes: _____

Arrowood Cabernet Sauvignon   **$**   **Pts**
Sonoma County, California 2004   50   84

The classic Sonoma Cab style, with wild blackberry fruit and lots of smoky oak. Decant or aerate, and serve with a big steak to tame the oak and tannin.

Kitchen Survivor™ Grade: B

Your notes: _____

Baron Philippe de Rothschild,   **$**   **Pts**
Escudo Rojo Cabernet Blend, Chile 2006   18   89

♉ ⚱ REALLY worth seeking out for its subtle complexity—smokiness, dried cumin, leather, coffee, figs, mint—and great balance. All that complexity demands a well-charred steak with a side of 'shrooms.

Kitchen Survivor™ Grade: B+

Your notes: _____

Beaulieu Vineyard (BV) Coastal Estates   **$**   **Pts**
Cabernet Sauvignon, California 2005   9   86

"Especially for the price," my Web tasters find it "tasty," with nice blackberry varietal character.

Kitchen Survivor™ Grade: C

Your notes: _____

Beaulieu Vineyard (BV) Georges   **$**   **Pts**
de Latour Private Reserve Cabernet   115   91
Sauvignon, Napa, California 2005

♉ "Amazing" say my Web tasters of this wine's licorice, cedar, black cherry, and tarry-mineral aromas, typical of the region's "Rutherford Dust" soil. Velvety, brooding, and worthy of the cellar.

Kitchen Survivor™ Grade: B

Your notes: _____

Beaulieu Vineyard (BV) Napa Valley   **$**   **Pts**
Cabernet Sauvignon, California 2005   19   86

Nice! Dusty, minty, earthy with subtle dark berry fruit. A great pairing with pesto pasta.

Kitchen Survivor™ Grade: B

Your notes: _____

Beaulieu Vineyard (BV) Rutherford   **$**   **Pts**
Cabernet Sauvignon, California 2005   27   88

♉ More than "a really solid trade-up" choice, this classic bottling is dusty and smoky with lead pencil, blackberry and crushed mint notes. Pair with a great cheese or simply a rare, well-charred steak.

Kitchen Survivor™ Grade: B

Your notes: _____

Beaulieu Vineyard (BV) Tapestry Reserve Red Blend, California 2005 $ 55 Pts 89

A blend of the Bordeaux grapes (Cab, Merlot, Cabernet Franc, Malbec and Petit Verdot) that shows layers of dusty earth, dark berry fruit, smoke and lead pencil, with a velvety texture. Ages well, too.

Kitchen Survivor™ Grade: B

Your notes: _____

Benziger Cabernet Sauvignon, Sonoma, California 2005 $ 18 Pts 89

An exemplary Sonoma Cab for the price, with succulent boysenberry and dark plum fruit, a whisper of licorice and a velvety-juicy, drink-me texture.

Kitchen Survivor™ Grade: B

Your notes: _____

Beringer Knights Valley Cabernet Sauvignon, California 2006 $ 27 Pts 88

The chewy cassis fruit with vanilla-scented oak are "as complex and balanced as a wine for twice the price." It "gets better" with age, too.

Kitchen Survivor™ Grade: A

Your notes: _____

Beringer Private Reserve Cabernet Sauvignon, California 2004 $ 116 Pts 90

Amazing aromas of cedar, olives, tobacco, and black currants, plus nice balance and ageability.

Kitchen Survivor™ Grade: B+

Your notes: _____

Blackstone Cabernet Sauvignon, California 2006 $ 12 Pts 85

☺ "Inexpensive for what you get"—namely, "delicious" blackberry and cocoa scents and flavors.

Kitchen Survivor™ Grade: B

Your notes: _____

Cain Cuvee Bordeaux Style Red,   **$**   **Pts**
California NV5   34   88

A "wow" versus more expensive California Cab blends. The cassis fruit and cedary oak "command your attention." NV5 indicates most of the wine is from the 2005 vintage. Pair with steak or a rich cheese.

Kitchen Survivor™ Grade: B+

Your notes: _____

Cakebread Cellars Napa Cabernet   **$**   **Pts**
Sauvignon, California 2004   75   87

The lead pencil, "cedar, blackberry, and anise" complexity draw raves for this "great name from Napa."

Kitchen Survivor™ Grade: B+

Your notes: _____

Caymus Napa Cabernet   **$**   **Pts**
Sauvignon, California 2005   70   89

Pricey, but one of the most sought-after Napa Cabs: jam-packed with huge dark fruit, sweet oak, and strapping tannins that make it cellar-worthy.

Kitchen Survivor™ Grade: B+

Your notes: _____

Chateau Clerc-Milon, Pauillac, Bordeaux,   **$**   **Pts**
France 2002   50   87

A great way to affordably buy Bordeaux is from a solid chateau without rockstar status, like this one. The 2004 vintage is beginning to show nicely, with scents of warm brick and flavors of warm berries, with a coffee finish. Pair with rare prime rib or lamb.

Kitchen Survivor™ Grade: B

Your notes: _____

Chateau Cos d'Estournel, Ste. Estephe,   **$**   **Pts**
Bordeaux, France 2004   130   89

Although the great 2005 vintage is impossibly expensive, this so-called "off" vintage makes a worthy splurge. Its dusty cedar, cassis, sweet tobacco, anise, and coffee bean character are classic Cos (rhymes with "boss"), as fans call it. Top vintages age 25+ years; lesser vintages still improve for a decade or so.

Kitchen Survivor™ Grade: B+

Your notes: _____

Chateau d'Issan Bordeaux, Margaux,   **$**   **Pts**
France 2005   **80**   **90**

♂ ♟ One of the more affordable 2005s that also happens to be awesome - power and elegance in perfect harmony. The seductive mocha, toast, blackcurrant and anise layers are luxuriant and long. If you can find the 2002, it is half the price, and also delicious.

Kitchen Survivor™ Grade: B+

Your notes: _____

Chateau Duhart-Milon Rothschild   **$**   **Pts**
Bordeaux, France 2004   **55**   **87**

♟ ♟ Another great bet for affordable Bordeaux. This wine is tightly-wound and intense, with chewy-dusty tannins, dark cherry and currant fruit, and lots of cedar and sandalwood in the scent and finish.

Kitchen Survivor™ Grade: B

Your notes: _____

Chateau Greysac Medoc, Bordeaux,   **$**   **Pts**
France 2005   **22**   **88**

♂ A fantastic wine from a world-class vintage. Textbook Medoc Bordeaux with autumn leaf pile, roasted espresso and cedar, and subtle blackcurrant fruit. Long, smoky, and tailor-made for a simple roast or aged cheese.

Kitchen Survivor™ Grade: B

Your notes: _____

Chateau Gruaud-Larose, St. Julien,   **$**   **Pts**
Bordeaux, France 2005   **75**   **89**

♟ "Pricey," but more affordable than many Bordeaux of comparable quality, with palate-coating tannins, dark cassis fruit, cedar-coffee scents, and a long finish.

Kitchen Survivor™ Grade: A

Your notes: _____

Chateau Lagrange, St. Julien,   **$**   **Pts**
Bordeaux, France 2005   **65**   **88**

♟ *Affordable* classic Bordeaux, with a textbook dusty, blackcurrant, and roasted coffee character. One of the few good ones that's fairly affordable in the highly-regarded 2005 vintage. Pair with braised shortribs.

Kitchen Survivor™ Grade: B+

Your notes: _____

Chateau Lascombes, Margaux,	$	Pts
Bordeaux, France 2003	59	87

🍎 Like so many 2003s (a ripe vintage), upfront and sexy now. Classic Medoc character of roasted coffee bean, mocha and cassis. Check my Web site for the complete note, and ageability recommendations.
Kitchen Survivor™ Grade: B

Your notes: _____

Chateau Les Ormes de Pez, Ste.	$	Pts
Estephe, Bordeaux, France 2004	40	85

♟ The "cassis and earthy" (autumn leaves and wet gravel) character is classic Bordeaux at a doable price.
Kitchen Survivor™ Grade: B

Your notes: _____

Chateau Lynch-Bages, Pauillac,	$	Pts
Bordeaux, France 2004	45	85

♟ A "deal and ready to drink" in so-so years, and always true to its style: cedar and lead-pencil scent, mineral-y cassis fruit, velvety-powerful texture. Pair with rosemary-roasted leg of lamb or a big cheese.
Kitchen Survivor™ Grade: B+

Your notes: _____

Chateau Meyney, Haut-Medoc,	$	Pts
Bordeaux, France 2005	24	88

♟ I think this will drink well for ten years or so, and it's nice now. The charry, smoky layers and fine core of dark cherry fruit lifted with cedar and lively acidity would pair deliciously with herb-crusted veal chops.
Kitchen Survivor™ Grade: B

Your notes: _____

Chateau Ste. Michelle Columbia	$	Pts
Valley Cabernet Sauvignon,	16	85
Washington 2005		

Great for the price, with a deep black cherry nose, soft blackberry flavors, and soft cedary oak.
Kitchen Survivor™ Grade: B

Your notes: _____

Chateau St. Jean Cinq Cepages   **$**   **Pts**
(*sank seh-PAHJH*) Cabernet   **75**   **89**
Blend, California 2005

♟ Needs aeration to show its classic suppleness and layers of pencil lead, tobacco, cedar and dark cherry.
Kitchen Survivor™ Grade: B

Your notes: _____

Clos du Bois Marlstone, Sonoma,   **$**   **Pts**
California 2004   **50**   **87**

Chewy and brooding, with a mineral, briary scent and layers of black olive, black cherry, and tobacco.
Kitchen Survivor™ Grade: B+

Your notes: _____

Clos du Bois Reserve Cabernet Sauvignon,   **$**   **Pts**
Alexander Valley, California 2005   **25**   **86**

The best of this bottling in a long time, with lots of blackberry fruit, anise, molasses and toasty oak.
Kitchen Survivor™ Grade: B

Your notes: _____

Clos du Bois Sonoma Cabernet   **$**   **Pts**
Sauvignon, California 2004   **18**   **83**

Although some of my Web tasters remember when it wasn't as "pricey," I think the wild berry and anise character beats their hugely popular Merlot.
Kitchen Survivor™ Grade: C

Your notes: _____

Clos du Val Napa Cabernet   **$**   **Pts**
Sauvignon, California 2004   **32**   **88**

Nice varietal character in the blackcurrant fruit, with the "Napa" stamp of cedar in the scent. Elegant, silky and well-made. Pair with steak and mushroom sauce.
Kitchen Survivor™ Grade: B

Your notes: _____

Columbia Crest Grand Estates Cabernet   **$**   **Pts**
Sauvignon, Columbia Valley, Washington 2005   **11**   **87**

☺ "Delicious" and "a 'wow' at this price" sums up the raves for this plush blackberry-and-earth Cab.
Kitchen Survivor™ Grade: B+

Your notes: _____

Concha y Toro Casillero del Diablo   **$**   **Pts**
Cabernet Sauvignon, Maipo, Chile 2005   12   87

♀ A lot of Cab character for the money, with dusty-blackberry, cocoa, and cedar, plus a meaty gaminess.

Kitchen Survivor™ Grade: C

Your notes: _____

Concha y Toro Don Melchor Cabernet   **$**   **Pts**
Cabernet Sauvignon Reserva, Maipo, Chile 2005   65   89

♀ You could mistake the subtle cedar, tobacco, vanilla, and dark fruit for Bordeaux. The fine-textured tannins, and the smoky minerality in the finish add to the sophistication. Pair with duck breast.

Kitchen Survivor™ Grade: A

Your notes: _____

Concha y Toro Marques de Casa   **$**   **Pts**
Concha Cabernet Sauvignon, Maipo, Chile 2005   14   86

♀ A little bit like a "baby Don Melchor," with subtle dustiness, cedar and lead pencil in the scent and a solid core of cassis fruit. Quite nice for the price.

Kitchen Survivor™ Grade: C

Your notes: _____

Cousino Macul Antiguas Reservas   **$**   **Pts**
Cabernet Sauvignon, Maipo, Chile 2006   18   87

♀ Another "terrific" for the price wine that shows what quality you can get if you trade up just a little in Chilean Cab: smoky-cocoa scent, blueberry nutmeg and cedar flavors, long finish. Pair with roast duck.

Kitchen Survivor™ Grade: B

Your notes: _____

Dynamite Vineyards Cabernet Sauvignon,   **$**   **Pts**
Red Hills, Lake County, California 2005   17   84

Cedar and blackberry scents and flavors, with a soft chocolatey-coconut character from the oak.

Kitchen Survivor™ Grade: C

Your notes: _____

Esser Cabernet Sauvignon,   **$**   **Pts**
California 2006   11   86

Nice varietal character that's a rare find at this price: blackberry, cedar, velvety texture.

Kitchen Survivor™ Grade: B

Your notes: _____

Estancia Paso Robles   **$**   **Pts**
Cabernet Sauvignon, California 2006   **15**   **84**

"Real-deal California Cabernet" flavor—mint and cassis—at a "good price" makes this a winner.

Kitchen Survivor™ Grade: B

Your notes: _____

Far Niente Cabernet Sauvignon,   **$**   **Pts**
California 2005   **125**   **88**

A "steakhouse classic" with a price to match. But it's classy, with the big dark fruit, licorice and chocolate notes its fans love. Pair it with blue cheese burgers.

Kitchen Survivor™ Grade: A

Your notes: _____

Fetzer Valley Oaks Cabernet   **$**   **Pts**
Sauvignon, California 2006   **9**   **84**

Just what a "bargain"-priced Cab should be: "generous fruit" (plum, berry) and "mild, food-friendly tannins." A smooth but flavorful everyday red choice.

Kitchen Survivor™ Grade: C

Your notes: _____

Ferrari Carano Cabernet Sauvignon,   **$**   **Pts**
Alexander Valley, California 2005   **38**   **86**

A big and showy wine, with toffee-vanilla oak, rich dark fruit, anise and molasses, and plush tannins.

Kitchen Survivor™ Grade: C

Your notes: _____

Flora Springs Trilogy Red Table Wine,   **$**   **Pts**
California 2005   **65**   **89**

♟ A Napa classic Bordeaux-style blend that's a fraction of the price of competitors, and ages great. It's subtle and cedary, with chewy dark cherry on the mid-palate and a dusty-cocoa finish.

Kitchen Survivor™ Grade: B+

Your notes: _____

Franciscan Magnificat Meritage, Napa, California 2005
$ 50 Pts 87

Althought it's no longer "a steal" in its category it still shows the "packed-in blackberry," cedar-vanilla, tobacco, and smokiness classic of Napa Cab blends.

Kitchen Survivor™ Grade: A

Your notes: _____

Franciscan Oakville Estate Cabernet Sauvignon, California 2005
$ 28 Pts 85

You get real Napa Cab character—a whiff of cedar-mint, dark cassis fruit, sweet vanilla from oak, and velvety tannins—that's subtle and not overblown.

Kitchen Survivor™ Grade: B

Your notes: _____

Francis Coppola Diamond Series Claret (*CLARE-ett*), California 2005
$ 19 Pts 89

Claret means it's a blend primarily of Cabernet and Merlot grapes. There's a lot here for the money: cedary, mocha scents and firm blackberry fruit and velvety tannins. Fantastic with pesto pasta.

Kitchen Survivor™ Grade: B

Your notes: _____

Frei Brothers Reserve Cabernet Sauvignon, Alexander Valley, California 2005
$ 25 Pts 87

The dusty-cassis-mint-tobacco style of this wine is textbook Alexander Valley Cab. It's graceful and subtle on the palate, making it a nice food partner.

Kitchen Survivor™ Grade: C

Your notes: _____

Frog's Leap Cabernet Sauvignon, Napa, California 2005
$ 38 Pts 90

One of Napa's most distinctive and worthy Cabs, jam-packed with blackberry flavor, kissed with vanilla, licorice, and black olive scents; impeccably balanced.

Kitchen Survivor™ Grade: B

Your notes: _____

Gallo Family Vineyards Barelli Creek Cabernet Sauvignon, California 2005
$ 28 Pts 85

Luxuriant blackberry, earth, coconut, and mint notes, with a hint of pepper. Pair it with jerk pork.

Kitchen Survivor™ Grade: B+

Your notes: _____

Gallo Family Vineyards Sonoma Reserve   **$**   **Pts**
Cabernet Sauvignon, California 2006   **15**   **87**

Although "it's gotten more oaky," there's still lots of big, dark berry and fig fruit intensity, and impressive concentration for the price. Pair it with grilled lamb chops.

Kitchen Survivor™ Grade: C

Your notes: _____

Geyser Peak Cabernet Sauvignon,   **$**   **Pts**
Alexander Valley, California 2005   **18**   **85**

This "textbook Sonoma Cab" "hits all the right notes"—cedar, dark berry fruit, fine tannins, for a good price. Great with fennel sausage pizza.

Kitchen Survivor™ Grade: B

Your notes: _____

Grgich Hills Estate Cabernet Sauvignon,   **$**   **Pts**
Napa, California 2004   **60**   **92**

🍴 👍 Grgich deftly eschews the "fruit bomb" model with this chewy and dense Cab that's built for aging. The dark cherry and blackcurrant fruit and tobacco character, plus a mushroomy earthiness, are almost old world in style. Pair it with slow-braised lamb or venison.

Kitchen Survivor™ Grade: A

Your notes: _____

Groth Napa Cabernet Sauvignon,   **$**   **Pts**
Oakville, California 2005   **58**   **88**

It's not cheap, but for a luxury Cab that ages well, it's reasonable. The plush tannins, deep cassis fruit, anise and licorice notes and lavish vanilla oak are classic Oakville. Pesto pasta is a great match-up.

Kitchen Survivor™ Grade: B+

Your notes: _____

Heitz Cellars Cabernet Sauvignon,   **$**   **Pts**
Napa, California 2004   **42**   **88**

👍 The "fabulous earthy-minty qualities" and powerful dark fruit that are Heitz signatures in the famous Martha's Vineyard bottling even come through in this basic Napa offering. Pair with herb-crusted lamb.

Kitchen Survivor™ Grade: B+

Your notes: _____

Hess Cabernet Sauvignon,   **$**   **Pts**
California 2005   **15**   **87**

☺ My Web tasters "love" this "always-reliable" Cabernet's plum and blackberry flavors and touch of earthy spiciness that "goes great with stuffed peppers." (Note that it used to be labeled Hess Select.)

Kitchen Survivor™ Grade: B

Your notes: _____

Hogue Cabernet Sauvignon,   **$**   **Pts**
Washington 2005   **9**   **85**

☺ Another "deal for the price" Cab from Washington, with earthy-cocoa scent and blackberry fruit.

Kitchen Survivor™ Grade: C

Your notes: _____

Jacob's Creek Reserve Cabernet   **$**   **Pts**
Sauvignon, Australia 2005   **12**   **88**

♟ The nice minty-berry fruit, soft tannin, and great price make this an "amazing value for the money."

Kitchen Survivor™ Grade: B

Your notes: _____

J. Lohr 7 Oaks Cabernet Sauvignon,   **$**   **Pts**
Paso Robles, California 2006   **17**   **84**

🍎 Always a solid price/value with wild berry fruit and luxurious coconut cream scent from American oak.

Kitchen Survivor™ Grade: B+

Your notes: _____

Jordan Cabernet Sauvignon,   **$**   **Pts**
California 2004   **50**   **85**

♙ The quality can vary by vintage, but the elegant leafy-earthy, red fruit style of this Cab distinguishes it from the huge "fruit and oak bomb" Cabs that critics love. Ages well in top years. Pair with duck

Kitchen Survivor™ Grade: B+

Your notes: _____

Joseph Phelps Insignia Cabernet   **$**   **Pts**
Blend, California 2005   **200**   **96**

♟ 🍎 👍 A Napa blockbuster, with potent black fruit, licorice, toasted-coconutty oak, and plush tannins. The wine wears its opulence with grace; while it's a decadent drink when young, it ages beautifully. One of the most "worth it" splurges out there.

Kitchen Survivor™ Grade: B+

Your notes: _____

Joseph Phelps Napa Cabernet   **$**   **Pts**
Sauvignon, California 2005   **54**   **89**

Real Napa Cab that's consistent every year for its nice structure, mint, cedar, coffee-spice, and black-berry fruit. Pair with pork or duck in red wine sauce.

Kitchen Survivor™ Grade: B

Your notes: _____

Justin Isosceles Cabernet Blend,   **$**   **Pts**
Paso Robles, California 2005   **60**   **88**

☞ This wine put Paso Robles on the map. Its dark berry, minty, and coffee aromas grow more refined with age. The meaty subtlety is tailor-made for pairing with roasted game birds or braised veal.

Kitchen Survivor™ Grade: C

Your notes: _____

Kendall-Jackson Vintner's Reserve   **$**   **Pts**
Cabernet Sauvignon, California 2005   **18**   **85**

Although all of K-Js' Vintner's Reserve reds have jumped in price, this bottling's Cab character—blackberry, earth, velvety tannin - is still exemplary.

Kitchen Survivor™ Grade: B

Your notes: _____

Kenwood Jack London Cabernet Sauvignon, **$**   **Pts**
Sonoma, California 2005   **38**   **87**

This wine's signature offers is savory sassafras and balsamic notes, chewy tannins, red currant fruit and coriander spice. A great pick for barbecued ribs.

Kitchen Survivor™ Grade: C

Your notes: _____

Liberty School Cabernet Sauvignon,   **$**   **Pts**
Paso Robles, California 2005   **18**   **85**

As it has for years, this wine offers good Cab character—dark plum fruit and spice—for the price.

Kitchen Survivor™ Grade: C

Your notes: _____

Los Vascos Cabernet Sauvignon, $ Pts
Chile 2006 10 85
One of Chile's best budget Cabernets, with dark
cherry fruit, a cedary scent, and smooth tannins.
Kitchen Survivor™ Grade: B
Your notes: _____

Louis Martini Alexander Valley Cabernet $ Pts
Sauvignon Reserve, California 2004 35 89
Tasted blind against Cabs at twice the price, this bot-
tling stands up tall, with coconutty-spicy oak, huge
but balanced blackberry fruit, mint, and eucalyptus.
Kitchen Survivor™ Grade: B+
Your notes: _____

Louis Martini Napa Valley Cabernet $ Pts
Sauvignon Reserve, Napa, California 2005 25 91
🍸 🍎 The gods of Cabernet must live at Martini; it
is where they keep their stash of incredibly affordable, drinkable-young-but-ageable, kicks expensive
Cabernets' butts Cab. Luckily they share some of the
velvety, blackcurrant, cedar-dusty juice with us. Why
pay more when you need not? Pair this with a great
steak and revel in the Napa-ness, for a great price.
Kitchen Survivor™ Grade: B+
Your notes: _____

Louis Martini Sonoma Cabernet $ Pts
Sauvignon, California 2006 17 88
Blackberry, fig, cocoa and coffee come on in subtle
layers, while the velvety texture coats your tongue.
The long, smoky finish screams for a charred burger.
Kitchen Survivor™ Grade: A
Your notes: _____

Markham Vineyards Cabernet Sauvignon, $ Pts
Napa, California 2003 29 87
☺ A "great wine list bet" because it offers nice black-
berry, cinnamon and cedar layers, at a decent price.
The tannins are soft, so pair with pork or even salmon.
Kitchen Survivor™ Grade: C
Your notes: _____

McWilliams Hanwood Estate $ Pts
Cabernet Sauvignon, Australia 2005 12 86
One of Australia's best value bottlings, offering lots of
layers for the price—mint, earth, ripe berries.

Kitchen Survivor™ Grade: B
Your notes: _____

Mt. Veeder Cabernet Sauvignon,   **$**   **Pts**
Napa, California 2005   **40**   **92**

One of my favorite Cabs, period—with firm tannins, dense fig fruit, tobacco and cedar, a long finish and good ageability. Pairing it with a charred steak or smoked brisket brings out the wine's tarry smokiness.

Kitchen Survivor™ Grade: A+
Your notes: _____

Oberon Hillside Reserve Cabernet   **$**   **Pts**
Sauvignon, Napa, California 2005   **20**   **89**

A textbook Napa Cab with rich blackcurrant and cassis fruit on the palate, and a dusty-cedar note in the scent and finish. Great with garlicky braised lamb.

Kitchen Survivor™ Grade: B
Your notes: _____

Opus One Cabernet Blend,   **$**   **Pts**
California 2004   **170**   **91**

A "powerful wine" with classy, toasty-mocha oak and blackcurrant-licorice flavors that are "so Napa," plus a coffee/lead-pencil scent that is Bordeaux-like."

Kitchen Survivor™ Grade: B
Your notes: _____

Penfolds Bin 389 Cabernet   **$**   **Pts**
Sauvignon/Shiraz, Australia 2005   **37**   **91**

This "awesome" wine delivers on all counts: complexity, the "yum" factor, and value. The vivid blueberry fruit and pepper/black olive/spice/coconut scent are delicious young, but the wine also cellars beautifully. Great with lamb, and even dark chocolate.

Kitchen Survivor™ Grade: A
Your notes: _____

Penfolds Koonunga Hill Cabernet/   **$**   **Pts**
Merlot, Australia 2006   **12**   **88**

☺ The cedar scent of Cabernet, plus the plummy softness of Merlot at a very good price for the quality.

Kitchen Survivor™ Grade: B
Your notes: _____

Pine Ridge Cabernet Sauvignon **$** **Pts**
Stag's Leap District, California 2003 80 87

While it's gotten price, it remains true to the classic Stag's Leap district Cab style, with earthy-cherry-cur-rant fruit, and soft scents of bay leaf and sandalwood.

Kitchen Survivor™ Grade: B

Your notes: _____

Provenance Vineyards Cabernet **$** **Pts**
Sauvignon, Rutherford, California 2005 42 91

If you want (affordable) Napa Cab opu-lence, this is your wine. The scent and palate drip with ripe, compoted blueberry-fig fruit, fragrant anise, dark chocolate and sweet vanilla. Speaking of chocolate, that's the food match. Cambazzola cheese is another great one.

Kitchen Survivor™ Grade: B

Your notes: _____

Quintessa Cabernet Blend, **$** **Pts**
California 2005 130 88

The price is high, but for fans of its elegance, deep cassis fruit flavor and subtle scents of autumn leaf pile and soft vanilla, it's worth the splurge.

Kitchen Survivor™ Grade: C

Your notes: _____

Raymond "R" Collection Cabernet **$** **Pts**
Sauvignon, Napa, California 2004 19 87

The Raymonds put quality and Napa character in the bottle for a great price. It's "minty and elegant," bal-anced and bright with lively red fruit that makes it a great pairing with baked pastas like lasagne.

Kitchen Survivor™ Grade: B

Your notes: _____

Raymond Reserve Cabernet **$** **Pts**
Sauvignon, Napa, California 2005 35 88

Here's to an affordable wine that really drinks like a reserve, with lots of dark-fruited richness, lavish vanilla and cinnamon spice, and a plush texture.

Kitchen Survivor™ Grade: B

Your notes: _____

Ray's Station Cabernet Sauvignon   **$**   **Pts**
Sonoma, California 2005   **15**   **86**

Nice Cab character for the price with blackberry, cocoa and cedar in a medium-bodied, drink-it-now style. Soft enough to pair with grilled salmon or tuna.

Kitchen Survivor™ Grade: C

Your notes: _____

Robert Mondavi Cabernet Sauvignon   **$**   **Pts**
Reserve, Napa, California 2005   **135**   **94**

A Napa blue chip sumptuously layered with eucalyptus, cedar, dark cherry and bittersweet chocolate; delicious young, but it ages incredibly well, too.

Kitchen Survivor™ Grade: B

Your notes: _____

Robert Mondavi Cabernet Sauvignon,   **$**   **Pts**
Napa, California 2005   **28**   **87**

The best vintage in years for this benchmark Napa Cab. There's a nice lift of acidity and fragrant cedar to the ripe cherry fruit, and softly earthy finish.

Kitchen Survivor™ Grade: C

Your notes: _____

Rodney Strong Sonoma Cabernet   **$**   **Pts**
Sauvignon, California 2005   **16**   **86**

My Web tasters "love" the coconutty oak and "huge berry fruit" that "tastes more expensive than it is." Exotic enough to pair with curry or teriyaki.

Kitchen Survivor™ Grade: B

Your notes: _____

Rosemount Diamond Label   **$**   **Pts**
Cabernet Sauvignon Australia 2006   **10**   **85**

☺ My Web tasters rave that this "jammy," "very-well-made" Aussie is "simply one of the best buys in wine."

Kitchen Survivor™ Grade: C

Your notes: _____

Rubicon Estate,   **$**   **Pts**
California 2004   **115**   **90**

🏆 I'm always struck by this wine's distinctive notes of balsamic-marinated cherries and lavendar. On the palate, plush tannins underpin the dark fruit, licorice and earth notes. Definitely a wine for the cellar.
Kitchen Survivor™ Grade: B+
Your notes: _____

Rust-en-Vrede Estate Red,   **$**   **Pts**
South Africa 2004   **40**   **89**

🏅🏆 "Like a good Bordeaux" in its complexity, but there's Shiraz mixed with the Cab and Merlot. It's "very characteristic" of South Africa reds, with velvety tannins and lusty meaty notes atop the ripe fig fruit.
Kitchen Survivor™ Grade: B+
Your notes: _____

St. Clement Cabernet Sauvignon,   **$**   **Pts**
Napa, California 2005   **35**   **89**

This Napa classic flies under the radar, hence the great price for what you get: classy real-deal Napa Cab. The cedar, violets, red cherry and warm brick scent unfolds to a palate of luxuriant dark fruit, velvety tannin and cinnamon spice. Delicious.
Kitchen Survivor™ Grade: B+
Your notes: _____

St. Francis Cabernet Sauvignon,   **$**   **Pts**
Sonoma, California 2005   **25**   **88**

🍎 Although it's gotten a little "pricey," this is the best St. Francis Cab yet, with dark wild berry, licorice and cinnamon spice. Pair with cumin-rubbed lamb.
Kitchen Survivor™ Grade: B
Your notes: _____

Santa Rita 120 Cabernet Sauvignon,   **$**   **Pts**
Rapel Valley, Chile 2007   **8**   **84**

☺ It is indeed "a price that's hard to believe" for the quality and flavor punch: soft blackberry fruit complimented by a meaty-spicy, dusty scent.
Kitchen Survivor™ Grade: C
Your notes: _____

Sebastiani Sonoma Cabernet | **$** | **Pts**
Sauvignon, California 2005 | **18** | **88**

🍎 I agree with this Web taster's comment: "This winery is doing things so well at such affordable prices." You just don't expect such complexity of "blackberry," "cassis," and spice at this price. Bravo!

Kitchen Survivor™ Grade: B

Your notes: _____

Sequoia Grove Cabernet Sauvignon | **$** | **Pts**
Napa, California 2005 | **40** | **89**

"Spend less, get more" Napa blackberry-cedar Cab character than from many of the pricier Cabs.

Kitchen Survivor™ Grade: B

Your notes: _____

Sequoia Grove Rutherford Bench Reserve | **$** | **Pts**
Cabernet Sauvignon, California 2004 | **60** | **93**

♟ A "reserve" that really earns the name, and is worth the trade-up. Dusty-cedar-smoke scents atop the dense, chewy blackcurrant fruit. In the finish, a hint of smoke and tobacco suggests the complexity will continue to mount with age. Pair with firm aged cheeses.

Kitchen Survivor™ Grade: B+

Your notes: _____

Silverado Napa Cabernet | **$** | **Pts**
Sauvignon, California 2005 | **43** | **90**

♟ 🏆 An iron fist in a velvet glove: this wine's all elegance, yet with plenty of stuffing. The style is subtle, with dense cassis, cedar, sweet-vanilla oak, and a leafy earthiness, all in seamless balance.

Kitchen Survivor™ Grade: B

Your notes: _____

Silver Oak Alexander Valley | **$** | **Pts**
Cabernet Sauvignon, California 2004 | **70** | **88**

♟ 🍎 This wine's die-hard devotees find its consistency and uniqueness "worth the price." You have to love the wild berry fruit, velvety tannins, a coconut-dill scent coming from American oak barrels, and impressive ageability.

Kitchen Survivor™ Grade: B

Your notes: _____

Silver Oak Napa Valley   **$**   **Pts**
Cabernet Sauvignon, California 2003   **100**   **90**

🍎 The more dark-fruited, violet-scented of the two Silver Oaks, with sumptuous blackcurrant fruit and lavish chocolate notes. In fact, you could pair it with dark chocolate; or grilled, rare blue cheese burgers.

Kitchen Survivor™ Grade: B

Your notes: _____

Simi Cabernet Sauvignon, Alexander   **$**   **Pts**
Valley, Sonoma, California 2005   **25**   **85**

Lavish vanilla oak frames the very Sonoma Cab flavors of warm wild berries and sweet spice.

Kitchen Survivor™ Grade: B

Your notes: _____

Souverain Alexander Valley   **$**   **Pts**
Cabernet Sauvignon, California 2005   **20**   **87**

🍎 "Cellar-worthy Cab" at this price is a rarity. It's got powerful fig fruit and balanced tannins and oak.

Kitchen Survivor™ Grade: B

Your notes: _____

Staglin Family "Salus" Estate Cabernet   **$**   **Pts**
Sauvignon, Napa, California 2005   **90**   **89**

🏆 👍 While Staglin's estate Cab commands cult status (and prices), this Salus is a splurge that lets you see how they walk the line between old world subtlety in the scent and layers, with new world density and ripeness. This is a meal in a glass, with eucalyptus, bay leaf, olive and balsamic notes layered with the dark cherry and red plum fruit flavor.

Kitchen Survivor™ Grade: B

Your notes: _____

Stag's Leap Artemis Cabernet Sauvignon,   **$**   **Pts**
Napa, California 2005   **55**   **86**

A mini-splurge compared to the winery's famous SLV, Cask 23 and Fay Vineyard bottlings. It's a good representation of the Stag's Leap style which emphasizes smooth aromatics - bay leaf, olive, cedar, and violets.

Kitchen Survivor™ Grade: C

Your notes: _____

Sterling Vineyards Cabernet Sauvignon $ Pts
Reserve, Napa, California 2005 75 89

Opulent vanilla, chocolate, and licorice with huge
mouth-coating cassis fruit and plush tannins.

Kitchen Survivor™ Grade: B+

Your notes: _____

Sterling Vineyards Napa Cabernet $ Pts
Sauvignon, California 2005 26 87

● The Web tasters praise this blue-chip Cab's "concentrated" "jammy fruits" and intensity. Velvety, elegant, and dusty, it needs a well-charred steak or a fine
hard cheese such as Manchego or Parmigiano.

Kitchen Survivor™ Grade: B

Your notes: _____

Sterling Vintner's Collection Cabernet $ Pts
Sauvignon, Central Coast, California 2006 15 85

☺ Soft and plump, with nice dusty blackberry fruit.

Kitchen Survivor™ Grade: C

Your notes: _____

Stonestreet Alexander Valley $ Pts
Cabernet Sauvignon, California 2005 42 85

The elegance and scents of vanilla, damp earth,
crushed mint, and blackberry are classic Alexander
Valley, and pair nicely with herb-crusted lamb chops.

Kitchen Survivor™ Grade: C

Your notes: _____

Toasted Head Cabernet Sauvignon, $ Pts
Sauvignon, California 2006 16 85

☺ My Web tasters like the "big Cab flavor for a good
price." Soft and juicy, with a spicy oakiness.

Kitchen Survivor™ Grade: C

Your notes: _____

Trefethen Estate Cabernet Sauvignon, $ Pts
Oak Knoll District, Napa California 2004 50 89

♨ ⚒ Such a stylish wine, and true to its signatures
of violets, black olive, dark plum, blackberry and
black pepper. All of that complexity makes it a wonderful match for steak au poivre or soy-marinated
duck, but this wine ages suprisingly well, too.

Kitchen Survivor™ Grade: B+

Your notes: _____

Twin Fin Cabernet Sauvignon,   **$**   **Pts**
California 2005   **12**   **85**

☺ "Gulpable," with red berry fruit and soft spice.

Kitchen Survivor™ Grade: C

Your notes: _____

Veramonte Cabernet Sauvignon,   **$**   **Pts**
Reserva, Colchagua Valley, Chile 2005   **13**   **85**

A "real value find for consumers," with licorice-berry fruit, chewy tannin, and savory spice and black olive notes; tastes like twice the price.

Kitchen Survivor™ Grade: C

Your notes: _____

Wente Vineyards Southern Hills Cabernet   **$**   **Pts**
Sauvignon, Livermore, California 2005   **15**   **88**

Dark cherry, chocolate, cedar and violets, with plush, soft tannins. A great match for smoked beef brisket.

Kitchen Survivor™ Grade: B+

Your notes: _____

William Hill Estate Cabernet   **$**   **Pts**
Sauvignon, California 2005   **25**   **88**

Incredibly elegant, layered scent of autumn leaves, smoke, cedar, blackberry. The palate is dense cassis with a hint of vanilla. Very classy.

Kitchen Survivor™ Grade: B+

Your notes: _____

Rioja, Ribera del Duero, and Other Spanish Reds

Category Profile: Like other classic European wines, it's the place—called a Denominación de Origen (DO)—rather than the grape on a Spanish wine label, in most cases. Spain's signature red grape, used in both the Rioja (*ree-OH-huh*) and the Ribera del Duero (*ree-BEAR-uh dell DWAIR-oh*) DOs, is called Tempranillo (*temp-rah-NEE-oh*). Depending on quality level, the style of Rioja ranges from easy drinking and spicy to seriously rich, leathery/toffee. Ribera del Duero is generally big and tannic. The other Spanish reds here are from Priorat (*pre-oh-RAHT*), known for strong, inky-dark cellar candidates (usually made from Tempranillo, Cabernet, and/or Grenache). Though not represented in the top red wine sellers, Penedes (*pen-eh-DESS*), which is better known for Cava sparkling wines, is also an outstanding source of values in every style and color.

Serve: Cool room temperature; as a rule Spanish reds are exemplary food wines, but basic reds from Penedes and Rioja (with the word *Cosecha* or *Crianza* on the label), and emerging regions like Navarra, Toro, and Somontano, are good "anytime" wines and tasty on their own.

When: If you dine out often in wine-focused restaurants, Spanish reds are *the* red wine category for world-class drinking that's also affordable.

With: The classic matches are pork and lamb, either roasted or grilled; also amazing with slow-roasted chicken or turkey and hams, sausages, and other cured meats. Finally, try a Spanish Ribera del Duero, Priorat, or Rioja Reserva or Gran Reserva with good-quality cheese. (Spanish Manchego is wonderful and available in supermarkets.)

In: An all-purpose wineglass or larger-bowled red wine stem.

Abadia Retuerta Seleccion Especial,   **$**   **Pts**
Sardon de Duero, Spain 2005   22   90

♈ ✒ This Tempranillo with a touch of Merlot and Cab has always offered nice complexity for the money. It's a nice mix of new world-style blackberry fruit and sweet oak, with old world notes of cedar and leather. Pair it with ratatouille or olive tapenade.

Kitchen Survivor™ Grade: A+

Your notes: _____

Alvaro Palacios Les Terrasses   **$**   **Pts**
(*ALL-vahr-oh puh-LAH-see-os lay*   33   91
***tear-AHSS*) Priorat, Spain 2005**

🍎 ✒ A great entry-level to the often pricey Priorat wines. Lush, intense, and inky, with beautiful black cherry flavors, wild herbs, toasty oak, and a long finish. Pair with slow-braised beef shortribs.

Kitchen Survivor™ Grade: B

Your notes: _____

Borsao Tinto Garnacha/Tempranillo,   **$**   **Pts**
Campo de Borja, Spain 2006   8   87

🍎 ☺ "Unexpectedly good" for the price. The fruit-bomb ripeness and nice spice let you "yum out" on the cheap. Pair this with chili, burritos or barbecue.

Kitchen Survivor™ Grade: B+

Your notes: _____

Comenge Ribera del Duero,   **$**   **Pts**
Spain 2000   30   88

♈ As is typical of Ribera del Duero, this is chewy and packed-in, with sour plum, balsamic and black pepper notes, and a leathery-fig finish. Mustard-crusted lamb chops would be a perfect match.

Kitchen Survivor™ Grade: B+

Your notes: _____

Marques de Arienzo Rioja Reserva,   **$**   **Pts**
Spain 2000   18   85

♈ A subtle style of Rioja—tobacco, toffee, and dried spice scent, with a dark berry and raisin fruit flavor. Pair with a simple pasta with garlic, olive oil and parmesan cheese.

Kitchen Survivor™ Grade: B

Your notes: _____

Marques de Caceres (*mahr-KESS* $ Pts
***deh CAH-sair-ess*) Rioja Crianza,**   12   85
Spain 2004

☺ With "lots of cherry fruit" and "toffee-spice," this is a favorite basic Rioja with my Web tasters.

Kitchen Survivor™ Grade: B

Your notes: _____

Marques de Caceres Rioja $ Pts
Reserva, Spain 2001   20   85

🏷 🍷 Some of my tasters would "skip the Crianza and trade up, for just a few bucks more." The complex flavors of "stawberry fruit leather" and black pepper make it "built for a rustic lamb dish."

Kitchen Survivor™ Grade: B

Your notes: _____

Marques de Riscal (*mahr-KESS* $ Pts
***deh ree-SKALL*) Rioja Crianza, Spain 2004**   8   85

This wine earns praise for its lovely spicy nose, silken texture, lively acidity and savory-strawberry flavor.

Kitchen Survivor™ Grade: B+

Your notes: _____

Marques de Riscal Rioja Gran $ Pts
Reserva, Spain 2000   35   89

Traditional Rioja at its best: date and dried figs; leather, chewy tannins; and great spice, with a long buttery-coconut finish. A great match for sauteed mushrooms with garlic, or grilled lamb chops.

Kitchen Survivor™ Grade: B

Your notes: _____

Marques de Riscal Rioja Reserva, $ Pts
Spain 2003   18   87

A "nice upgrade from the Crianza" (the base-level Riscal), with more oak aging that gives toffee/coconut scents to match the raisiny and chocolatey flavor.

Kitchen Survivor™ Grade: B

Your notes: _____

Montecillo (*mohn-teh-SEE-yoh*) $ Pts
Rioja Crianza, Spain 2004   11   85

🍴 Another favorite of wine aficionados, for its Old-World pepper-on-strawberries flavors and snappy texture that loves food. Great with grilled eggplant or roasted peppers stuffed with Manchego cheese.

Kitchen Survivor™ Grade: C

Your notes: _____

Montecillo Rioja Gran Reserva, $ Pts
Spain 2001   27   89

🏆 Earthy, mushroomy dustiness and leathery-tobacco scents give complexity to the chewy dark cherry fruit spiked with pepper and cumin. Pair with smoked pork.

Kitchen Survivor™ Grade: B+

Your notes: _____

Montecillo Rioja Reserva, $ Pts
Spain 2002   20   88

🏆 Extra oak aging creates layers of tobacco, toffee, and sweet spice alongside the fig and raisin fruit.

Kitchen Survivor™ Grade: B+

Your notes: _____

Muga (*MOO-guh*) Rioja Reserva, $ Pts
Spain 2004   24   90

🍷🏆👍 A world-class wine and a relative value in that realm, with stunning fig, prune, and dried cherry fruit and dense but suede-smooth tannins.

Kitchen Survivor™ Grade: A+

Your notes: _____

Osborne Solaz Tempranillo-Cabernet, $ Pts
Tierra de Castilla, Spain 2005   9   85

A great way to get to know Spain's signature Tempranillo grape (here blended with Cab). It's got a smoky scent, lots of pretty plum fruit, and soft tannin.

Kitchen Survivor™ Grade: C

Your notes: _____

Palacios Remondo La Montesa Rioja $ Pts
Crianza, Spain 2004   20   89

👍 Unusually for Rioja, this is a Garnacha-dominated blend (45%), with 40% Tempranillo plus Mazuelo and Graciano. The result is liveliness and character, with scents and flavors of both red and dark berries, orange peel, and soft cedar. Spicy and textured, it's a great match for pork chops with mustard sauce.

Kitchen Survivor™ Grade: C

Your notes: _____

Palacios Remondo La Vendimia Rioja,   **$**   **Pts**
Spain 2006   **14**   **87**

This 50/50 blend of Garnacha and Tempranillo showcases the fun of the *joven* (young) style of Rioja, with its frisky red fruits and bright spicy-herb notes just made for pairing with barbecued chicken or ribs.

Kitchen Survivor™ Grade: C

Your notes: _____

Pesquera (*pess-CARE-uh*) Crianza, Ribera   **$**   **Pts**
del Duero, Spain 2005   **35**   **91**

A big and brooding wine. The scents of violets, tar and dark berries, and palate of dense tannins and plum liqueur, will harmonize with cellaring. When young, pair with roast game or rich cheeses.

Kitchen Survivor™ Grade: B

Your notes: _____

Senoria de Laredo Rioja Gran Reserva,   **$**   **Pts**
Rioja, Spain 1998   **22**   **89**

Complexity! Vanilla, cinnamon, pepper, tar and roasted coffee layered with the very ripe dark plum fruit. The meaty texture is tailor-made for rich meat stews or fine cheeses such as Manchego or Idiazabal.

Kitchen Survivor™ Grade: B

Your notes: _____

Val Llach Embruix (*em-BROOSH*) Priorat,   **$**   **Pts**
Spain 2005   **34**   **89**

Classic Priorat without the sticker shock This one's heady with dark fig, olive, molasses and allspice notes, with meaty-mushroomy undertones. Pair it with rich meats such as braised duck or lamb shanks.

Kitchen Survivor™ Grade: B+

Your notes: _____

Vinicola del Priorat Onix   **$**   **Pts**
(*veen-EE-co-lah dell PREE-oh-raht*   **16**   **85**
***OH-nix*), Spain 2006**

♟ Among Priorat wines, this one's "more affordable than most," with tangy berry fruit, a tarry scent, and chewy tannins.

Kitchen Survivor™ Grade: A

Your notes: _____

Uncommon Red Grapes and Blends

Category Profile: As with the whites, this isn't a cohesive category but rather a spot to put worthy, popular reds that don't neatly fit a grape or region category—namely, proprietary blends, and uncommon varietals.

> Proprietary Blends—These may be tasty, inexpensive blends or ambitious signature blends at luxury prices.

> Uncommon Varietals—These are quite exciting. I introduced Malbec and Carmenere in the Merlot section, because I think they are distinctive and delicious alternatives for Merlot lovers. Although the names and even the style (bold and a little peppery) are similar, Petite Sirah and Syrah (Shiraz) are not the same grape.

Serve: Cool room temperature, or even slightly chilled.

When: Anytime you need an interesting, value-priced red.

With: Snacks and everyday meals for the budget-priced wines.

In: An all-purpose wineglass.

Arboleda Carmenere, Colchagua,   **$**   **Pts**
Chile 2006   **19**   **90**

🗲 Arboleda achieves awesome character for the price. This Carmenere is a meaty meal-in-a-glass, with notes of cumin, prosciutto, rosemary, blackberry and leather. Pair with meaty, mushroomy pastas.

Kitchen Survivor™ Grade: A+

Your notes: _____

Bogle Petite Sirah,	$	Pts
California 2006	12	87

🍎 A black pepper and berries mouthful that my Web tasters call an "awesome value." It's also awesome with cheeseburgers and barbecue.

Kitchen Survivor™ Grade: B

Your notes: _____

Catena Malbec, Mendoza,	$	Pts
Argentina 2005	24	90

♀ 🍎 An Argentina pioneer. The dense blackberry fruit, velvet texture, vanilla-sweet oak and peppery-mineral finish are at once sleek and powerful.

Kitchen Survivor™ Grade: B

Your notes: _____

Cline Ancient Vines Mourvedre,	$	Pts
California 2006	18	88

"Very rich" dark fig-plum fruit with "spice and depth." A unique, and perfect, pairing for Thanksgiving.

Kitchen Survivor™ Grade: B+

Your notes: _____

Cline Cashmere Grenache-Syrah-	$	Pts
Mourvedre, Contra Costa, California 2006	18	89

♀ 🍎 Christmas pudding and Devil's-food cake in a glass? Pretty much! Blueberry, allspice, chocolate, velvet texture. You could pair it with chocolate, or exotic meat dishes such as teriyaki or jerk pork.

Kitchen Survivor™ Grade: B+

Your notes: _____

Concannon Petite Sirah, Central Coast,	$	Pts
California 2005	16	88

🍎 Take a black pepper and berry scent, add burst-in-your-mouth fruit-pie flavor, plump tannins, and a licorice finish, and you've got this unique, fun wine.

Kitchen Survivor™ Grade: B+

Your notes: _____

Concha y Toro Casillero del Diablo	$	Pts
Carmenere, Chile 2005	10	88

The wine is spicy, raisiny, and oozing with character, with a heady scent like molasses-cured bacon. Just try it! Awesome with meaty stews and cheesy pastas.

Kitchen Survivor™ Grade: B

Your notes: _____

Concha y Toro Terrunyo　　　　　　**$**　**Pts**
Carmenere, Chile 2004　　　　　　　**40**　**94**

One of the most expensive Chilean Carmeneres, but something special. It's like the concentrated essence of wild berries (huckleberries, raspberries), with a velvety-plush texture and sweet spice-cola scents. Worth a search!

Kitchen Survivor™ Grade: B

Your notes: _____

MontGras Carmenere Reserva,　　　　**$**　**Pts**
Colchagua, Chile 2007　　　　　　　**14**　**88**

Attention-getting flavors and scents of cumin, smoke, meat stock and dark cherry. Have it with hard cheeses or a beefy roast to showcase the layers.

Kitchen Survivor™ Grade: C

Your notes: _____

Navarro Correas Malbec, Mendoza,　　**$**　**Pts**
Argentina 2006　　　　　　　　　　**13**　**87**

Rustic but really inviting, with an earthy, leathery, savory spice scent, and silky, subtle plum fruit.

Kitchen Survivor™ Grade: B

Your notes: _____

Salentein Malbec Reserve,　　　　　**$**　**Pts**
Argentina 2006　　　　　　　　　　**20**　**90**

Richer, more sophisticated and more complex than most Argentinian Malbecs. Dark boysenberry fruit with varietally-typical notes of pen ink, roast beef and leather underneath the soft vanilla and spice. A real attention-getter. Pair with a great steak.

Kitchen Survivor™ Grade: B+

Your notes: _____

Stags' Leap Winery Petite Sirah,　　　**$**　**Pts**
Napa, California 2005　　　　　　　**38**　**89**

One of "the best" Petite Sirahs available, with licorice and blackberry scents and flavors, chewy tannins, and a smoky-tar finish. Pair it with black olive and fennel sausage pizza, or rare burgers with blue cheese.

Kitchen Survivor™ Grade: B

Your notes: _____

Terrazas Alto Malbec, Mendoza,   **$**   **Pts**
Argentina 2006   **10**   **85**

This "juicy, plummy, spicy" Malbec gets "great value" marks from my Web tasters.

Kitchen Survivor™ Grade: C

Your notes: _____

Veramonte Primus,   **$**   **Pts**
Chile 2005   **22**   **89**

This pioneer Carmenere blend is still one of the best, with a lot of exotic berry fruit, both savory and sweet spices, and a smoky-meaty note.

Kitchen Survivor™ Grade: B

Your notes: _____

Syrah/Shiraz and Other Rhone-Style Reds

Category Profile: The varietal Shiraz, Australia's signature red, is so hot that many pros say it has unseated Merlot as consumers' go-to grape. Popularity has its price for Shiraz lovers, though, because many of the biggest brands have begun to taste like generic red wine rather than the spunky-spicy Shiraz with which we fell in love. I've focused on brands that have stayed true to the Shiraz taste. The same grape, under the French spelling *Syrah*, also forms the backbone for France's revered Rhone Valley reds with centuries-old reputations. These include Cotes-du-Rhone (*coat-duh-ROAN*), Cote-Rotie (*ro-TEE*), Hermitage (*uhr-muh-TAHJ*), and Chateauneuf-du-Pape (*shah-toe-NUFF-duh-POP*). Like basic Shiraz, Cotes-du-Rhone, with its lovely spicy fruit character, is a value star. The latter three are true French classics and, in my view, currently lead that elite group in quality for the money. They are full-bodied, powerful, peppery, earthy, concentrated, and oak aged. Finally, most major American wineries, and many smaller players, are bottling California or Washington State versions, often labeled with the Aussie spelling *Shiraz* rather than the French *Syrah*.

Serve: Cool room temperature; aeration enhances the aroma and flavor.

When: Basic Syrah/Shiraz and Cotes-du-Rhone are great everyday drinking wines; in restaurants, these are great go-to categories for relative value.

With: Grilled, barbecued, or roasted anything (including fish and vegetables); outstanding with steaks, fine cheeses, and other dishes that call for a full red wine; I also love these styles with traditional Thanksgiving fare.

In: An all-purpose wineglass or a larger-bowled red wine stem.

	$	Pts
Alice White Shiraz, Australia 2007	8	85

☺ "A lot of bang for the buck" thanks to its "spicy scent and wild raspberry fruit." Bring on the BBQ!

Kitchen Survivor™ Grade: B

Your notes: _____

	$	Pts
Andrew Murray Syrah Tous Les Jours, Central Coast, California 2006	16	89

One of the tastiest bets in CA Syrah for the money, with luscious raspberry-pomegranate fruit and a hint of white pepper spiciness. Great with pizza.

Kitchen Survivor™ Grade: B

Your notes: _____

	$	Pts
Beaulieu Vineyard (BV) Coastal Estates Shiraz, California 2006	9	86

☺ Meaty, juicy dark plum and berries; a yummy steal that's the perfect house red if you like 'em lush.

Kitchen Survivor™ Grade: B

Your notes: _____

	$	Pts
Beaulieu Vineyard (BV) Napa Valley Syrah, California 2005	15	88

A chewy mouthful of dark fig and raspberry, vanilla, licorice, and tobacco. Great with rich, cheesy pastas.

Kitchen Survivor™ Grade: B

Your notes: _____

Black Opal Shiraz, $ Pts
Australia 2006 8 85
☺ "Always a great value," with juicy fruit and a soft
texture that makes it a great "house red."
Kitchen Survivor™ Grade: C
Your notes: _____

Blackstone Syrah, $ Pts
California 2006 12 86
🍎"Very rich, dark fruit with a nice spice at the end."
Kitchen Survivor™ Grade: C
Your notes: _____

Bonny Doon Cigare Volant, $ Pts
California 2004 30 88
More Grenache-dominated in this vintage, which
gives the wine a pomegranate, orange peel and rhu-
barb character that compliments the savory white
pepper spice nicely. A great match for ratatouille.
Kitchen Survivor™ Grade: C
Your notes: _____

Brokenwood Shiraz, McLaren Vale, $ Pts
Australia 2006 27 88
🍎 "Soft tannins," a licorice scent, "chocolate and
black cherries" on the palate, and good ageability
Kitchen Survivor™ Grade: B+
Your notes: _____

Burgess Napa Syrah, Napa, $ Pts
California 2004 20 89
A winner with my tough-customer husband, for its
chewy sassafras-fig fruit and smoky-tarry finish.
Kitchen Survivor™ Grade: B
Your notes: _____

Chalone Vineyard Estate Syrah, $ Pts
Chalone, California 2005 30 91
Power and subtlety: tarry, dark fig and black raspberry
fruit. Very smoky, firm and velvety. Loooong finish.
Kitchen Survivor™ Grade: B
Your notes: _____

Chapoutier Chateauneuf-du-Pape   **$**   **Pts**
Le Bernardine, Rhone, France 2004   35   89

♟ The scent of sun-warmed figs, leather, pepper, and touch of rosemary transports you to the south of France. Pair with rich lamb stew or goat cheese.

Kitchen Survivor™ Grade: B

Your notes: _____

Chapoutier Cotes-du-Rhone Rouge,   **$**   **Pts**
Rhone, France 2004   14   87

🌾 Rustic pepper-cumin scent, silky strawberry-rhubarb flavor; awesome with herbed ham quiche.

Kitchen Survivor™ Grade: B

Your notes: _____

Chateau de Beaucastel   **$**   **Pts**
Chateauneuf-du-Pape, France 2005   100   93

👍 Although it's "expensive," the Asian spiced tea and pepper scent and powerful fig and dark berry fruit are fabulous. Cellars beautifully. Pair with braised beef.

Kitchen Survivor™ Grade: A+

Your notes: _____

Chateau La Nerthe (*shah-TOE lah*   **$**   **Pts**
***NAIRT*) Chateauneuf-du-Pape,**   42   88
Rhone, France 2004

🌾 ♟ The pepper/spicy/leathery scents, gripping tannins, and dried cranberry-anise flavors are textbook Chateauneuf, built for rich meats and stews.

Kitchen Survivor™ Grade: A

Your notes: _____

Cline Syrah,   **$**   **Pts**
California 2005   12   87

☺ Cline puts vibrant berry fruit flavor and spicy-zingy scent in the bottle for a great price.

Kitchen Survivor™ Grade: B+

Your notes: _____

D'Arenberg The Footbolt Shiraz,   **$**   **Pts**
Australia 2005   20   89

"Intense and well balanced" wine: meaty-smoky, tangy berries, savory and sweet spices, all at a "nice price." An ideal match for barbecue or pizza.

Kitchen Survivor™ Grade: B

Your notes: _____

Domaine de la Griveliere Cotes-du-Rhone   **$**   **Pts**
(*coat-duh-ROAN*), Rhone, France 2006   **13**   **88**

More Grenache than Syrah (with some Mourvedre) but I include it in the section with other Cotes du Rhones. This one's lively with pomegranate, floral and pepper notes, and red currant jelly flavors. Great with goat cheese, steak au poivre, or an herbed omelet.
Kitchen Survivor™ Grade: B

Your notes: _____

Duboeuf (Georges) Cotes-du-Rhone   **$**   **Pts**
(*du-BUFF coat-duh-ROAN*), France 2004   **10**   **86**

Juicy and fresh, with red cherry and spicy pomegranate flavors that make your mouthwater. Delicious with most any food, but especially tomato-sauced dishes, goat cheese and grilled fish, chicken or pork..
Kitchen Survivor™ Grade: B

Your notes: _____

E & M Guigal (*ghee-GALL*)   **$**   **Pts**
Cotes-du-Rhone, Rhone, France 2004   **15**   **89**

A value from the famous Guigal name, with strawberry fruit, rose potpourri, and pepper-spice notes. Delicious with herbed goat cheese.
Kitchen Survivor™ Grade: A

Your notes: _____

E & M Guigal Cote-Rotie Brune et   **$**   **Pts**
Blonde, Rhone, France 2003   **75**   **93**

Is it the texture ("liquid velvet"), the scent ("pepper and lavender"), or flavor ("blackberry") that's most compelling? My Web tasters note: it "will age 20 years." If you can't wait, pair it with braised shortribs.
Kitchen Survivor™ Grade: B+

Your notes: _____

Gallo Family Vineyards Sonoma   **$**   **Pts**
Reserve Syrah, California 2005   **15**   **88**

The best Syrah at this price—deep berry-fig fruit, with an alluring meaty quality. A meal in a glass! A great wine for pizza, lasagne or spaghetti.
Kitchen Survivor™ Grade: B

Your notes: _____

Goats Do Roam Red, Paarl $ Pts
South Africa 2005 8 88
♀� A tongue-in-cheek take on French Cotes-du-Rhone, with a South African flair from Pinotage in the blend. The result is snappy and alluring meaty-pepper and soft red fruit flavors, for a great price.
Kitchen Survivor™ Grade: C
Your notes: _____

Greg Norman Shiraz, $ Pts
Australia 2005 14 85
It wasn't for everyone on my panel, but many liked the "smooth," "spicy" character at a "good price."
Kitchen Survivor™ Grade: C
Your notes: _____

Hill of Content Grenache/Shiraz, $ Pts
Australia 2006 14 87
♀☏ The raspberry scent, the ripe, jammy berry fruit taste, and juicy texture are de-lish!
Kitchen Survivor™ Grade: A
Your notes: _____

Jaboulet (*jhah-boo-LAY***) Parallele 45** $ Pts
Cotes-du-Rhone, France 2006 17 88
🗲 ♟ A classic Rhone with earthy red-plum fruit and smoky black pepper scents. Great with tapenade crostini, stuffed peppers, or pasta Bolognese.
Kitchen Survivor™ Grade: B
Your notes: _____

Jacob's Creek Shiraz/Cabernet $ Pts
Sauvignon, Australia 2007 8 87
☺ "Great taste and great value," with exotic raspberry and eucalyptus notes and a plump texture.
Kitchen Survivor™ Grade: B+
Your notes: _____

Jade Mountain Napa Syrah, $ Pts
California 2004 28 92
♀☏ 👍 The best California Syrah on the market? It's got rich raspberry fruit, a pepper-cumin-rosemary scent and an irresistible meaty-gaminess and mint on the palate. Bring on the leg of lamb or BBQ'd ribs!
Kitchen Survivor™ Grade: B+
Your notes: _____

Joseph Phelps Le Mistral, Monterey,   **$**   **Pts**
California 2005   **40**   **89**

This mainly Syrah-Grenache blend is "excellent,"
with strawberry-rhubarb fruit and zippy spice.

Kitchen Survivor™ Grade: B+

Your notes: _____

Joseph Phelps Pastiche (pah-STEESH)   **$**   **Pts**
Rouge, California 2004   **18**   **85**

Just yummy wine: it's a mixture of grapes similar to
French Cotes-du-Rhone, with peppery spice and
juicy strawberry-pomegranate fruit. It's pizza-perfect.

Kitchen Survivor™ Grade: B

Your notes: _____

La Vieille Ferme (*lah vee-yay*   **$**   **Pts**
***FAIRM;* means "the old farm")**   **11**   **87**
Cotes-du-Ventoux, France 2006

☺ This raspberry-ripe, lively red is a tasting panel
favorite, with "great character" and spice for the price.

Kitchen Survivor™ Grade: B+

Your notes: _____

Lindemans Bin 50 Shiraz,   **$**   **Pts**
Australia 2007   **7**   **86**

☺ Soft, ripe raspberry fruit and a black pepper scent;
an all-around great drink and great buy.

Kitchen Survivor™ Grade: B+

Your notes: _____

Marquis Philips Sarah's Blend,   **$**   **Pts**
Australia 2006   **18**   **88**

🍎 Shiraz, Cab, and Merlot, with "explosive fruit and
spiciness" and "velvety" tannins.

Kitchen Survivor™ Grade: B

Your notes: _____

Morgan Syrah, Monterey,   **$**   **Pts**
California 2006   **18**   **88**

Savory and alluring, with raspberry fruit and a an
olive-y charred note in the scent and finish. Pair it
with grilled eggplant or roasted peppers.

Kitchen Survivor™ Grade: B

Your notes: _____

Penfolds Kalimna Shiraz Bin 28, $ Pts
Australia 2006 26 89

♉ I serve this to my wine students to teach them about real-deal Aussie Shiraz—it's full of black pepper, plum compote flavors, and thick velvety tannins. Fantastic with jerk-spiced chicken or steak au poivre.

Kitchen Survivor™ Grade: B

Your notes: _____

Penfolds Koonunga Hill Shiraz $ Pts
Cabernet, Australia 2007 12 86

☺ You can't beat this plummy, slightly spicy red for easy drinkability, yet with some nice tannic grip.

Kitchen Survivor™ Grade: C

Your notes: _____

Qupe Central Coast Syrah, Central $ Pts
Coast, California 2006 18 87

A "favorite" with my Web tasters (and me) that's tasting better than ever. It's signature is a lush raspberry-vanilla-white pepper style that says "fire up the grill!"

Kitchen Survivor™ Grade: B

Your notes: _____

Red Bicyclette Syrah, Vin de Pays d'Oc, $ Pts
France 2005 12 84

This is Red Bicyclette's best foot forward; it's peppery and lively with rustic dried fruit flavor.

Kitchen Survivor™ Grade: C

Your notes: _____

Rosemount Diamond Label Shiraz, $ Pts
Australia 2006 10 86

☺ Still a "best buy" that counts legions of devotees to its signature raspberry fruit and soft spice scent.

Kitchen Survivor™ Grade: B

Your notes: _____

Rosemount Diamond Label Shiraz/ $ Pts
Cabernet Sauvignon, Australia 2005 8 87

♉ My favorite of the Diamond Label reds. It's got juicy, mouthwatering berry fruit, a touch of mint in the scent, and a gentle tug of tannin.

Kitchen Survivor™ Grade: B

Your notes: _____

Rosemount Show Reserve McLarenVale
GSM (Grenache-Shiraz-Mourvedre),   **$**   **Pts**
Australia 2004   **24**   **88**

🍎 This "wow" wine shows all the hallmarks of blends from these three Rhone red grapes—both savory and sweet spices; smoky/meaty scent, and rich, jammy black cherry and blueberry flavors.

Kitchen Survivor™ Grade: A

Your notes: _____

Shingleback McLaren Vale Shiraz,   **$**   **Pts**
Australia, California 2005   **20**   **85**

🍎 Real McLaren Vale character: clove spice, raspberry fruit, vanilla-coconut-licorice finish.

Kitchen Survivor™ Grade: C

Your notes: _____

Sterling Vintner's Collection   **$**   **Pts**
Shiraz, Central Coast, California 2006   **10**   **87**

Balsamic-y fig fruit, vanilla, and licorice. A tasty buy.

Kitchen Survivor™ Grade: C

Your notes: _____

Wakefield Promised Land Shiraz/Cabernet, **$**   **Pts**
South Australia 2005   **13**   **90**

♉ A luxuriant expression of pretty Aussie Shiraz character - eucalyptus, raspberry and coconut - balanced by the cocoa, cedar and velvety tannins of the Cab in the blend. What a value! Pair with herbed lamb, or tandoori or Moroccan-spiced chicken.

Kitchen Survivor™ Grade: B

Your notes: _____

Wente Livermore Syrah,   **$**   **Pts**
California 2005   **10**   **87**

♉ A real surprise for its complex "animal" scent. There is also fragrant violet and jasmine and on the palate, plummy juiciness and good structure.

Kitchen Survivor™ Grade: C

Your notes: _____

The Wishing Tree Shiraz,   **$**   **Pts**
Australia, California 2004   **13**   **87**

Lovely raspberry-coconut flavors and scents with a touch of baking spices. Succulent and plump.

Kitchen Survivor™ Grade: B

Your notes: _____

Wolf Blass Yellow Label   **$**   **Pts**
Shiraz, Australia 2006   **13**   **89**

♀ The black cherry and black pepper complexity, with a velvety texture make this a top "best buy" among Aussie Shirazes. A great house wine bet.

Kitchen Survivor™ Grade: C

Your notes: _____

Yellowtail Shiraz,   **$**   **Pts**
Australia 2006   **7**   **85**

While it's "not as good as their Chardonnay," most of my Web tasters call it a "good quaff" at an "unbeatable price." Great with pizza or barbecue.

Kitchen Survivor™ Grade: C

Your notes: _____

Red Zinfandel

Category Profile: *Groupie* is the apt moniker for devotees of this California specialty, which ranges in style from medium-bodied, with bright and juicy raspberry flavors, to lush, full-bodied, and high in alcohol with intense blueberry, licorice, and even chocolate scents and flavors. Many of the best vineyards have old vines that produce some amazingly intense, complex wines. Zins usually are oaky—a little or a lot, depending on the intensity of the grapes used. The grape intensity is a function of the vineyard—its age and its location. California's most famous red Zinfandel areas are Sonoma (especially the Dry Creek Valley subdistrict), Napa, Amador, and the Sierra foothills. Lodi, in California's Central Valley, is also a good source.

Serve: Room temperature; aeration enhances the aroma and flavor.

When: Value Zinfandels are excellent for everyday drinking; good restaurant lists usually have a selection worth exploring across the price spectrum.

With: Burgers, pizza, lamb (especially with Indian or Moroccan spices), and quality cheeses are favorites—even dark chocolate!

In: An all-purpose wineglass or a larger-bowled red wine stem.

7 Deadly Zins Zinfandel, Lodi,   **$**   **Pts**
California 2006   **15**   **83**

"Packs the wallop" of huge licorice and black fruits that many Zin lovers clamor for.

Kitchen Survivor™ Grade: C

Your notes: _____

Alexander Valley Vineyards Sin Zin,   **$**   **Pts**
Alexander Valley, California 2006   **20**   **87**

What Zin should be - wild boysenberry fruit, black pepper, licorice and violets, without excessive alcohol. Nice with dark chocolate, burgers, big cheeses.

Kitchen Survivor™ Grade: C

Your notes: _____

Artezin Zinfandel,   **$**   **Pts**
California 2006   **18**   **86**

A nice effort from Hess, with briary wild berry fruit and a hint of smoke and pepper.

Kitchen Survivor™ Grade: C

Your notes: _____

Beaulieu Vineyard Napa Valley   **$**   **Pts**
Zinfandel, California 2006   **15**   **87**

🍎 My Web tasters recommend this wine's "jammy" fruit flavors "with grilled steaks."

Kitchen Survivor™ Grade: C

Your notes: _____

Blackstone Zinfandel,   **$**   **Pts**
California 2006   **12**   **86**

🍎 "Molasses and fig" scent, with powerful plum jam fruit. Quite nice for the price.

Kitchen Survivor™ Grade: C

Your notes: _____

Bogle Old Vines Zinfandel,   **$**   **Pts**
California 2006   **12**   **87**

The "great fruit and berry flavor" and "kind of chewy texture" are typical of old-vines Zinfandel.

Kitchen Survivor™ Grade: C

Your notes: _____

C G Di Arie Zinfandel, Shenandoah Valley, California 2006 $ 25 Pts 89

♀ Delish, and full of character, with blackberry, black pepper, clove, black olive and licorice notes, all in balance and without excessive alcohol. Bravo!

Kitchen Survivor™ Grade: B

Your notes: _____

Cline Zinfandel, California 2006 $ 10 Pts 87

Lots of spice and fruit "for a great price" prompted Web tasters to call this "the perfect house wine."

Kitchen Survivor™ Grade: C

Your notes: _____

Clos du Bois Sonoma Zinfandel, California 2005 $ 15 Pts 85

Sweet oak in the scent, raspberry fruit, soft tannins. To me, it tops their more popular Merlot, and it's cheaper.

Kitchen Survivor™ Grade: B

Your notes: _____

Dancing Bull Zinfandel, California 2006 $ 12 Pts 86

The "nice fruit and spice" are great every day for sipping, and pairing with bold foods like barbecue.

Kitchen Survivor™ Grade: C

Your notes: _____

Dashe Cellars Dry Creek Zinfandel, California 2006 $ 22 Pts 88

"Phenomenal" inky complexity that "makes you want to crawl inside the glass" of ripe fig, spice, and licorice. Pair with barbecued ribs, or even dark chocolate.

Kitchen Survivor™ Grade: C

Your notes: _____

Deloach Vneyards Zinfandel, Russian River Valley, California 2006 $ 18 Pts 89

♀ A yum-fest, with lush raspberry and boysenberrry flavors and medium body. Delicious on its own and with strawberries with balsamic and black pepper.

Kitchen Survivor™ Grade: B

Your notes: _____

Dry Creek Vineyard Old Vine $ Pts
Zinfandel, Sonoma, California 2005 28 85

🍎 A perfect introduction to old-vines Zin—
"blueberries and chocolate," as one of my sommelier
buddies describes the flavor, with thick and velvety
tannins. Serve with braised shortribs.

Kitchen Survivor™ Grade: A

Your notes: _____

Fetzer Valley Oaks Zinfandel, $ Pts
California 2006 9 85

☺ Juicy, spicy, nice cherry flavors and the consistency you can count on from Fetzer's Valley Oaks line.

Kitchen Survivor™ Grade: B+

Your notes: _____

Francis Ford Coppola Directors Cut $ Pts
Zinfandel, California 2006 20 91

♟ A super Zin, with blueberry, chocolate, licorice
and black olive notes all in a velvety, balanced package. Pair it with braised shortribs or barbecue.

Kitchen Survivor™ Grade: C

Your notes: _____

Frog's Leap Zinfandel, Napa, $ Pts
California 2006 28 90

♟ Classy and stylish, with complex black cherry,
blueberry, sassafras and cedar, and a tangy finish.

Kitchen Survivor™ Grade: B

Your notes: _____

Gallo Family Vineyards Sonoma $ Pts
Reserve Zinfandel, California 2006 15 87

One of the most delicious, spice & blueberry jam Zins
at this price. Pair it with juicy blue cheese burgers.

Kitchen Survivor™ Grade: B+

Your notes: _____

Girard Old Vine Zinfandel, $ Pts
California 2006 24 89

"Earthy, loaded with pepper" and ripe fig fruit, and a
lot better balanced than most big California Zins
these days.

Kitchen Survivor™ Grade: B+

Your notes: _____

Grgich Hills Estate Zinfandel,   **$**   **Pts**
California 2003   **28**   **91**

This wine's complexity, firm structure, and restraint deliver the power of Zin, with a subtle scent and flavor—wild berry fruit, sundried tomato, spice, and cedary oak. A fantastic partner for crispy duck, braised shortribs or classic cheeses.

Kitchen Survivor™ Grade: B+

Your notes: _____

Joel Gott Zinfandel,   **$**   **Pts**
California 2006   **14**   **86**

The exotic style—blueberry pie filling and licorice—might make you think "pricey," but not so. Yay!

Kitchen Survivor™ Grade: B+

Your notes: _____

Kendall-Jackson Vintner's Reserve   **$**   **Pts**
Zinfandel, California 2006   **16**   **85**

The Web tasters call it a "solid" Zin, and I like the balance of ripe dark fruit and peppery notes. Drinks great by itself and with bold food from the grill.

Kitchen Survivor™ Grade: B

Your notes: _____

Kenwood Jack London Zinfandel,   **$**   **Pts**
California 2005   **24**   **85**

Big and chewy, with blueberry, licorice, and raisin flavors, with a splash of spicy oak.

Kitchen Survivor™ Grade: C

Your notes: _____

Kunde EstateZinfandel, Sonoma,   **$**   **Pts**
California 2006   **18**   **85**

I like the medium body, soft tannins and nice red fruit with a little spice; great with tomato-basil pasta.

Kitchen Survivor™ Grade: C

Your notes: _____

Laurel Glen Reds, Lodi,   **$**   **Pts**
California 2006   **10**   **87**

As one taster put it: "Fabulous flavor in a Zin 'field blend'. Great with food, great alone, great value."

Kitchen Survivor™ Grade: B

Your notes: _____

Louis Martini Monte Rosso Gnarly Vines Zinfandel, California 2005

	$	Pts
	50	88

A big Zin for a big price, but the intense spice and fig fruit and powerful structure are quite impressive.

Kitchen Survivor™ Grade: B

Your notes: _____

Montevina Terra d'Oro Zinfandel, Amador, California 2005

	$	Pts
	14	85

Classic Amador Zin: leathery, savory-spice scent (think cumin and cardamom), prune and licorice flavors, and a firm tannic grip.

Kitchen Survivor™ Grade: B+

Your notes: _____

Pezzi King Zinfandel, Dry Creek Valley, California

	$	Pts
	18	88

This Zin specialist does it right, delivering blueberry-chocolate flavor with a hint of herb and spice, all in balance and delish. Great with big cheeseburgers.

Kitchen Survivor™ Grade: B

Your notes: _____

Quivira Zinfandel, Dry Creek Valley, Sonoma, California 2006

	$	Pts
	20	89

Super-classy and almost Bordeaux-like, but with the boysenberry and bay leaf complexity of Zin. Bravo!

Kitchen Survivor™ Grade: B

Your notes: _____

Rabbit Ridge Paso Robles Zinfandel, California 2006

	$	Pts
	14	86

Formerly a Sonoma Zin specialist now in Paso Robles. Look for "gulpable" wild berry fruit, spice, and smooth tannins.

Kitchen Survivor™ Grade: C

Your notes: _____

Rancho Zabaco Dry Creek Valley Reserve Zinfandel, Sonoma, California 2004

	$	Pts
	24	88

This is textbook Dry Creek Zin—blueberry compote flavors, sweet spice, thick and juicy texture.

Kitchen Survivor™ Grade: C

Your notes: _____

Rancho Zabaco Heritage Vines Zinfandel, Sonoma, California 2006

$ 18   **Pts** 86

Nice dried-cherry fruit and tobacco, with a touch of black pepper. Pair it with barbecue or grilled eggplant, mozzarella and sundried tomato sandwiches.

Kitchen Survivor™ Grade: B

Your notes: _____

Rancho Zabaco Russian River Valley Zinfandel, California 2005

$ 28   **Pts** 89

A tasty Zin mouthful: raspberry jam, sweet cardamom spice, red licorice and vanilla. It's delicious with barbecue, jerk pork, teriyaki, and even dark chocolate.

Kitchen Survivor™ Grade: B+

Your notes: _____

Ravenswood Lodi Old Vines Zinfandel, California 2006

$ 17   **Pts** 87

Chock-full of "spice," "zest," and almost Port-like fig fruit, this is a "can't go wrong" bottling from one of California's best Zin producers.

Kitchen Survivor™ Grade: B

Your notes: _____

Ravenswood Vintner's Blend Zinfandel, California 2005

$ 12   **Pts** 85

☺ This value classic gets high marks for consistency, with blueberry and spice flavors and a "yummy juiciness" that's true to the Zin varietal character.

Kitchen Survivor™ Grade: A

Your notes: _____

Renwood Zinfandel, Shenandoah California 2005

$ 20   **Pts** 89

Renwood's Zins are justly revered among Zin lovers; this one's lusciously jammy, with a savory backnote of black pepper. Pair it with herb-crusted lamb chops or steak with peppercorn sauce.

Kitchen Survivor™ Grade: ?

Your notes: _____

Ridge Geyserville (Zinfandel), Sonoma, California 2005

$ 32   **Pts** 92

This wine garners raves from my Web tasters. The scent is complex cedar, savory-sweet spice, and dark fruit that's very intense and velvety, but not heavy.

Kitchen Survivor™ Grade: A+

Your notes: _____

Rodney Strong Zinfandel, Sonoma, California 2006	$ 14	Pts 85

🍎 It's hard to go wrong with the jammy berry fruit and sweet coconut-eucalyptus notes on this wine.

Kitchen Survivor™ Grade: C

Your notes: _____

Rombauer Zinfandel, California 2005	$ 22	Pts 85

A "big fruit forward" Zin with "succulent dark cherry."

Kitchen Survivor™ Grade: B

Your notes: _____

Rosenblum Zinfandel Vintner's Cuvee, California NV	$ 12	Pts 87

🍎 The luscious blueberry fruit makes this "slurpable" and a "best buy."

Kitchen Survivor™ Grade: B

Your notes: _____

St. Francis Old Vines Zinfandel, Sonoma, California 2005	$ 25	Pts 85

"Big, but not over-the-top," so the Zin character - dark fig, blueberry, balsamic and black pepper - can come through. Pair it with game or a meaty stew.

Kitchen Survivor™ Grade: B

Your notes: _____

Seghesio Sonoma Zinfandel, California 2006	$ 19	Pts 85

"What a great deal," say my Web tasters because it offers real Sonoma character—wild-berry fruit, dried spices—at an affordable price. I like the balance and finesse, which make it a nice partner for grilled salmon or rare seared tuna.

Kitchen Survivor™ Grade: C

Your notes: _____

Simi Zinfandel, Sonoma,   **$**   **Pts**
California 2006   **20**   **87**

One of Simi's best reds, with lots of ripe boysenberry and raspberry fruit, lavish sweet-spicy oak, and a succulent texture. A great partner for pesto pasta.

Kitchen Survivor™ Grade: C

Your notes: _____

Sterling Vintner's Collection Zinfandel,   **$**   **Pts**
Central Coast, California 2006   **10**   **85**

A best buy Zin in the "slurpable berries" style. Yum!

Kitchen Survivor™ Grade: C

Your notes: _____

Woodbridge Fish Net Creek Old   **$**   **Pts**
Vine Zinfandel, California 2006   **12**   **88**

For the price, amazingly plush and complex, with scents of fig preserves, anise, sweet spice, and savory herbs. Pair it with jerk Chicken or teriyaki.

Kitchen Survivor™ Grade: B

Your notes: _____

Woodbridge (Robert Mondavi)   **$**   **Pts**
Zinfandel, California 2006   **7**   **85**

The best varietal in the Woodbridge line, with nice ripe plump fruit.

Kitchen Survivor™ Grade: C

Your notes: _____

DESSERT WINES

Category Profile: There are plenty of great and available dessert wines to choose from, many of them affordable enough to enjoy often, with or instead of dessert (they're fat free!). These are dessert selections suggested by my Web tasters and by me. I hope you'll try them, because they will really jazz up your wine and food life. They are fantastic for entertaining, because they are unique and memorable, putting a distinctive mark on your dinner parties and cocktail gatherings.

Serve: Serving temperature depends on the wine, so see the individual entries.

When: With dessert, or as dessert; the lighter ones also make nice aperitifs. If you like to entertain, they're great. Add fruit, cheese, or some cookies, and you have a very classy end to a meal with very low hassle.

With: Blue cheese, chocolate, or simple cookies (like biscotti or shortbread) are classic.

In: An all-purpose wineglass or a smaller wineglass (the standard serving is 3 ounces rather than the traditional 6 for most wines).

	$	Pts
Baron Philippe de Rothschild **Sauternes, France 2002**	40	87

The classic and beautiful honeyed, crème brûlée, and peach scent and flavors of true Sauternes. Serve cool.
Kitchen Survivor™ Grade: A
Your notes: _____

	$	Pts
Blandy's 10-Year-Old Malmsey **Madeira, Portugal NV**	35	85

♟ Caramel, burnt sugar, toffee, burnt orange, toasted nuts, spice, and a cut of tangy acidity. Pair it with caramel or nut desserts or, best of all, dark chocolate!
Kitchen Survivor™ Grade: A+
Your notes: _____

	$	Pts
Bonny Doon Muscat Vin de **Glaciere (*van duh glahss-YAIR*),** **California 2007 (half bottle)**	20	87

Lush passion fruit and peach flavor and fabulous acidity. Chill, and serve with fruit tart or cheesecake.
Kitchen Survivor™ Grade: A
Your notes: _____

	$	Pts
Broadbent 3 Year Fine Rich **Madeira, Portugal NV**	18	88

A great starter Madeira, with classic candied orange peel–toffee-caramel character at an easy price. Serve room temp, and the wine stays fresh for months.
Kitchen Survivor™ Grade: A+
Your notes: _____

Campbell's Rutherglen Muscat,   **$**   **Pts**
Australia NV (half bottle)   **20**   **90**

"Liquid Fig Newtons!" Stunning with chocolate or aged cheddar cheese. Serve at cool room temp.

Kitchen Survivor™ Grade: A+

Your notes: _____

Castello Banfi Brachetto d'Acqui,   **$**   **Pts**
Piedmont, Italy 2007   **20**   **89**

☺ This "great for a summer afternoon with chocolate" has delicious juicy-berry flavor and an alluring rose petal scent that seems to always surprise and delight. Serve chilled; also great as an aperitif.

Kitchen Survivor™ Grade: B

Your notes: _____

Chambers Rosewood Vineyards Rutherglen   **$**   **Pts**
Muscadelle, Australia NV (half bottle)   **15**   **89**

A deep, viscous flavor of dried figs and toasted nuts. Serve at cool room temp, with chocolate or cheeses.

Kitchen Survivor™ Grade: A+

Your notes: _____

Chateau Ste. Michelle Reserve Late Harvest   **$**   **Pts**
Riesling, Washington 2006 (half bottle)   **18**   **93**

Pineapple and peach pie flavors, with floral honeysuckle nectar notes. Incredible concentration makes it delicious on its own, but also luscious with creme brulee, ice cream, or fruit tarts. Serve chilled.

Kitchen Survivor™ Grade: B

Your notes: _____

Cockburn's Fine Ruby Port,   **$**   **Pts**
Portugal NV   **16**   **85**

Enjoy this fig-and-spice-flavored dessert wine at room temp over many weeks, as the leftovers hold up well.

Kitchen Survivor™ Grade: A+

Your notes: _____

Domaine de Coyeaux Muscat de   **$**   **Pts**
Beaume de Venise, France 2004   **28**   **89**

What an alluring mandarin orange and honeysuckle scent and peach flavor! Serve lightly chilled with fruit or cream desserts, pound cake, or shortbread cookies.

Kitchen Survivor™ Grade: B

Your notes: _____

Dow's Colheita Tawny Port,   **$**   **Pts**
Portugal 1992   **40**   **85**

Vintage tawny is rare, yet still a steal for the quality; toasted walnuts, caramel, toffee—wow! Serve cool room temperature with holiday desserts: pumpkin pie, apple pie or gingerbread.

Kitchen Survivor™ Grade: A

Your notes: _____

Emilio Lustau Pedro Ximenez   **$**   **Pts**
"San Emilio" (*eh-MEE-lee-oh*   **22**   **85**
LOO-stau Pedro Hee-MEN-ez san
***eh-MEE-lee-oh*) Sherry, Spain NV**

Redolent with fig flavors and "lovely with all chocolate desserts." In Spain they pour it over vanilla ice cream. Serve at cool room temp. It's also nice with biscotti cookies, banana bread, or apple tart.

Kitchen Survivor™ Grade: A+

Your notes: _____

Ferreira Doña Antonia Port,   **$**   **Pts**
Portugal NV   **19**   **88**

Tawny-style Port—all amber gold color, toasted nut, cinnamon sugar, cappuccino, and maple scents and flavors. Beautiful with milk chocolate or nut desserts.

Kitchen Survivor™ Grade: A+

Your notes: _____

Ficklin Tinta "Port,"   **$**   **Pts**
California NV   **18**   **87**

A very worthy version of the Port style, with flavors of chocolate, nuts, dried figs, and sweet spices.

Kitchen Survivor™ Grade: A+

Your notes: _____

Fonseca Bin 27 Port,   **$**   **Pts**
Portugal NV   **18**   **85**

This is Port in the ruby style, with flavors of ripest figs, licorice, and allspice. Delicious at cool room temp with blue cheeses, nut bread and fruit.

Kitchen Survivor™ Grade: A+

Your notes: _____

Graham's Late Bottled Vintage Port,   **$**   **Pts**
Portugal 1996   **24**   **88**

The dense chocolate-dipped fig and spicy plum pudding notes are perfect with blue cheese or chocolate.

Kitchen Survivor™ Grade: A+

Your notes: _____

Hogue Late Harvest Riesling,   **$**   **Pts**
Washington 2006   **12**   **87**

Lightly sweet with a "hint of malt flavor." Great price and convenient screw-top package. Chill and serve with sponge cake or creamy desserts.

Kitchen Survivor™ Grade: C

Your notes: _____

Inniskillin Riesling Ice Wine,   **$**   **Pts**
Canada 2005 (half bottle)   **70**   **92**

"Pricey" but "worth it," with "creamy, rich" stone fruits and tree fruits. Serve lightly chilled with ice cream, fruit tarts or cheesecake; or, a fine blue cheese.

Kitchen Survivor™ Grade: A

Your notes: _____

Leacock's Rainwater Madeira,   **$**   **Pts**
Portugal NV   **18**   **87**

"Rainwater" refers to the style - light, with just a touch of sweetness. Toffee and orange zest flavors with a tangy lemon drop finish. Serve cool room temperature with cookies or pineapple upside down cake.

Kitchen Survivor™ Grade: A

Your notes: _____

Michele Chiarlo Nivole ("Clouds")   **$**   **Pts**
Moscato d'Asti, Piedmont, Italy 2007   **15**   **86**

Honeysuckle-scented, low in alcohol, high in apricot-orange fruit and refreshment. Served chilled, it makes a great brunch wine or light, festive aperitif.

Kitchen Survivor™ Grade: B

Your notes: _____

Paolo Saracco Moscato d'Asti,   **$**   **Pts**
Piedmont, Italy 2007   **16**   **90**

Nutmeg spice, orange blossom, honeysuckle and peach, plus a light and delicate bubble, make this an irresistible quaff. The light sweetness cuts through spicy heat, compliments brunch fare perfectly, and makes a wonderful, unique aperitif.

Kitchen Survivor™ Grade: B

Your notes: _____

Plunkett's Blackwood Ridge Botrytis Semillon, Australia NV

	$	Pts
	17	89

Honeyed and mushroomey, with a syrupy texture and flavors of quince paste. Serve lightly chilled, with aged cheddar or nut desserts such as pecan pie.

Kitchen Survivor™ Grade: A

Your notes: _____

Rivetti Moscato d'Asti La Spinetta, Italy 2007

	$	Pts
	20	89

To many of my tasters it's the "gold standard by which all others should be judged" in the category of Moscato d'Asti (the Moscato grape from the town of Asti). The honeysuckle, orange blossom, and apricot scent and flavor are gorgeous, and the light alcohol makes it a "great brunch wine."

Kitchen Survivor™ Grade: B

Your notes: _____

RL Buller Fine Muscat, Australia 2005 (half bottle)

	$	Pts
	16	89

The syrupy "toffee, coffee, and caramel" flavor makes it "the perfect soak for pound cake."

Kitchen Survivor™ Grade: A

Your notes: _____

St. Supery Moscato, California 2006

	$	Pts
	18	88

"A wonderful dessert wine" with the scent of honeysuckles and the flavor of spiced apricots. Serve chilled with fruit tarts or cheesecake.

Kitchen Survivor™ Grade: B

Your notes: _____

Smith Woodhouse Lodge Reserve Port, Portugal NV

	$	Pts
	22	85

The flavors of dried figs, dates, and berry syrup and long finish make this great for sipping with Stilton cheese. Serve cool room temp; it stays fresh for weeks.

Kitchen Survivor™ Grade: A

Your notes: _____

Taylor Fladgate 20 Year Tawny $ Pts
Port, Portugal NV 60 92

"Pricey" due to the decades of aging, but complex—
toasted walnuts, streusel, and caramel. Lovely for
sipping at cool room temp on its own, or with milk
chocolate desserts, nut cookies or flan.

Kitchen Survivor™ Grade: A

Your notes: _____

Warre 10-Year-Old Otima Tawny $ Pts
Port, Portugal NV 28 85

The "nut flavor" and "smooth, warming texture" are
classic to tawny Port; a touch sweet but not at all
cloying. Serve cool room temp with banana nut cake.

Kitchen Survivor™ Grade: A+

Your notes: _____

THE
COMPLETE WINE COURSE MINI-COURSE: A WINE CLASS IN A GLASS

How do you go about choosing wine? The best way to ensure you'll be happy with your wine choices is to learn your taste.

Here are two quick wine lessons, adapted from my *Complete Wine Course* DVD, that will let you do exactly that. You're probably thinking, Will there be a test? In a way, every pulled cork is a test, but for the *wine:* Are you happy with what you got for the price you paid, and would you buy it again? This mini-course will teach you to pick wines that pass muster by helping you learn what styles and tastes you like in a wine and how to use the label to help you find them.

If you want, you can complete each lesson in a matter of minutes. As with food, tasting impressions form quickly with wine. Then you can get dinner on the table, accompanied by your wine picks. Start by doing the first lesson, "White Wine Made Simple," one evening, and then Lesson 2, "Red Wine Made Simple," another time. Or you can invite friends over and make it a party. Everyone will learn a little bit about wine, while having fun.

Setup
Glassware: You will need three glasses per taster. A simple all-purpose wineglass is ideal, but clear disposables are fine, too.

Pouring: Start with a tasting portion (about an ounce of each wine). Tasters can repour more of their favorite to enjoy with hors d'oeuvres or dinner.

Flights: Taste the Lesson 1 whites first and then the Lesson 2 reds (pros call each sequence of wine a *flight*). There is no need to wash or rinse the glasses.

To Taste It Is to Know It
Tasting is the fastest way to learn about wine. My wine students tell me this all the time: They know

what wines they like when they try them. The trick is in understanding the style and knowing how to ask for it and get it again: "I'd like a Chardonnay with lots of buttery, toasty oak and gobs of creamy, tropical fruit flavors." If you don't know what it means, you might feel silly offering a description like that when wine shopping. But those words really are in the glass, and these easy-to-follow tasting lessons will help you recognize the styles and learn which ones are your favorites.

The Lessons

What You'll Do:
For Lesson 1, "White Wine Made Simple," you will comparison-taste three major white wine grapes: Riesling, Sauvignon Blanc, and Chardonnay. For Lesson 2, "Red Wine Made Simple," you will compare three major reds: Pinot Noir, Merlot, and Cabernet Sauvignon. Follow these easy steps:

1. Buy your wines. Make your choice from the varietal sections of this book. It's best to choose wines in the same price category—for example, all under-$15 wines.
2. Chill (even the reds can take a light chill; they warm up quickly and can taste out of balance if too warm), pour, and taste the wines in the order of body, light to full, as shown in the tasting notes.
3. Use the tasting notes as a guide, and record your own if you want.

What You'll Learn:
Body styles of the major grapes—light, medium, or full. You'll see that Riesling is lighter (less heavy) than Chardonnay, in the same way that, for example, skim milk is lighter than heavy cream.

What the major grapes taste like—When tasted side by side, the grapes are quite distinctive, just as a pear tastes different from an apple, a strawberry tastes different from a blueberry, and so on.

What other wine flavor words taste like—Specifically, you'll experience these tastes: oaky, tannic, crisp, and fruity. Knowing them is helpful because they're used a lot in this book, on wine bottle labels, and by sellers of wine—merchants, waiters, and so on.

Getting comfortable with these basics will equip you to describe the wine styles you like to a waiter or wine merchant and to use the information on a bottle label to find those styles on your own. In the "Buying Lingo" section that follows, I've defined lots of other style words and listed some wine types you can try to experience them.

Tasting Lesson 1
WHITE WINE MADE SIMPLE

Instructions: Taste the wines in numbered order. Note your impressions of:

Color: Which is lightest and which is darkest? Whites can range from pale straw to deep yellow-gold. The darker the color, the fuller the body.

Scent: While they all smell like white wine, the aromas differ, from delicate and tangy to rich and fruity.

Taste and Body: In the same way that fruits range from crisp and tart (like apples) to ripe and lush (like mangoes), the wine tastes will vary along with the body styles of the grapes, from light to full.

Which grape and style do you like best? If you like more than one style, that's great, too!

The White Wines

Grape 1: Riesling (any region)—light bodied

Description: Crisp and refreshing, with vibrant fruit flavor ranging from apple to peach.

Brand name:_____

Your notes: _____

_____

Grape 2: Sauvignon Blanc (France or New Zealand)—medium bodied

Description: Very distinctive! The smell is exotically pungent, the taste tangy and mouthwatering, like citrus fruit (lime and grapefruit).

Brand name:_____

Your notes: _____

_____

Grape 3: Chardonnay (California)—full bodied

Description: The richest scent and taste, with fruit flavor ranging from ripe apples to peaches to tropical fruits. You can feel the full-bodied texture, too. "Oaky" scents come through as a sweet, buttery, or toasty impression.

Brand name:_____

Your notes: _____

_____

Tasting Lesson 2
RED WINE MADE SIMPLE

Instructions: Again, taste the wines in numbered order and note your impressions.

Color: Red wines range in color from transparent ruby, like the Pinot Noir, to inky dark purple—the darker the color, the fuller the body.

Scent: In addition to the smell of "red wine," you'll get the cherrylike smell of Pinot Noir, perhaps plum character in the Merlot, and a rich dark-berry smell in the Cabernet. There are other scents, too, so enjoy them. You can also compare your impressions with those included in the reviews section of the book.

Taste and Body: Like white wines, red wines range from light and delicate to rich and intense. You'll note the differences in body from light to full and the distinctive taste character of each grape. As you can see, tasting them side by side makes it easy to detect and compare the differences.

The Red Wines

Grape 1: Pinot Noir (any region)—light bodied

Description: Delicate cherrylike fruit flavor, silky-smooth texture, mouthwatering acidity, all of which make Pinot Noir a versatile wine for most types of food.

Brand name:_____

Your notes: _____

_____

Grape 2: Merlot (California, Chile, or Washington)—medium bodied

Description: More intense than Pinot Noir: rich "red wine" flavor, yet not too heavy. That's probably why it's so popular!

Brand name:_____

Your notes: _____

_____

Grape 3: Cabernet Sauvignon (Chile or California)—full bodied

Description: The fullest-bodied, most intense taste. Notice the drying sensation it leaves on your tongue? That's tannin, a natural grape component that, like color, comes from the skin. As you can see, more color and more tannin come together. Tasting high-tannin wines with fat or protein counters that drying sensation (that's why Cabernet and red meat are considered classic partners). In reds, an "oaky" character comes through as one or more of these scents: spice, cedar, smoke, toastiness, vanilla, and coconut. No wonder buyers love it!

Brand name: _____

Your notes: _____

_____

Wine Glossary

Here are the meanings of some of the major wine style words that you see in this book, on wine bottles and in wine shops.

Acidity—The tangy, tart, crisp, mouthwatering component in wine. It's a prominent characteristic of Riesling, Sauvignon Blanc, and Pinot Grigio whites and Pinot Noir and Chianti/Sangiovese reds.

Bag-in-a-Box—A box with a wine-filled bag inside that deflates as the wine is consumed, preventing oxidation.

Balance—The harmony of all the wine's main components: fruit, alcohol, and acidity, plus sweetness (if any), oak (if used in the wine making), and tannin (in reds). As with food, balance in the wine is important to your enjoyment, and a sign of quality. But it's also a matter of taste—the dish may taste "too salty" and the wine "too oaky" for one person but be fine to another.

Barrel aged / barrel fermented—The wine was aged or fermented (or both) in oak barrels. The barrels give fuller body as well as an "oaky" character to the wine's scent and flavor, making it seem richer. "Oaky" scents are often in the sweet family—but *not* sugary. Rather, *toasty, spicy, vanilla, buttery,* and *coconut* are the common wine words to describe "oaky" character. Other label signals that mean "oaky": Barrel Fermented, Barrel Select, Barrel Cuvee, Cask Fermented.

Bouquet—All of the wine's scents, which come from the grape(s) used, the techniques (like oak aging), the age of the wine, and the vineyard characteristics (like soil and climate).

Bright—Vivid and vibrant. Usually used as a modifier, like "bright fruit" or "bright acidity."

Buttery—Literally, the creamy-sweet smell of butter. One by-product of fermentation is an ester that mimics the butter smell, so you may well notice this in some wines, especially barrel-fermented Chardonnays.

Corked, corky—Refers to a wine whose scent or taste has been tainted by corks or wine-making equipment infected with a bacteria called TCA. While not harmful to health, TCA gives wines a musty smell and taste.

Creamy—Can mean a smell similar to fresh cream or a smooth and lush texture. In sparkling wines, it's a textural delicacy and smoothness of the bubbles.

Crisp—See ACIDITY.

Dry—A wine without sweetness (though not without fruit; see FRUITY for more on this).

Earthy—As with cheeses, potatoes, mushrooms, and other good consumables, wines can have scents and flavors reminiscent of, or owing to, the soil. The "earth" terms commonly attributed to wine include *mushrooms, truffles, flint, dusty, gravelly, chalky, slaty, wet leaves,* and even *barnyard.*

Exotic—Just as it applies to other things, this description suggests unusual and alluring characteristics in wine. Quite often refers to wines with a floral or spicy style or flavors beyond your typical fruit bowl, such as tropical fruits or rare berries.

Floral—Having scents that mimic flower scents, whether fresh (as in the honeysuckle scent of some Rieslings) or dried (as in the wilted rose petal scent of some Gewurztraminers).

Food friendly—Food-friendly wines have taste characteristics that pair well with a wide variety of foods without clashing or overpowering— namely, good acidity and moderate (not too heavy) body. The food-friendly whites include Riesling and Sauvignon Blanc; the reds include

Chianti, Spanish Rioja, red Rhone, and Pinot Noir wines.

Fruity—Marked by a prominent smell and taste of fruit. In whites the fruit tastes can range from lean and tangy (like lemons and crisp apples) to medium (like melons and peaches) to lush (like mangoes and pineapples). In reds, think cranberries and cherries, plums and blueberries, figs and prunes. Note that *fruity* doesn't mean "sweet." The taste and smell of ripe fruit are perceived as sweet, but they're not sugary. Most wines on the market are at once dry (meaning not sweet) and fruity, with lots of fruit flavor.

Grassy—Describes a wine marked with scents of fresh-cut grass or herbs or even green vegetables (like green pepper and asparagus). It's a signature of Sauvignon Blanc wines, especially those grown in New Zealand and France. *Herbal* and *herbaceous* are close synonyms.

Herbal, herbaceous—See GRASSY.

Legs—The drips running down the inside of the wineglass after you swirl it. Not a sign of quality (as in "good legs") but of viscosity. Fast-running legs indicate a low-viscosity wine and slow legs a high-viscosity wine. The higher the viscosity, the richer and fuller the wine feels in your mouth.

Nose—The smell of the wine. Isn't it interesting how wines have a nose, legs, and body? As you've no doubt discovered, they have personalities, too!

Oaky—See BARREL AGED.

Off-dry—A lightly sweet wine.

Old vines—Refers to wine from vines significantly older than average, usually at least 30 years old and sometimes far older. Older vines yield a smaller, but often more intensely flavored, crop of grapes.

Regional wine—A wine named for the region where the grapes are grown, such as Champagne, Chianti, and Pouilly-Fuisse.

Spicy—A wine with scents and flavors reminiscent of spices, both sweet (cinnamon, ginger, cardamom, clove) and savory (pepper, cumin, curry).

Sweet—A wine that has perceptible sugar, called *residual sugar* because it is left over from fermentation and not converted to alcohol. A wine can be lightly sweet like a Moscato or very sweet like a Port or Sauternes.

Tannic—A red wine whose tannin is noticeable—a little or a lot—as a drying sensation on your tongue ranging from gentle (lightly tannic) to velvety (richly tannic) to harsh (too tannic).

Terroir—The distinctive flavors, scents, and character of a wine owing to its vineyard source. For example, the terroir of French red Burgundies is sometimes described as *earthy*.

Toasty—Wines with a toasty, roasted, caramelized, or smoky scent reminiscent of coffee beans, toasted nuts or spices, or burnt sugar.

Unfiltered—A wine that has not been filtered before bottling (which is common practice). Some say filtering the wine strips out flavor, but not everyone agrees. I think most tasters cannot tell the difference.

Varietal wine—A wine named for the grape used to make it, such as Chardonnay or Merlot.

Handling Wine Leftovers

I developed the Kitchen Survivor™ grades to give you an idea of how long each wine stays in good drinking condition if you don't finish the bottle. In the same way that resealing the cereal box or wrapping and refrigerating leftovers will extend their freshness window, you can do the same for wine by handling the leftovers as follows:

Still Wines

Recork—At a minimum, close the bottle with its original cork. Most wines will stay fresh a day or two at normal room temperature. To extend that freshness-window, purchase a vacuum-sealer (available in kitchenware shops and wine shops). You simply cork the bottle with the purchased rubber stopper, which has a one-way valve. The accompanying plastic vacuum pump is then placed on top of the stopper; you pump the handle repeatedly until the resistance tightens, indicating the air has been pumped out of the bottle. (Note: A few wine experts don't think rubber stoppers work, but I have used them for years. In my restaurants, I have found they extended the life of bottles opened for by-the-glass service at least two days longer than just sealing with the original cork.)

Refrigerate stoppered (and vacuum-sealed) bottles, whether white, pink, or red. Refrigeration of anything slows the spoilage, and your red wine, once removed from the fridge and poured in the glass, will quickly come to serving temperature.

For even longer shelf-life, you can preserve partial bottles with inert gas. I recommend this especially for more expensive wines. Wine Life and Private Preserve are two brands that I have used (sold in wine shops and accessories catalogs). They come in a can that feels light, as if it were empty. Inside is an inert gas mixture that is heavier than air. The can's spray nozzle is inserted into the bottle. A one-second spray fills the empty bottle space with the inert gas, displacing the air inside, which is the key because no air in contact with the wine means no oxidation. Then you quickly replace the cork (make sure the fit is tight). My experience in restaurants using gas systems for very upscale wines by the glass is that they keep well for a week or more.

Sparkling Wines

Your best bet is to purchase "clam shell" Champagne stoppers, with one or two hinged metal clamps attached to a stopper top that has a rubber or plastic gasket for a tight seal. You place the stopper on top, press down, and then anchor the clamps to the bottle lip. If you open your sparkler carefully and don't "pop" the cork, losing precious carbonation, a stoppered partial bottle will keep its effervescence for at least a few days, and sometimes much longer.

SAVVY SHOPPER:
RETAIL WINE BUYING

Supermarkets, pharmacies, price clubs, catalogs, state stores, megastores, dot.coms, and boutiques . . . where you shop for wine depends a lot on the state where you live, because selling wine requires a state license. What many people don't realize is how much the wine laws vary from one state to the next.

In most states, the regulations affect the prices you pay for wine, what wines are available, and how you get your hands on them (ideally, they are delivered to your door or poured at your table, but this isn't always legal). Here is a quick summary of the retail scene to help you make the most of your buying power wherever you live.

Wine Availability The single biggest frustration for every wine buyer and winery is bureaucracy. To ensure the collection of excise taxes, in nearly all states every single wine must be registered and approved in some way before it can be sold. If a wine you're seeking isn't available in your area, this is probably the reason. For many small boutique wineries, it just isn't worth the bother and expense to get legal approval for the few cases of wine they would sell in a particular state. One extreme example is Pennsylvania, a "control state" where wine is sold exclusively by a state-run monopoly that, without competition, has little incentive to source a lot of boutique wines. By contrast, California, New York, and Chicago, with high demand and competition, are good markets for wine availability.

Wine Prices and Discounts Wine prices can vary from one state to the next due to different tax rates. And in general, prices are lower in competitive markets, where stores can use discounts, sale prices, and so on to vie for your business.

Where they are legal, case discounts of 10% to 15% are a great way to get the best possible prices for your favorite wines. On the more expensive wines, many people I know coordinate their buying with friends and family so they can buy full cases and get these discounts.

Delivery and Wine-by-Mail In many states, it is not legal for stores or other retailers to deliver wine to the purchaser.

Many catalogs and Web sites sell wine by mail. Some are affiliated with retail stores or wineries, whereas others are strictly virtual stores. The conveniences include shopping on your own time and terms, from home or office, helpful buying recommendations and information, and usually home delivery. Keep in mind that the laws governing such shipping are complex, and vary from state to state (in some states it is completely prohibited).

Mail-order wine clubs are an interesting option when you are looking for new wines to try. For information on my own wine club, Andrea's A-List,™ visit my Web site, www.andreawine.com.

Where Should I Shop? That depends on what you're buying. If you know what you want, then price is your main consideration, and you'll get your best deals at venues that concentrate on volume sales—discount stores, price clubs, and so on. If you want buying advice, or are buying rare wines, you're better off in a wine shop or merchant specializing in collectible wines. These stores have trained buyers who taste and know their inventory well; they can help you with your decision. The better stores also have temperature-controlled storage for their rare wines, which is critical to ensure you get a product in good condition. There are also Web-based fine and rare wine specialists, but that is a fairly new market. I suggest you purchase fine and rare wines only through sources with a good track record of customer service. In that way, if you have problems with a shipment, you will have some recourse.

Can I Take That Bottle on the Wine List Home with Me? In most states, restaurants' wine licenses allow for sale and consumption "on-premise" only, meaning they cannot sell you a bottle to take home.

Burgundy Buyers, Beware With the exception of volume categories such as Beaujolais, Macon, and

Pouilly-Fuissé, buyers of French white and red Burgundy should shop only at fine wine merchants, preferably those that specialize in Burgundy, for two reasons. First, Burgundy is simply too fragile to handle the storage conditions in most stores. Burgundy specialists ensure temperature-controlled storage. Second, selection is a major factor, because quality varies a lot from one winery to the next, and from one vintage to the next. Specialist stores have the needed buying expertise to ensure the quality of their offerings.

Is That a Deal or a Disaster? Floor stacks, "end caps," private labels, and bin ends can be a boon for the buyer, or a bust, depending on where you are shopping. Here's what you need to know about them:

"Floor Stacks" of large-volume categories and brands (e.g., branded varietal wines)—These are a best bet in supermarkets and other volume-based venues, where they're used to draw your attention to a price markdown. Take advantage of it to stock up for everyday or party wines.

"End Cap" wine displays featured at the ends of aisles—A good bet, especially in fine wine shops. You may not have heard of the wine, but they're usually "hidden gems" that the buyer discovered and bought in volume, to offer you quality and uniqueness at a savings.

"Bin Ends"—Retailers often clear out the last few bottles of something by discounting the price. In reputable retail stores, they are usually still good quality, and thus a good bet. Otherwise, steer clear.

Private labels—These are wines blended and bottled exclusively for the retailer—again, good bets in reputable stores, who stake their reputation on your satisfaction with their private labels.

"Shelf-talkers"—Written signs, reviews, and ratings. Good shops offer their own recommendations in lieu of, or along with, critics' scores. If the only information is a critic's score, check to be sure that the vintage being sold matches that of the wine that was reviewed.

BUYING WINE IN RESTAURANTS

Wine List Strategy Session

A lot of us have a love–hate relationship with the wine list. On the one hand, we know it holds the potential to enhance the evening, impress the date or client, broaden our horizons, or all three. But it also makes us feel intimidated, inadequate, overwhelmed, and . . .

Panicked by prices—That goes for both the cheapest wines *and* the most expensive ones; we're leery of extremes.

Pressured by pairing—Will this wine "go with" our food?

Overwhelmed by options—Can this wine I've never heard of possibly be any good? Does my selection measure up? (Remember, the restaurant is supposed to impress *you,* not the other way around.) This "phone book" wine list makes me want to dial 911.

Stumped by Styles—Food menus are easy because we understand the key terms: appetizer, entree, dessert, salad, soup, fish, meat, and so on. But after *white* and *red,* most of us get lost pretty quickly with wine categories. (Burgundy . . . is that a style, a color, a place, or all three?)

Let's deal with the first three above. For the lowdown on wine list terms, use the decoder that follows to pinpoint the grapes and styles behind all the major wine names.

Wine List Prices
The prices on wine lists reflect three things:

- *The dining-out experience*—The restaurant wine markup is higher than in retail stores because the decor is (usually) nicer, and you get to stay a while, during which time they open the wine, serve it in a nice glass, and clean up afterward. They also may have invested in the cost and expertise to select and store the wine properly. Consequently those who enjoy drinking wine in restaurants are accustomed to being charged more for the wine than you would pay to drink the same bottle at home. That said, exorbitant mark-ups are, in my opinion, the biggest deterrent to more guests enjoying wine in restaurants (which is both good for the guests and good for business). You can always vote with your wallet and dine in restaurants with guest-friendly wine pricing.

- *Location*—Restaurants in exclusive resorts, in urban centers with a business clientele, or with a star chef behind them, tend toward higher wine markups, because they can get away with it. The logic, so to speak, is that if you're on vacation, it's on the company, or it's just the "in" place, high markups (on everything) are part of the price of admission. However, I don't really think that's right, and I do think these places would sell more wine with lower markups.

- *The rarity of the wine*—Often, the rarer the wine (either because it's in high demand due to critics' hype or because it's old and just a few bottles remain), the higher the markup. It's a form of rationing in the face of high demand/low supply. Food can be the same way (lobsters, truffles, caviar, etc.).

Getting the Most Restaurant Wine for Your Money

Seeking value doesn't make you a cheapskate. Here are the best strategies to keep in mind:

1. Take the road less traveled—Chardonnay and Cabernet Sauvignon are what I call "comfort wines" because they're so well known. But their prices often reflect a "comfort premium" (in the same way that a name-brand toothpaste costs more than the store brand). These spectacular wine styles often give better value for the money, because they're less widely known:

   Whites
   Riesling
   Sauvignon Blanc and Fume Blanc
   Sancerre (a French Loire Valley wine made from the Sauvignon Blanc grape)
   Anything from Washington State or New Zealand

Reds
Cotes-du-Rhone and other French Rhone
   Valley reds
Red Zinfandel from California
Spanish Rioja and other reds from Spain
Cabernet Sauvignon from Chile

2. Savvy Splurging—There's no doubt about it: nothing commemorates, celebrates, or impresses better than a special wine. Since splurging on wine in a restaurant can mean especially big bucks, here are the "trophy" wine styles that give you the most for your money on wine lists:

> French Champagne—I think that Champagne (the real stuff from France's Champagne region) is among the most affordable luxuries on the planet, and its wine list prices are often among the best of all the "badge" wine categories (such as French Bordeaux and Burgundy, cult California Cabernets, and boutique Italian wines).

> California's Blue Chip Cabernets—I don't mean the tiny-production cult-movement Cabernets but rather the classics that have been around for decades, and still make world-class wine at a fair price. Names like Beringer, BV, Franciscan, Mt. Veeder, Robert Mondavi, Silver Oak, Simi, and Stag's Leap all made the survey, and for good reason: they're excellent and available.

> Italian Chianti Classico Riserva—This recommendation may surprise you, but I include it because the quality for the price is better than ever, and recent vintages have been great. I also think that across the country a lot of people celebrate and do business in steak houses and Italian restaurants, which tend to carry this wine category because it complements their food.

3. The Midprice/Midstyle "Safety Zone"—This is a strategy I first developed not for dining guests but for our *waiters* trying to help diners choose

a bottle, usually with very little to go on (many people aren't comfortable describing their taste preference, and they rarely broadcast their budget for fear of looking cheap). The mid-price/midstyle strategy is this: in any wine list category (e.g., Chardonnays and Italian reds), if you go for the midprice range in that section, odds are good the wine will be midstyle. Mid-style is my shorthand for the most typical, crowd-pleasing version, likely to satisfy a high proportion of guests and to be sticker shock free. The fact is that the more expensive the wine is, the more distinctive and even unusual its style is likely to be. If it's not to your taste *and* you've spent a lot, you're doubly disap-pointed.

4. Ask—With wine more popular than ever, res-taurants are the most proactive they've ever been in seeking to put quality and value on their wine lists. So ask for it: "What's the best red wine deal on your list right now?" Or, if you have a style preference, say something like "We want to spend $XX. Which of these Chardon-nays do you think is the best for the money?"

Pairing Wine and Food

Worrying a lot about this is a big waste of time, because most wines complement most foods, regard-less of wine color, center-of-the-plate protein, and all that other stuff. How well? Their affinity can range from "fine" to "Omigod." You can pretty much expect at least a nice combination every time you have wine with food and great matches from time to time (of course, frequent experimentation ups your odds). The point is, your style preference is a lot more important than the pairing, per se, because if you hate the dish or the wine, you're hardly likely to enjoy the pairing. That said, here is a list of wine styles that are especially favored by sommeliers and chefs for their exceptional food affinity and versatility, along with a few best-bet food recommendations:

Favorite "Food Wines" White	Best-Bet Food Matches
Champagne and Sparkling Wine—So many people save bubbly just for toasts, but it's an amazing "food wine"	Sushi All shellfish Cheeses (even stinky ones) Omelets and other egg dishes Mushroom sauces (on risotto, pasta or whatever)
Riesling from Germany, Alsace (France), America, Australia	Mexican, southwestern, and other spicy foods Shellfish Cured meats and sausages
Alsace (France) White Wines—Riesling, Pinot Gris, and Gewurztraminer	Pacific Rim foods—Japanese, Thai, Korean, Chinese Indian food Smoked meats and charcuterie Meat stews (really!)
Sauvignon Blanc and wines made from it (French Sancerre, Pouilly-Fume, and white Bordeaux)	Goat cheese Salads Herbed sauces (like pesto) Tomato dishes (salads, soups, sauces)

Red	
Beaujolais (from France)	Mushroom dishes
Pinot Noir	Fish (especially rich ones like tuna, salmon, and cod) Smoked meats Grilled vegetables Duck
Chianti, Rosso di Montalcino, and other Italian reds made from the Sangiovese grape	Pizza, eggplant parmigiana (and other Italian-American–inspired tastes) Cheesy dishes Spicy sausages
Rioja from Spain	Roasted and grilled meats

Choosing from the Wine List

You've got the wine list. Unless you know a lot about wine, you now face at least one of these dilemmas:

- You've never heard of any of the wines listed or at least none of those in your price range. (Okay, maybe you've heard of Dom Pérignon, but let's be real.) Or the names you do recognize don't interest you.

- You have no idea how much a decent selection should cost. But you *do* know you want to keep to your budget, without broadcasting it to your guests and the entire dining room.
- The wine list is so huge you don't even want to open it.

Wine List Playbook

Remember, you're the buyer. Good restaurants want you to enjoy wine and to feel comfortable with the list, your budget, and so on. As far as the wine-snobby ones go, what are you doing there anyway? (Okay, if you took a gamble on a new place or somebody else picked it, the strategies here can help.)

The basics:

1. *Don't worry if you haven't heard of the names.* There are literally thousands of worthy wines beyond the big brand names, and many restaurants feature them to spice up their selection.
2. *Determine what you want to spend.* I think most people want the best deal they can get. With that in mind, here are some price/value rules of thumb. In most restaurants the wine prices tend to relate to the food prices, as follows:
   - Wines by-the-glass: The price window for good-quality wines that please a high percentage of diners usually parallels the restaurant's mid- to top-priced appetizers. So if the Caesar salad (or wings or whatever) is $5.95, expect to spend that, plus or minus a dollar or two, for a good glass of wine. This goes for dessert wine, too. Champagne and sparkling wines can be more, due to the cost of the product and greater waste because it goes flat.
   - Bottles: This is far more variable, but in general most restaurants try to offer an ample selection of good-quality bottles priced in what I call a "selling zone" that's benchmarked to their highest entree price, plus a margin. That's the variable part. It can range from $5–10 on average in national chain restaurants and their peers to at least $10–20 in luxury and destination restaurants. So if the

casual chain's steak-and-shrimp-scampi combo costs $17.95, the $20–30 zone on their wine list will likely hold plenty of good bottle choices. In an urban restaurant where the star chef's signature herb-crusted lamb costs $28, you could expect a cluster of worthy bottles in the $35–55 range.

We in the trade find it funny, and nearly universal, that guests shy away from the least expensive wines on our lists, suspicious that there's something "wrong" with the wine. But any restaurant that's committed to wine, whether casual chain or destination eatery, puts extra effort into finding top-quality wines at the lowest price points. They may come from grapes or regions you don't know, but my advice is to muster your sense of adventure and try them. In the worst-case scenario, you'll be underwhelmed, but since tastes vary, this can happen with wine at any price. I think the odds are better that you'll enjoy one of the best deals on the wine list.

The wine list transaction: You've set your budget. Now it's time to zero in on a selection. You've got two choices—go it alone or ask for help. In either case, here's what to do:

1. Ask for the wine list right away. It's a pet peeve of mine that guests even *need* to ask (rather than getting the list automatically with the food menus), because that can cause both service delays and anxiety. Many people are scared to request the list for fear it "commits" them to a purchase, before they can determine whether they'll be comfortable with the prices and choices available. As you're being handed the menus, say "We'll take a look at the wine list, too" to indicate you want a copy to review, not a pushy sales job. *Tip:* I always ask that the wine-by-the-glass list be brought, too. Since many places change them often, they may be on a separate card or a specials board. (I think verbal listings are the worst, because often key information, like the price or winery, can get lost in translation.)

2. Determine any style particulars you're in the mood for:
   - White or red?
   - A particular grape, region, or body style?

   If the table can't reach a consensus, look at wine-by-the-glass and half-bottle options. This can happen when preferences differ or food choices are all over the map ("I'm having the oysters, he's having the wild boar, we want one wine . . ." is a stumper I've actually faced!).
3. Find your style zone in the list. Turn to the section that represents your chosen category—e.g., whites, the wine-by-the-glass section, Chardonnays, Italian reds, or whatever—or let the server know what style particulars you have in mind.
4. Match your budget. Pick a wine priced accordingly, keeping in mind these "safety zones":
   - The wines recommended in this book
   - Winery or region names that you remember liking or hearing good things about (e.g., Chianti in Italy or a different offering from your favorite white Zinfandel producer)
   - The midprice/midstyle zone (as I explained earlier, many lists have this "sweet spot" of well-made, moderately priced offerings)
   - Featured wine specials, if they meet your price parameters

   You can communicate your budget while keeping your dignity with this easy trick I teach waiters:
   - Find your style zone—e.g., Pinot Grigios—in the wine list.
   - With both you and the server looking at the list, *point to the price* of a wine that's close to what you want to spend and then say, "We were looking at this one. What do you think?"
   - Keep pointing long enough for the server to see the price, and you'll be understood without having to say (in front of your date or client), "No more than thirty bucks, okay?"

I ask my waiters to point to the price, starting at a moderate level, with their first wine suggestion. From there the guest's reaction shows his or her intentions, without the embarrassment of having to talk price.

There's no formula, but the bottom line is this: whether glass or bottle, it's hard to go wrong with popular grapes and styles, moderate prices, the "signature" or featured wine(s) of the restaurant, and/or the waiter's enthusiastic recommendation. If you don't like it, chalk it up to experience—the same could happen with a first-time food choice, right? Most of the time, experimentation pays off. So enjoy!

Wine List Decoder

Wine is like food—it's easy to choose from among the styles with which you're familiar. That's why wines like Pinot Grigio, Chardonnay, Chianti, and Merlot are such big sellers. But when navigating other parts of the list, namely less-common grape varieties and the classic European regional wines, I think many of us get lost pretty quickly. And yet these are major players in the wine world, without which buyers miss out on a whole array of delicious options, from classic to cutting edge.

This decoder gives you the tools you need to explore them. It reveals:

> *The grapes used* to make the classic wines—If it's a grape you've tried, then you'll have an idea of what the wine tastes like.
>
> *The body styles from light to full* of every major wine category—The waiters and wine students with whom I work always find this extremely helpful, because it breaks up the wine world into broad, logical categories that are easy to understand and similar to the way we classify other things. With food, for example, we have vegetables, meat, fish, and so on.
>
> *The taste profile,* in simple terms—The exact taste of any wine is subjective (I say apple, you say pear), but knowing how the tastes *compare* is a great tool to help you identify your preferred style.

The names are set up just as you might see them on a wine list, under the key country and region headings, and in each section they are arranged by body style from light to full. (For whites, Italy comes before France in body style, overall. Their order is reversed for reds.) Finally, where applicable I've highlighted the major grapes in italics in the column on the left to help you quickly see just how widely used these grapes are and thus how much you already know about these heretofore mystifying wine names.

Sparkling Wines

- **Italy**

Asti Spumante	Muscat (Moscato)	Light; floral, hint of sweetness
Prosecco	Prosecco	Delicate; crisp, tangy, the wine used in Bellini cocktails

- **Spain**

Cava	Locals: Xarel-lo, Parellada, Macabeo plus Chardonnay	Light; crisp, refreshing

- **France**

Champagne	The red (yes!) grapes Pinot Noir and Pinot Meunier, plus Chardonnay	To me, all are heavenly, but check the style on the label: Blanc de Blancs—delicate and tangy Brut NV, vintage and luxury—range from soft and creamy to rich and toasty

White Wines

- **Germany**

Riesling	Riesling rules Germany's quality wine scene	Feather-light but flavor-packed: fruit salad in a glass

- **Italy**

Frascati	Trebbiano, Malvasia	As you've noticed, mostly local grapes are used in Italy's whites. But the style of all these is easy to remember: light, tangy, and refreshing. Pinot Grigio, the best known, is also more distinctive—pleasant pear and lemon flavors, tasty but not heavy. The less common Pinot Bianco is similar.
Soave	Garganega, Trebbiano	
Orvieto	Grechetto, Procanico, and many others	
Gavi	Cortese	
Vernaccia	Vernaccia	
Pinot Grigio		

- **France**
  - *Alsace—Grape names are on the label:*

	Pinot Blanc	Light; tangy, pleasant
Riesling	Riesling	Fuller than German Riesling but not heavy; citrus, apples, subtle but layered
	Pinot Gris	Smooth, richer texture; fruit compote flavors
	Gewurztraminer	Sweet spices, apricots, lychee fruit

  - *Loire Valley*

Vouvray	Chenin Blanc	Look for the style name: Sec—dry and tangy; Demi-sec—baked apple, hint of sweetness; Moelleux—honeyed dessert style

Sauvignon Blanc

Sancerre and Pouilly-Fume	Sauvignon Blanc	Light to medium; subtle fruit, racy acidity

  - *White Bordeaux*

Sauvignon Blanc & Semillon

Entre-Deux-Mers	Sauvignon Blanc and Semillon	Tangy, crisp, light
Graves Pessac-Leognan		Medium to full; ranging from creamy lemon-lime to lush fig flavors; pricey ones are usually oaky

  - *Burgundy White*

Chardonnay

Macon St.-Veran Pouilly-Fuisse	Every Chardonnay in the world is modeled on white French Burgundy	Light; refreshing, citrus-apple flavors
Chablis		Subtle, mineral, green apple
St. Aubin Meursault Puligny-Montrachet Chassagne-Montrachet Corton-Charlemagne		Medium; pear, dried apple, nutty; complexity ranging from simple to sublime

Red Wines

- **France**
  - ***Red Burgundy***

Beaujolais Beaujolais-Villages	Gamay	Uncomplicated, light; fruity, pleasant
Beaujolais Cru: Morgon, Moulin-a-Vent, etc.		More complex, plum-berry taste, smooth (the wines are named for their village)

Pinot Noir

Cote de Beaune Santenay Volnay Pommard Nuits-St.-Georges Vosne-Romanee Gevrey-Chambertin Clos de Vougeot, etc.	Pinot Noir	Ranging from light body, pretty cherry taste to extraordinary complexity: captivating spice, berry and earth scents, silky texture, berries and plums flavor

  - ***Red Bordeaux***

Merlot

Pomerol St. Emilion	Merlot, plus Cabernet Franc and Cabernet Sauvignon	Medium to full; oaky-vanilla scent, plum flavor

Cabernet Sauvignon

Medoc Margaux Pauillac St-Estephe	Cabernet Sauvignon, plus Merlot, Cabernet Franc, and Petit Verdot	Full; chunky-velvety texture; cedar-spice-toasty scent; dark berry flavor

  - ***Rhone Red***

Syrah, aka Shiraz

Cotes-du-Rhone	Mainly Grenache, Syrah, Cinsault, Mourvedre	Medium to full; juicy texture; spicy raspberry scent and taste
Cote-Rotie	Syrah, plus a splash of white Viognier	Full; brawny texture; peppery scent; plum and dark berry taste

Hermitage	Syrah, plus a touch of the white grapes Marsanne and Roussane	Similar to Cote-Rotie
Chateauneuf-du-Pape	Mainly Syrah, Grenache, Cinsault, Mourvedre	Full; exotic leathery-spicy scent; spiced fig and berry compote taste

(Red Zinfandel is here in the light-to-full body spectrum)

- **Spain**
  - *Rioja*

Rioja Crianza, Reserva and Gran Reserva	Tempranillo, plus Garnacha, aka Grenache, and other local grapes	Ranging from soft and smooth, juicy strawberry character (Crianza); to full, caramel-leather scent, spicy-dried fruit taste (Reserva and Gran Reserva)

  - *Ribera del Duero*

	Mostly Tempranillo	Full; mouth-filling texture; toasty-spice scent; anise and plum taste

  - *Priorat*

Sometimes Cabernet Sauvignon

Priorat	Varied blends may include Cabernet Sauvignon, Garnacha, and other local grapes	Full; gripping texture; meaty-leathery-fig scent; superconcentrated plum and dark berry taste

- **Italy**

  As you'll notice from the left column, Italy's classic regions mostly march to their own *bellissimo* beat.

  - *Veneto*

Valpolicella	Corvina plus other local grapes	Light; mouthwatering, tangy cherry taste and scent
Amarone della Valpolicella	Corvina; same vineyards as Valpolicella	Full; rich, velvety texture; toasted almond/prune scent; intense dark raisin and dried fig taste (think Fig Newtons)

- *Piedmont*

Dolcetto d'Alba (the best known of the Dolcettos, but others are good, too)	Dolcetto	Light; zesty, spicy, cranberry-sour cherry taste
Barbera d'Alba (look for Barbera d'Asti and others)	Barbera	Medium; licorice-spice-berry scent; earth and berry taste
Barolo Barbaresco	Nebbiolo	Full; "chewy" texture; exotic earth, licorice, tar scent; strawberry-spice taste

- *Tuscany*

Chianti/ Chianti Classico	Sangiovese	Ranges from light, easy, lip-smacking strawberry-spice character to intense, gripping texture; plum, licorice, and earth scent and taste
Vino Nobile di Monte-pulciano	Prugnolo (a type of Sangiovese)	Medium-to-full; velvety texture, earth-spice, stewed plum taste
Brunello di Montalcino	Brunello (a type of Sangiovese)	Very full; "chewy" in the mouth; powerful dark-fruit flavor

Sometimes Cabernet Sauvignon

"Super Tuscans"— not a region but an important category	Usually a blend of Sangiovese and Cabernet Sauvignon	Modeled to be a classy cross between French red Bordeaux and Italian Chianti; usually full, spicy, and intense, with deep plum and berry flavors

The bottom line on restaurant wine lists: In my opinion, it's not the size of the list that matters but rather the restaurant's effort to make enjoying wine as easy as possible for its guests. How? As always, it comes down to the basics:

Top Ten Tip-Offs You're in a Wine-Wise Restaurant

1. You're *never* made to feel you have to spend a lot to get something good.

2. Wine by the glass is taken as seriously as bottles, with a good range of styles and prices, listed prominently so you don't have to "hunt" to find them.

3. The wine list is presented automatically, so you don't have to ask for it (and wait while the waiter searches for a copy).

4. There are lots of quality bottle choices in the moderate price zone.

5. Wine service, whether glass or bottle, is helpful, speedy, and proficient.

6. Waiters draw your attention to "great values" rather than just the expensive stuff.

7. *Affordable* wine pairings are offered for the signature dishes—either on the menu or by servers.

8. You can ask for a taste before you choose a wine by the glass if you're not sure which you want.

9. It's no problem to split a glass, or get just a half-glass, of by-the-glass offerings. (Great for situations when you want only a little wine or want to try a range of different wines.)

10. There's no such thing as no-name "house white and red." (House-featured wines are fine, but they, and you, merit a name or grape and a region.)

Best Bottles in the Whole Book...

Tear out this page, fold it, and put it into your wallet. As the section title states, these are my personal picks for the best wines in the book. They are go-to wines that you can always count on to deliver outstanding quality for the price.

Best of the Big Brands—In supermarkets, chain restaurants, and hotels.

Alice White—Much better than Yellowtail in the same price point.

Beaulieu Vineyard (BV)—From their basic Coastal Estates line to their top-of-the-line bottlings, you get amazing quality for the money. They've been around so long you might have forgotten about them. If so, you are missing out.

Columbia Crest—Across-the-board quality for cheap.

Blackstone—Nice reds but everything they make is good for the price.

Gallo Family Vineyards Sonoma Reserve—Used to be Gallo of Sonoma. I don't know how they do it for the price, but just excellent across the board.

Kendall-Jackson Vintner's Reserve—Outstanding quality and varietal character across the whole line, for a very good price.

Lindemans—Their value-priced bin series is fantastic for the money.

Sebastiani—Their Sonoma County varietals, at under $20, beat most wineries' $40 wines.

Sterling Vintner's Collection—In many cases, as good as, and cheaper than, their Napa line. That said, the Napa bottlings are tasting better than ever.

Wente—Their basic Livermore varietals are super price/value.

Specialists—These are wineries with particular focus on a certain grape or style. They are worth the search.

Sparkling—Iron Horse, Domaine Carneros, Schramsberg, J Vineyard & Winery

Riesling—Eroica, Trimbach, Wakefield Wines

Sauvignon Blanc—Frog's Leap, St. Supery, Robert Mondavi Fume Blanc, Brancott

Chardonnay—Chalone, Chateau St. Jean, Cuvaison, Grgich Hills, Souverain, Matanzas Creek

Pinot Noir—Au Bon Climat, Etude, MacMurray Ranch, Domaine Drouhin, Cristom, Sokol-Blosser, Truchard

Merlot—Duckhorn, Chateau Ste. Michelle, Franciscan

Cabernet Sauvignon and Blends—Mt. Veeder, St. Clement, Flora Springs, Louis Martini

Syrah/Shiraz—Penfolds, D'Arenberg, Wolf Blass, Jacob's Creek, Andrew Murray, Jade Mountain

Zinfandel—Ridge, Ravenswood, Quivira

Italy and Tuscan Reds—Badia a Coltibuono, Castello di Gabbiano (the best Chiantis for the money), Frescobaldi

Spanish Reds—Montecillo, Marques de Riscal, Muga, Palacios Remondo

Worth the Splurge—For a special occasion, these are the wines that repay the investment in pleasure, and wow factor.

Brut NV Champagne

Charles Heidsieck—decadent and toasty

Moët & Chandon—outstanding, medium-bodied

Perrier-Jouët—elegant, long finish

Luxury Champagne

Bollinger RD—toasty-nutty, extraordinary

Dom Perignon—better than ever

Krug Grande Cuvee—like you've died and awoken in heaven's croissant bakery

Sauvignon Blanc

Grgich Hills—truly special, complex melon flavors and great concentration

Chardonnay

Talbott—very ripe, rich, decadent

Grgich Hills—very classy and Burgundian, ageable

Pinot Noir

Au Bon Climat single vineyards—sexy, meaty, silky, good agers

Rochioli—deep, pure spiced cherry, long finish

Williams-Selyem—always concentrated, pure, layered and complex

Merlot

Duckhorn—opulent, lush, intense

Shafer—gorgeous succulent fruit, licorice, chocolate

Cabernet Sauvignon and Blends

BV Georges de Latour Private Reserve—thick, rich, classy, ages great

Caymus—powerful, rich, like-no-other coconut scent

Opus One—opulent, classy, one of the best-aging CA Cab blends I know of

Joseph Phelps Insignia - always kicks butt in my blind tastings

Robert Mondavi Reserve—World-class complexity and ageability

Spain

Muga Rioja—leather, tobacco, great intensity

Pesquera Ribera del Duero—spice, concentrated fruit, good ageability

Overlooked and Underrated—That means the prices are great for the quality.

Bogle—especially the Petite Sirah

Cline—Zins and Syrahs

Los Vascos and Veramonte—two of Chile's best at great budget prices

Spanish Rioja Reds—look for Marques de Riscal, Marques de Caceres, and Montecillo; don't be afraid to try other brands because this region offers a lot for the money

Souverain—amazing wines in the $15–25 range

Wente - great quality from the basics to the reserves

Wolf-Blass and Jacob's Creek—so much more character for the money in Aussie varietals than most of the competition

Woodbridge single vineyard series—small lots of vineyard-designated wines that are only slightly more expensive, but dramatically more exciting, than the base Woodbridge line

Andrea's Best Bets: Wines for Every Occasion

Best "House" Wines for Every Day—Sparkling, White, and Red

(*House* means *your* house.) These are great go-to wines to keep around for every day and company, too, because they're tasty, *very* inexpensive, and go with everything from takeout to Sunday dinner. They're also wines that got high Kitchen Survivor™ grades, so you don't have to worry if you don't finish the bottle right away. (Selections are listed by body style—lightest to fullest.)

House Sparkling
Segura Viudas Aria Cava Brut Sparkling, Spain
Domaine Ste. Michelle Brut Sparkling, Washington

House Whites
Big House White, California
Robert Mondavi Private Selection Riesling, California
Lindemans Bin 65 Chardonnay, Australia
Gallo Family Vineyards Sonoma Reserve Chardonnay, California
Dry Creek Fume Blanc, California

House Reds
Castle Rock Pinot Noir, California
Duboeuf (Georges) Cotes-du-Rhone, France
Montecillo Rioja Crianza, Spain
Wolf Blass Yellow Label Shiraz, Australia
Los Vascos Cabernet Sauvignon, Chile
Columbia Crest Grand Estates Merlot, Washington
Falesco Vitiano Rosso, Italy

Impress the Date—Hip Wines

White
Bonny Doon Pacific Rim Riesling, USA/Germany
Frog's Leap Sauvignon Blanc, California
Monkey Bay Sauvignon Blanc, New Zealand
Toasted Head Chardonnay, California
Soliloquy Sauvignon Blanc, California

Red

Firesteed Pinot Noir, Oregon

Joel Gott Zinfandel, California

Baron Philippe de Rothschild, Escudo Rojo Cabernet Blend, Chile

Catena Malbec, Argentina

D'Arenberg The Footbolt Shiraz, Australia

Impress the Client—Blue Chip Wines

Sparkling/White

Taittinger Brut La Francaise Champagne, France

Cloudy Bay Sauvignon Blanc, New Zealand

Grgich Hills Fume Blanc, California

Robert Mondavi Napa Fume Blanc, California

Sonoma-Cutrer Russian River Ranches Chardonnay, California

Talbott (Robert) Sleepy Hollow Vineyard Chardonnay, California

Red

Etude Carneros Pinot Noir, California

Domaine Drouhin Willamette Valley Pinot Noir, Oregon

Duckhorn Napa Merlot, California

Ridge Geyserville (Zinfandel), California

BV Private Reserve Cabernet Sauvignon, California

Silver Oak Napa Cabernet Sauvignon, California

You're Invited—Unimpeachable Bottles to Bring to Dinner

(You *do* still have to send a note the next day.)

Trimbach Riesling, Alsace, France

St. Supery Sauvignon Blanc, California

Louis Jadot Pouilly-Fuisse, France

Beringer Napa Chardonnay, California

Calera Central Coast Pinot Noir, California

Ruffino Chianti Classico Riserva Ducale Gold Label, Italy

Penfolds Bin 389 Cabernet Sauvignon/Shiraz, Australia

Franciscan Napa Cabernet Sauvignon, California

Mt. Veeder Napa Cabernet Sauvignon, California

Affordable Agers

Like many wine geeks, my husband John and I especially like wines with bottle age. For certain wines, a little bottle age or even a lot brings in flavors that simply can't exist in a young wine. For reds, that's often flavors of leather and mushrooms; for whites it's often a nutty-toasty, caramelized flavor. For both, the overall wine becomes more subtle and more complex at the same time. For me, there's nothing like a great wine with the right amout of bottle age.

Like many parents, we want to buy some wine to commemorate the birth year of our children, to hopefully share with them when they reach the legal age. The problem is that the best-known wines for reliable aging are often very expensive. So to help solve that problem, we have put together our list of "affordable agers." Of course, what is "affordable" depends on the person, and since there are so few wines that age well below $20, we have come up with three ager categories:

> Affordable agers - Wines under $50 that age gracefully
>
> Splurge-worthy agers - Wines between $50 and $150 that age well
>
> The Big Guns - Elite, classic wines over $150 that age well, and typically appreciate in value, with age (Chateau Latour, Romanee-Conti, Harlan Estate, etc.)

Below is a selection of the most broadly available bottles from this year's list. We taste aged wine as often as we can, and will update this section of the book every year. (The complete list, including The Big Guns and the latest updates, is on my Web site.)

Note that we have included some "agers" for medium-term cellaring, because we like to put bottles aside to mark annual milestones like anniversaries and birthdays. When appropriate I have indicated the number of years the wine will age gracefully if stored in reasonably cool cellar conditions.

Region	Affordable Agers*	Splurge-worthy Agers
Bordeaux red* Graves	Domaine de Chevalier	Smith-Haut-Lafitte
	Cantenac-Brown	Palmer, d'Issan
Margaux	Clerc-Milon	Lynch-Bages
Pauillac	Lagrange, Gruaud-Larose, Talbot	Leoville-Barton
St. Julien		
		Calon Segur
Ste. Estephe	Simard	Figeac, Clos Fourtet
St. Emilion	Cantemerle	La Lagune
Rhone red	Alain Graillot Crozes-Hermitage	Guigal Cote-Rotie Brune et Blonde, Chapoutier Hermitage
Burgundy Red (7-10 yr)	Joblot Givry, Faiveley Mercurey	LeClerc Gevrey-Chambertin, Engel Nuits St. Georges
Burgundy White (5-7 yr)	Chablis 1er Cru/Grand Cru (Laroche, Louis Moreau)	Domaine Leflaive Puligny-Montrachet
California Cabernet Sauvignon	Mt. Veeder, Robert Mondavi Napa, St. Clement	Mondavi Reserve, Ridge Montebello, Grgich Hills Estate, Beringer Private Reserve, BV Georges de Latour
Pinot Noir (7-10 yr)	Etude, Lynmar	Williams-Selyem, Rochioli, Calera (single vineyards)
Chardonnay (6-8 yr)	Chalk Hill, Chalone, Franciscan Cuvee Sauvage	Kistler, Hanzell, Williams-Selyem
Oregon Pinot Noir (7-10 yr)	Cristom, Sokol-Blosser	Domaine Drouhin Oregon
Italy (8-12 yr)	Frescobaldi Chianti Rufina Riserva	Solengo, Badia a Coltibuono Sangioveto
Australia	Penfolds Bin 389 Cabernet-Shiraz	Leeuwin Cabernet Sauvignon
Spain	La Rioja Alta Gran Reserva, Teofilo Reyes Ribera del Duero	Torre Muga Rioja, Capafons-Osso Priorat

*The great chateaus of Bordeaux are an expensive category; as such we have defined "affordable" as under $100.

CUISINE COMPLEMENTS

Whether you're dining out, ordering in, or whipping it up yourself, the following wine recommendations will help you choose a wine to flatter the food in question. If your store doesn't carry that specific wine bottle, ask for a similar selection.

Thanksgiving Wines

More than any other meal, the traditional Thanksgiving lineup features a pretty far-flung range of flavors—from gooey-sweet yams to spicy stuffing to tangy cranberry sauce and everything in between. These wines are like a group hug for all the flavors at the table and the guests around it. My tip: choose a white and a red, put them on the table, and let the diners taste and help themselves to whichever they care to drink. (Selections are listed by body style—lightest to fullest.)

	White	Red
S T E A L	Cavit Pinot Grigio, Italy Bonny Doon Pacific Rim Riesling (USA/Germany) Chateau St. Jean Fume Blanc, California Pierre Sparr Alsace-One, France Chateau Ste. Michelle Gewurztraminer, Washington Gallo Family Vineyards Reserve Chardonnay, California	Louis Jadot Beaujolais-Villages, France Falesco Vitiano, Italy Castle Rock Pinot Noir, California Duboeuf Cotes-du-Rhone, France Marques de Caceres Rioja Crianza, Spain Cline Zinfandel, California Wolf Blass Yellow Label Shiraz, Australia
S P L U R G E	Maso Canali Pinot Grigio, Italy Trimbach Riesling, France Robert Mondavi To-Ka-Lon Reserve Fume Blanc, California Paul Blanck Gewurztraminer, France Matanzas Creek Chardonnay, California	Etude Pinot Noir, California Chateau de Beaucastel Chateauneuf-du-Pape, France Penfolds Bin 389 Cabernet Sauvignon/Shiraz, Australia Teofilo Reyes Ribera del Duero, Spain Ridge Geyserville (Zinfandel), California

Barbecue
Goats do Rome Rose, South Africa
Dry Creek Fume Blanc, California
Jacob's Creek Shiraz, Australia
Hill of Content Grenache/Shiraz, Australia
Jaboulet Parallele 45 Cotes-du-Rhone, France
Montevina Amador Zinfandel, California

Chinese Food
Saint M Riesling, Washington
Ken Forrester Petit Chenin, South Africa
Jolivet Sancerre, France
Castle Rock Pinot Noir, California
Palacios Remondo La Vendimia Rioja, Spain
Ravenswood Vintner's Blend Zinfandel, California
Louis Jadot Beaujolais-Villages, France
Allegrini Valpolicella, Italy

Nuevo Latino (Cuban, Caribbean, South American)
Freixenet Brut de Noirs Cava Rose, Spain
Robert Mondavi Private Selection Pinot Grigio, California
Hermanos Lurton Rueda Verdejo, Spain
Terrazas Alto Malbec, Argentina
Los Vascos Cabernet Sauvignon, Chile
Woodbridge (Robert Mondavi) Zinfandel, California

Picnics
Danzante Pinot Grigio, Italy
Domaine Ste. Michelle Brut Sparkling, Washington
Beringer White Zinfandel, California
Lindemans Bin 65 Chardonnay, Australia
Citra Montepulciano d'Abruzzo, Italy
Duboeuf (Georges) Beaujolais-Villages, France

Sushi
Moët & Chandon White Star Champagne, France
Trimbach Riesling, France
Burgans Albarino, Spain
Jolivet Sancerre, France
Monkey Bay Sauvignon Blanc, New Zealand
Frog's Leap Sauvignon Blanc, California
Louis Jadot Pouilly-Fuisse, France
Duboeuf Beaujolais-Villages, France

Mark West Pinot Noir, California
Calera Central Coast Pinot Noir, California

Clambake/Lobster Bake
Gallo Family Vineyards Sonoma Reserve Chardonnay, California
Beringer Napa Chardonnay, California
Cambria Katherine's Vineyard Chardonnay, California
Borsao Tinto, Spain
Erath Pinot Noir, Oregon

Mexican Food
Pierre Sparr Alsace-One, France
Veramonte Sauvignon Blanc, Chile
Hugel Gewurztraminer, France
Beringer White Zinfandel, California
Duboeuf (Georges) Cotes-du-Rhone, France
Cline Syrah, California
Ravenswood Vintner's Blend Zinfandel, California

Pizza
Citra Montepulciano d'Abruzzo, Italy
Cantina Zaccagnini Montepulciano, Italy
Montecillo Rioja Crianza, Spain
D'Arenberg The Footbolt Shiraz, Australia
Montevina Amador Zinfandel, California
Woodbridge (Robert Mondavi) Zinfandel, California

The Cheese Course
Frescobaldi Nippozano Chianti Rufina Riserva, Italy
Penfolds Bin 389 Cabernet Sauvignon/Shiraz, Australia
Chateau de Beaucastel Chateauneuf-du-Pape, France
Muga Rioja Reserva, Spain
Pesquera Ribera del Duero, Spain
Ridge Geyserville (Zinfandel), California
Rosemount GSM (Grenache-Shiraz-Mourvedre), Australia
Grgich Hills Napa Zinfandel, California
Mt. Veeder Napa Cabernet Sauvignon, California
Chateau Gruaud-Larose Bordeaux, France
Banfi Brunello di Montalcino, Italy
Alvaro Palacios Les Terrasses Priorat, Spain

Steak

Ferrari-Carano Alexander Valley Chardonnay, California

Talbott (Robert) Sleepy Hollow Vineyard Chardonnay, California

Domaine Drouhin Willamette Valley Pinot Noir, Oregon

Ruffino Chianti Classico Riserva Ducale Gold Label, Italy

Marchesi di Barolo Barolo, Italy

Shafer Merlot, California

Cakebread Napa Cabernet Sauvignon, California

Beringer Knights Valley Cabernet Sauvignon, California

Robert Mondavi Cabernet Sauvignon Reserve, California

Groth Napa Cabernet Sauvignon, California

Staglin Salus Napa Cabernet Sauvignon, California

Joseph Phelps Napa Cabernet Sauvignon, California

Rancho Zabaco Dry Creek Valley Zinfandel, California

Salad

Ruffino Orvieto, Italy

Hugel Pinot Blanc, France

Trimbach Riesling, France

Louis Jadot Macon-Villages Chardonnay, France

Allegrini Valpolicella, Italy

Calera Central Coast Pinot Noir, California

Vegetarian

Gallo Family Vineyards Reserve Pinot Gris, California

Hess Chardonnay, California

Estancia Pinnacles Pinot Noir, California

Castello di Gabbiano Chianti, Italy

Jaboulet Parallele 45 Cotes-du-Rhone, France

ENTERTAINING WITH WINE

In my experience, people stress a lot about the wine aspect of entertaining—what to choose, how much to buy, and serving savvy. *Relax*, because the wine part is easy. There's no prep involved other than popping the cork, and wine can really make a gathering memorable. Here are my top ten tips for pulling it off with ease.

1. Set your budget to fit the occasion, and your comfort zone. At large or casual gatherings, any wine in this book with the crowd pleaser symbol ☺ will do you proud. For a dinner party with a special menu or a guest of honor, it's nice to trade up a little, and theme your choices to the dishes on the menu.

2. Serve one white and one red (at least). Even if your party menu is geared to a particular wine style (e.g., a burger bash & red wine), offer the other color, too, for those guests who strongly prefer it.

3. Offer a unique aperitif. Champagne is the classic aperitif (pre-dinner pour, usually with hors d'oeuvres), but you don't have to go with something expensive. Prosecco and Spanish cava are worthy budget bubblies. Rose wines and lighter whites like Riesling and Pinot Grigio also make great aperitifs.

4. Serve white before red, light before heavy, dry before sweet. For both wine and food, the fullest and sweetest flavors get served last, so they don't overpower the lighter dishes and wines.

5. Open the wines ahead of time. As long as you re-cork and keep them cool, the wines will taste great and you won't have last-minute stress.

6. An all-purpose glass is fine. Unless you are having a serious wine gathering, you don't need lots of different wine glasses. A good-quality glass with an ample bowl and thin rim will showcase most wines nicely.

7. Give guests a printout of the wines. A printed menu with the wine names is a nice touch, so guests can remember the names of the wines they enjoyed.

8. Don't fill glasses to the top. Pros leave plenty of head space in the glass for swirling the wine, which enhances the aromas. Many good wine glasses are designed so that a 5-6 ounce standard pour reaches the widest part of the bowl. At cocktail parties and wine tastings I go with smaller pours of 2-3 ounces, so guests have the opportunity to try different tastes, and then pour more of what they like best.

9. Calculate how much wine you will need. Each standard (750 ml) wine bottle contains about five 5-ounce glasses of wine. For a dinner party plan on consumption of about 2-3 glasses per guest. Multiply that times the number of guests, then divide by 5 to determine the number of bottles needed. For a cocktail party where you are only serving wine, estimate consumption of 1 1/2 per glasses per guest for the first hour, and 1 glass per guest for each hour after that. Divide the total number of glasses you think your guests will drink by five to determine the number of bottles needed. If a full bar is available at the cocktail party, figure that one-third of your guests will drink wine and then make the above calculations. A good rule of thumb is to assume guests will consume 60% white wine, and 40% red. Always have water and other nonalcoholic drinks available, too. For a bubbly toast, buy one bottle for every eight guests.

10. Host the easiest wine tasting cocktail party ever. Serve one selection from each of the Big Six grapes paired with a simple appetizer (e.g., Riesling & eggrolls, Sauvignon Blanc and goat cheese, Chardonnay and popcorn, Pinot Noir and stuffed mushrooms, Cab/Merlot and pesto bruschetta, Syrah/Shiraz and Buffalo wings. Arrange the paired wines and appetizers next to each other, buffet style. Give each guest a wine glass and menu/note sheet, and let them enjoy tasting their way through the different matchups. It's a blast!

Food & Wine Pairing Basics

Whether you are a wary wine novice or a certified wine geek, "What wine should I drink with...?" is a constant question. Why? I think it is simply that those of us who enjoy wine love food even more. And we intuitively sense the possibilities to enhance what we're eating by pairing it with wine.

But a lot of people think that getting it "right" when it comes to pairing takes a big budget and a lot of wine knowledge. Far from it. Isn't it true that in Europe, the simplest of country lunches and bistro suppers, with wine, are often among the most memorable meals?

Back home, wine can transform your everyday dinners. Whether it's takeout, leftovers, or your best kitchen creation, you can just pour a glass of whatever wine you have handy and as long as it's one you like, you're bound to enjoy the match. That said, a well-chosen match can take the experience from nice, to knock-your-socks-off. To see for yourself, try some of my simple pairing pointers. They're a lot of fun and no hassle, so you won't need to wait for a special occasion to try them. In fact that's the whole point: everyday dinner *is* the occasion. Here's to making the most of it!

Pairing Basics

When I started as a sommelier, the pairing rule was "red wine with red meat, and white wine with fish." And in those days red wine meant Cabernet Sauvignon and Merlot, and white wine meant Chardonnay. "Meat" was beef, and fish was flounder or sole. Then along came...Malbec, and Shiraz, Pinot Noir, Riesling, Pinot Grigio...and a host of global grapes whose varied styles and flavors invited all kinds of new foods to the wine lover's table. Salmon and shrimp morphed from "special-occasion" to staple, pork and lamb gained new prominence, and exotic techniques and seasonings like stirfrying, smoking, Asian accents, and southwestern salsas evolved into simply everyday fare. Since then I've had a ball playing matchmaker for all of these grapes and food flavors. And like any good couple, the best matches are based on either complement or contrast.

Complement simply means linking up common traits. For wine and food, that can mean matching body or flavors: if the wine and food are on a par, neither gets overpowered and the character of each can shine. For contrasting matches, pairing disparate flavors in the food and the wine can showcase the complexity of each. For example, a slightly sweet or tangy wine with a spicy-hot dish gives the palate a reprieve from the heat, priming your mouth for the next tasty forkful. A rich, creamy or buttery dish can find new balance and flavor complexity when paired with a crisp, tangy wine to cut through the heaviness and showcase the flavor layers. Here are some specific ways to put these ideas into practice.

Pairing Principles for White Wines...

When it comes to complementing matches, I focus on the body of the wine and the dish. Simply put, that means light-bodied whites with light-bodied dishes, and fuller-bodied whites with heavy or rich dishes. For example, the best wines for crisp salads are the light and crisp ones, particularly Pinot Grigio and Sauvignon Blanc. Richer salads such as Caesar or tunafish call for a richer white like Chardonnay. In the same vein, lighter cheeses like goat and feta love a sparkling wine or Sauvignon Blanc. Heavier cheeses such as Parmigiano Reggiano or aged cheddar, match marvelously with a rich Chardonnay or Viognier. For seafood dishes think about the body of both the core fish or seafood, and the heaviness of the preparation. For example, lighter Asian stirfry preparation I'd match a crisp white; with a cream sauce or buttery dish (like Shrimp Scampi), I'd go with a richer white. On that note, generally the tangy/gingery/sweet flavors of Asian-accented dishes are well-suited to white wines with vibrant acidity, and even a touch of sweetness (think Riesling, and Sauvignon Blancs from New Zealand). This point can illustrate either complement (tangy dish with tangy wine) or contrast (spicy-hot dish with sweet wine). And what about meat with whites? As a sommelier I've even served big Chardonnays to my guests ordering steak, pork and game. Remember, no matter what the pairing rulebook says, the most important rule of all is: drink what you like.

...and for Red Wines

For red wines, again body is the basis for complementing matches. For example, a big Napa Valley Cab or Italian Super Tuscan red stands up to a big steak or a rich cheese like Parmigiano Reggiano or Camembert, but a delicate Pinot Noir or Beaujolais (based on the Gamay grape) is better suited to lighter grilled salmon, pork or chicken, and to goat cheeses. Beyond body, it's fun to also explore some complementing flavor matches for red wines. For example, the peppery spice of an Aussie Shiraz is the perfect flavor compliment to spicy dishes like barbecue or steak au poivre. Earthy wines such as Italian Chianti, Spanish Rioja, or Oregon or French Pinot Noir wines, are a great complement to earthy dishes based on mushrooms, grains such as barley and polenta, or legumes like lentils and chickpeas.

For contrasting matches, both tangy and tannic qualities in red wine can cut through richness in food. For example, tangy Chianti with cheesy tortellini, or tannic red Bordeaux with richly-marbled steak or prime rib, are great matches. Herbal flavors such as basil pesto, or a rosemary crust for lamb, make a fabulous contrast with the rich blackberry compote fruit flavors of Californian, Chilean and Washington Cabernets and Merlots. And finally, the ultimate contrasting match for me is a big, fruity red wine such as California Syrah, with dark chocolate.

When you put these opposites together, they bring out the best in each other. And that's really the whole point of pairing wine and food anyway.

WINERY INDEX

Beckmen, California
  Grenache Rose   79

Belguardo, Italy
  Serrata Maremma Super Tuscan   98

Benton Lane, Oregon
  Pinot Noir   85

Benziger, California
  Cabernet Sauvignon   119
  Chardonnay   57
  Sauvignon Blanc   43

Beringer, California
  Founders' Estate Chardonnay   58
  Knights Valley Cabernet Sauvignon   119
  Napa Valley Chardonnay   58
  Napa Valley Dry Riesling   35
  Napa Valley Merlot   106
  Napa Valley Pinot Noir   84
  Napa Valley Sauvignon Blanc   43
  Private Reserve Cabernet Sauvignon   119
  Private Reserve Chardonnay   58
  Third Century Merlot   106
  Third Century Pinot Noir   84
  White Zinfandel   79

Benton Lane, Oregon
  Pinot Noir Willamette Valley   84

Bethel Heights, Oregon
  Pinot Gris Willamette Valley   29

Big House, California
  Pinot Grigio   29
  Pink   79
  White   72

Black Box 3L, California
  California Merlot   107

Black Opal, Australia
  Shiraz   149

Blackstone, California
  Cabernet Sauvignon   119
  Monterey Chardonnay   58
  Merlot   107
  Sonoma Reserve Merlot   107
  Syrah   149
  Zinfandel   157

Blandy's, Portugal
  10-Year-Old Malmsey Madeira   165

Blue Fish, Germany
  Sweet Riesling   36

Bodegas Ochoa, Spain
  Garnacha Rosado   79

Calera, California
Central Coast Pinot Noir   85

Cambria, California
Julia's Vineyard Pinot Noir   85
Katherine's Vineyard Chardonnay   59

Campbell's, Australia
Rutherglen Muscat   166

Canoe Ridge, Washington
Columbia Valley Merlot   107

Cantina Zaccagnini, Italy
Montepulciano d'Abruzzo   98

Casa Lapostolle, Chile
Cuvee Alexandre Cabernet Sauvignon   115
Cuvee Alexandre Chardonnay   59
Cuvee Alexandre Merlot   107
Sauvignon Blanc   44

Castello Banfi, Italy
Brachetto d'Acqui   166
Brunello di Montalcino   99
Chianti Classico Riserva   99
Le Rime Pinot Grigio/Chardonnay   32
San Angelo Pinot Grigio   29

Castello di Gabbiano, Italy
Alleanza   99
Chianti Classico   99
Chianti Classico Riserva   99

Castle Rock, California
Pinot Noir Mendocino   85

Catena, Argentina
Chardonnay   59
Malbec   145

Cavit, Italy
Pinot Grigio   30

Caymus, California
Napa Cabernet Sauvignon   120

C.G. DeArie, California
Shenandoah Zinfandel   158

Chalk Hill, California
Estate Chardonnay   59
Estate Sauvignon Blanc   44

Chalone, California
Estate Chardonnay   59
Estate Pinot Noir   86
Estate Syrah   149

Chambers, Australia
Rosewood Vineyards Rutherglen Muscadelle   166

Deloach, California
Russian River Valley Pinot Noir   87
Russian River Valley Zinfandel   158

Domaine Carneros, California
Brut   21
Le Reve   21
Pinot Noir   87

Domaine Chandon, California
Brut Classic   21
Riche   21
Rose   21

Domaine de Coyeaux, France
Muscat Beaumes de Venise   166

Domaine Drouhin, Oregon
Willamette Valley Pinot Noir   87

Domaine Ott, France
Bandol Rose   80

Domaine Ste. Michelle, Washington
Brut   22

Domaine Vincent Delaporte, France
Sancerre   46

Dom Perignon, Champagne, France
Brut   22

Dr. Konstantin Frank, New York
Dry Riesling   37

Dr. Loosen, Germany
Riesling Kabinett Estate   37

Dow's Colheita, Portugal
Tawny Port 1992   167

Dry Creek Vineyard, California
Chenin Blanc   74
Fume Blanc   46
Old Vine Zinfandel   159

Drylands, New Zealand
Sauvignon Blanc   46

Duboeuf (Georges), France
Beaujolais-Villages   81
Cotes-du-Rhone   151
Moulin-a-Vent   82

Duckhorn, California
Napa Merlot   107
Sauvignon Blanc   46

Duck Pond, Oregon
Pinot Noir   87

Duval-Leroy, France
Brut NV   22

Dynamite Wines, California
Cabernet Sauvignon 124
Chardonnay 61
Merlot 107

E & M Guigal, France
Cote-Rotie Brune et Blonde 151
Cotes-du-Rhone 151

Ecco Domani, Italy
Pinot Grigio 30

Echelon, California
Vin de Pays Pinot Noir 87

Edna Valley Vineyard, California
Paragon Chardonnay 61
Paragon Pinot Noir 88
Paragon Sauvignon Blanc 46
San Luis Obispo Merlot 107

Emilio Lustau, Spain
Pedro Ximenez "San Emilio" Sherry 167

Emmolo, California
Sauvignon Blanc 46

Erath, Oregon
Pinot Gris 31
Pinot Noir 88

Eroica, Washington
Riesling 37

Esser, California
Cabernet Sauvignon 124

Estancia, California
Central Coast Merlot 107
Paso Robles Cabernet Sauvignon 125
Pinot Grigio 31
Pinnacles Ranches Chardonnay 61
Pinnacles Ranches Pinot Noir 88

Etude, California
Carneros Pinot Noir 88

Falesco, Italy
Montiano 109
Vitiano Rosso 100

Fall Creek, Texas
Chenin Blanc 74

Far Niente, California
Cabernet Sauvignon 125
Chardonnay 61

Felsina Berardenga, Italy
Chianti Classico 100

Ferrari-Carano, California
Alexander Valley Cabernet Sauvignon 125
Alexander Valley Chardonnay 61
Fume Blanc 47
Sonoma Merlot 110

Ferreira, Portugal
Doña Antonia Port 167

Fess Parker, California
Santa Barbara Pinot Noir 88

Fetzer, California
Valley Oaks Cabernet Sauvignon 125
Valley Oaks Chardonnay 62
Valley Oaks Gewurztraminer 74
Valley Oaks Johannisberg Riesling 38
Valley Oaks Merlot 110
Valley Oaks Zinfandel 159

Ficklin, California
Tinta "Port" 167

Firesteed, Oregon
Pinot Gris 31
Pinot Noir 88

Five Rivers Ranch, California
Pinot Noir 89

Firestone, California
Riesling 38

Flora Springs, California
Barrel Fermented Chardonnay 62
Pinot Grigio 31
Soliloquy 47
Triology 125

Folie a Deux, California
Menage a Trois, White Blend 74

Folonari, Italy
Pinot Grigio 31

Fonseca, Portugal
Bin 27 Port 167

Fonterutoli, Italy
Chianti Classico 100

Franciscan, California
Magnificat Meritage 126
Oakville Chardonnay 62
Oakville Estate Cabernet Sauvignon 126
Oakville Estate Merlot 110

Francis Coppola, California
Diamond Series Blue Label Merlot 110
Diamond Series Claret 126
Director's Cut Zinfandel 159

Grgich Hills, California
Fume Blanc   48
Napa Estate Cabernet Sauvignon   127
Napa Estate Chardonnay   63
Napa Estate Merlot   111
Napa Estate Zinfandel   160

Groth, California
Napa Cabernet Sauvignon   127
Napa Sauvignon Blanc   48

Gruet, New Mexico
Brut St. Vincent   23

Gunderloch, Germany
Riesling Estate   38

Gunn Estate, New Zealand
Sauvignon Blanc   48

Hall Wines, California
Sauvignon Blanc   48

Hanna, California
Sauvignon Blanc   48

Heitz, California
Napa Cabernet Sauvignon   127

Hermanos Lurton, Spain
Rueda Verdejo   75

Hess, California
Cabernet Sauvignon   128
Chardonnay   63

Hidalgo, Spain
La Gitana Manzanilla Sherry   75

Hill of Content, Australia
Grenache/Shiraz   152

Hirsch, Austria
Gruner Veltliner #1   75

Hogue, Washington
Cabernet Sauvignon   128
Fume Blanc   49
Gewurztraminer   75
Johannisberg Riesling   38
Late Harvest Riesling   168

Honig, California
Sauvignon Blanc   49

Hugel, Alsace, France
Gewurztraminer   75
Pinot Blanc Cuvee Les Amours   75

Il Poggione, Italy
Brunello di Montalcino   101

Russian River Pinot Noir 90
Cuvee 20 Brut Sparkling 23

Kendall-Jackson, California
Vintner's Reserve Cabernet Sauvignon 129
Vintner's Reserve Chardonnay 64
Vintner's Reserve Merlot 111
Vintner's Reserve Pinot Noir 90
Vintner's Reserve Riesling 39
Vintner's Reserve Sauvignon Blanc 49
Vintner's Reserve Zinfandel 160

Ken Forrester, South Africa
Petit Chenin 76

Kenwood, California
Jack London Cabernet Sauvignon 129
Jack London Zinfandel 160
Merlot 112
Sauvignon Blanc 50

Kesselstatt, Germany
RK Riesling 39

Kim Crawford, New Zealand
Sauvignon Blanc 50
Unoaked Chardonnay 64

King Estate, Oregon
Pinot Gris 34
Pinot Noir 90

Krug, France
Grande Cuvee Multivintage 23

Kunde Estate, California
Magnolia Lane Sauvignon Blanc 50
Sonoma Zinfandel 160

L'Ecole No. 41, Washington
Walla Walla Valley Merlot 112

La Crema, California
Russian River Valley Chardonnay 64
Sonoma Coast Pinot Noir 90

Landmark Vineyards, California
Overlook Chardonnay 64

Laurel Glen, California
Reds 160

Laurent-Perrier, Champagne, France
Brut LP 24

La Vieille Ferme, France
Cotes-du-Ventoux Rose 80
Cotes-du-Ventoux Rouge 153

La Vite Lucente, Italy
Super Tuscan 101

Merlot	112
Sauvignon Blanc	50

Mark West, California
Central Coast Pinot Noir	91

Marques de Arienzo, Spain
Rioja Reserva	140

Marques de Caceres, Spain
Rioja Crianza	141
Rioja Reserva	141
Rioja Rosado	80

Marques de Riscal, Spain
Rioja Crianza	141
Rioja Gran Reserva	141
Rioja Reserva	141
Rueda White	76

Marquis Philips, Australia
Sarah's Blend	153

Martin Codax, Spain
Albarino	76

Martinsancho, Spain
Verdejo	76

Maso Canali, Italy
Pinot Grigio	32

Mason, California
Sauvignon Blanc	50

Matanzas Creek, California
Bennett Valley Merlot	112
Sonoma Chardonnay	65
Sonoma Sauvignon Blanc	51

Maximin Grunhauser, Germany
Abtsberg Riesling Kabinett	39

McWilliams Hanwood Estate, Australia
Cabernet Sauvignon	130

Meridian, California
Pinot Noir	91

Merry Edwards, California
Russian River Valley Pinot Noir	91

Merryvale, California
Starmont Chardonnay	66
Starmont Merlot	113
Starmont Sauvignon Blanc	51

Mer Soleil, California
Chardonnay	66

Michele Chiarlo, Italy
Le Orme Barbera d'Asti	102
Nivole ("Clouds") Moscato d'Asti	168

Sea Smoke, California
  Botella Pinot Noir   93

Sebastiani, California
  Sonoma County Cabernet Sauvignon   135
  Sonoma County Chardonnay   68
  Sonoma County Merlot   114
  Sonoma Coast Pinot Noir   94

Seghesio, California
  Zinfandel   163

Segura Viudas, Spain
  Aria Estate Cava Brut   27
  Reserva Heredad Cava Brut   27

Selbach-Oster, Germany
  Fish Label Riesling   43

Sella & Mosca, Italy
  Vermentino La Cala   77

Sequoia Grove, California
  Napa Cabernet Sauvignon   135
  Reserve Cabernet Sauvignon   135

Shafer, California
  Merlot   114

Shingleback, Australia
  McLaren Vale Shiraz   155

Silverado, California
  Cabernet Sauvignon   135
  Chardonnay   68
  Miller Ranch Sauvignon Blanc   53

Silver Oak
  Alexander Valley Cabernet Sauvignon   135
  Napa Valley Cabernet Sauvignon   136

Simi, California
  Cabernet Sauvignon   136
  Chardonnay   68
  Merlot   114
  Sauvignon Blanc   53
  Zinfandel   164

Smith Woodhouse, Portugal
  Lodge Reserve Port   169

Sofia, California
  Blanc de Blancs   30

Sokol Blosser, Oregon
  Evolution   78
  Willamette Valley Pinot Noir   94

Solorosa, California
  Rose   80

Sonoma-Cutrer, California
  Russian River Ranches Chardonnay   68